THE BEDFORD SERIES IN HISTORY AND CULTURE

The Federalist

by Alexander Hamilton,
James Madison, and John Jay

THE ESSENTIAL ESSAYS

THE BEDFORD SERIES IN HISTORY AND CULTURE

The Federalist

by Alexander Hamilton, James Madison, and John Jay

THE ESSENTIAL ESSAYS

Edited with an Introduction by

Jack N. Rakove

Stanford University

BEDFORD/ST. MARTIN'S   Boston ◆ New York

To the memory of James Kettner, my colleague on two coasts.

For Bedford/St. Martin's

Publisher for History: Patricia A. Rossi
Director of Development for History: Jane Knetzger
Developmental Editor: Gretchen Boger
Associate Editor, Publishing Services: Maria Teresa Burwell
Production Supervisor: Jennifer Wetzel
Marketing Manager: Jenna Bookin Barry
Project Management: Books By Design, Inc.
Text Design: Claire Seng-Niemoeller
Indexer: Books By Design, Inc.
Cover Design: Billy Boardman
Cover Photo: First Chief Justice John Jay; Portrait of James Madison;
  Alexander Hamilton Portrait. Courtesy Bettmann/CORBIS.
Composition: Stratford Publishing Services, Inc.
Printing and Binding: Haddon Craftsmen, an RR Donnelley & Sons Company

President: Joan E. Feinberg
Editorial Director: Denise B. Wydra
Director of Marketing: Karen R. Melton
Director of Editing, Design, and Production: Marcia Cohen
Manager, Publishing Services: Emily Berleth

Library of Congress Control Number: 2002109899

Manufactured in the United States of America.

5 4 3 2 1
f e d

For information, write: Bedford/St. Martin's, 75 Arlington Street, Boston, MA 02116
(617-399-4000)

ISBN: 978-0-312-24732-4

Foreword

The Bedford Series in History and Culture is designed so that readers can study the past as historians do.

The historian's first task is finding the evidence. Documents, letters, memoirs, interviews, pictures, movies, novels, or poems can provide facts and clues. Then the historian questions and compares the sources. There is more to do than in a courtroom, for hearsay evidence is welcome, and the historian is usually looking for answers beyond act and motive. Different views of an event may be as important as a single verdict. How a story is told may yield as much information as what it says.

Along the way the historian seeks help from other historians and perhaps from specialists in other disciplines. Finally, it is time to write, to decide on an interpretation and how to arrange the evidence for readers.

Each book in this series contains an important historical document or group of documents, each document a witness from the past and open to interpretation in different ways. The documents are combined with some element of historical narrative—an introduction or a biographical essay, for example—that provides students with an analysis of the primary source material and important background information about the world in which it was produced.

Each book in the series focuses on a specific topic within a specific historical period. Each provides a basis for lively thought and discussion about several aspects of the topic and the historian's role. Each is short enough (and inexpensive enough) to be a reasonable one-week assignment in a college course. Whether as classroom or personal reading, each book in the series provides firsthand experience of the challenge—and fun—of discovering, recreating, and interpreting the past.

Natalie Zemon Davis
Ernest R. May
Lynn Hunt
David W. Blight

Preface

A long time ago, in a university far away from my current posting, I drew the assignment in my first graduate seminar of tracing the uses of *The Federalist* in the constitutional disputes of the period that historians call the Early Republic—roughly 1789 to 1850. In the course of writing that paper, I learned that this text, like others, has its own history. Some of the essays that modern scholars value most, notably *Federalist* 10, received little attention during the post-Revolutionary decades, while others now neglected, notably *Federalist* 32, were read and cited with some frequency.

This shift provides an important clue to the ways in which *The Federalist* is usually read. Although it is possible to view the eighty-five essays as a single sustained treatise, and useful to ask how its different series of topics fit together, the dominant mode of reading tends to be highly focused and selective. Three essays in particular have nearly cornered the market in critical commentary: the exposition of the theory of the extended republic in *Federalist* 10, the summation of the separation of powers in *Federalist* 51, and the account of judicial review in *Federalist* 78. A second tier of modestly less important essays could be identified without great difficulty. And then there are all those other essays that bear closely on particular provisions of the Constitution whose adoption *The Federalist* was written to support. Interest in these pieces ebbs and flows, waxes and wanes, as contemporary controversies remind us that constitutional interpretation in the United States involves the ongoing enterprise of making sense of a document that contains a surprising number of provisions that lie dormant for long periods and then flare into sudden importance.

This pattern of use of *The Federalist* justifies, I believe, a decision that historians would ordinarily shrink from taking: to publish a select edition of the essays that cannot do justice to the richness of the original complete set, but that can still answer the needs of classroom use. Of course, historians generally prefer to have more evidence available than less, just as they are reluctant to excise material that promises to enlarge our understanding of the larger subject. But in practice, the teaching of *The Federalist* is selective and focused in just the way that this volume has been prepared. Although scholars would probably compile somewhat different lists of what might be called their top-twenty *Federalist* favorites, I am confident that the contents selected for this volume will meet general approval, even if my colleagues might substitute other picks of their own for some of those presented here.

The introduction to this volume establishes the historical and political context within which these essays should be located. Some scholars stress the intellectual context within which *The Federalist* should be read, comparing and contrasting its assumptions about human nature and society with those of earlier political philosophers. I adopt a different perspective, more political than intellectual, that begins by recognizing that *The Federalist* was written as a contribution to a specific political debate. To establish the context within which its arguments were framed, one has to know how the Constitution it defended came to be written, why the debates at the Federal Convention of 1787 took the course they did, and how the objections raised by the Constitution's Anti-Federalist opponents shaped the responses that *The Federalist* and other Federalists were driven to offer. One also has to know something of the distinctive political careers and concerns of its authors, Alexander Hamilton, James Madison, and John Jay.

In addition to the introduction, the editorial apparatus to this volume includes headnotes for each of the essays. These notes identify the aspect of the larger constitutional debate to which each essay is responding, relate the provision being analyzed to the debates at the Federal Convention, or explain how the argument of the essay illustrates distinctive elements of the political ideas and concerns of its author. A chronology of the adoption of the Constitution, questions for consideration, and an annotated bibliography close the volume.

A NOTE ABOUT THE TEXT

Any select edition of *The Federalist* is likely to do its leading author, Alexander Hamilton, a serious injustice. Hamilton conceived the project and wrote exactly three-fifths of the essays. Yet for modern scholarly interpreters, Publius (the collective pseudonym used by all three authors) is first and foremost James Madison. Although no authoritative poll of the top-ten, all-time *Federalist* favorites has yet to be compiled, a plausible list of the most important or influential essays would feature seven by Madison (10, 14, 39, 45, 46, 48, and 51) and only three by Hamilton (1, 70, and 78). Other lists could be prepared to even the balance, but the commanding stature of *Federalist* 10 and 51 would still give Madison the advantage. It was his literary fortune to draw the assignments to discuss the possibility of an extended national republic and the reformulation of the problem of separation of powers. By contrast, Hamilton's great contribution to the project was to carry the burden, primarily in the opening series of essays, of explaining why a vigorous Union was necessary. At the time, and well into the nineteenth century, it remained an open question whether the United States could become, or should remain, a single nation. Today, when Americans take their nationhood for granted, that question is far less urgent.

In one sense, the essays selected for this edition of *The Federalist* reflect the Madisonian bias of modern constitutional commentary. Although the two main authors contribute roughly the same number of essays, this means that proportionally more of Madison's essays appear than Hamilton's. (The third author, John Jay, is represented here by a single essay.)

Several criteria have guided the selection of essays. First, and most important, I have selected those that reflect the general scholarly consensus as to which essays best represent the critical contributions that Publius made to constitutional theory in general and the doctrines of American constitutionalism in particular. These include essays 9 and 10 on the extended republic; 15, 39, 45, and 46 on federalism; 47–51 on the separation of powers; and 78 on judicial review. A second criterion was to include essays that illuminate how the authors thought about the process of reasoning about politics in general, including especially *Federalist* 1, 14, 23, and 37. A third set consists of especially incisive analyses of the distinctive characteristics of institutions: essays 53, 62, 63, 70–72, and 84. A fourth criterion was to identify essays that concern topics of enduring constitutional importance or historical interest: 32 and 35 on taxation; 54 on the three-fifths clause; 64 and 75 on the allocation of authority over foreign relations; and 84 on the value of a bill of rights. Finally, Publius deserved to be able to write his own conclusion to this volume, so it seemed only fair to include the final summation of *Federalist* 85. It goes almost without saying that this list will not be completely satisfactory to every scholar, but taken together, I believe the essays selected illustrate why *The Federalist* is widely regarded as the new republic's preeminent contribution to political theory.

In selecting the exact texts to be printed here, I have followed the editorial practice of Jacob Cooke in the scholarly edition of *The Federalist* published in 1961:[1] that is, to follow the initial newspaper printing for essays 1–77, and the McLean edition of 1788 for essays 78–85, while making minor changes to the former set of essays on the basis of corrections that already appeared in McLean. The intention is thus to present *The Federalist* essentially as its first audience would have read it, but with slight adjustments made for the first round of corrections. Footnotes that the authors added to their original essays are also reprinted, and will be identified in the text with the typographical symbols (such as asterisks) that they used. I have added a limited number of explanatory notes to identify persons and events and to define unfamiliar terms; these notes are numbered.

ACKNOWLEDGMENTS

This project began under the editorial tutelage of Katherine Kurzman, and continued under the guidance of Patricia Rossi, Jane Knetzger, Julie Mooza, and Gretchen Boger (who I hope does not regret too much relinquishing her opportunity to study on the Stanford farm). Their assistance is deeply appreciated, as is the long-suffering patience of Chuck Christensen and Joan Feinberg. I have also derived great benefit from the friends and colleagues who read the editorial apparatus and commented on the selections: Saul Cornell, Joanne Freeman, Herbert Sloan, Jean Yarbrough, Melvin Yazawa, and Rosemarie Zagarri. I regret only that cruel but not unusual exigencies of space prevented me from heeding all their valuable suggestions. At a pressing moment, my fellow Chicagoan Rachel Aliyah Shapiro lent me her unflappable assistance, encouraging me once again to forgive her mistaken loyalty to the White Sox. She is only one of the many Stanford students who helped me prepare this book by taking the courses in which we pondered Publius and the other sources that make the study of the formative era of American constitutional thinking so rewarding.

This book is dedicated to the memory of my late colleague James Kettner. News of his untimely death reached me as I was completing the last details of preparing this manuscript for publication. My own memory always returns to the sight of Jim seated at a table in the

---

[1] Jacob Cooke, ed., *The Federalist* (Middletown, Conn.: Wesleyan University Press, 1961), xii.

main reading room of Widener Library, patiently working over the notes that became his pathbreaking study of *The Development of American Citizenship,* in just the same way that his students and colleagues at Berkeley would see him in his office, door always open for anyone seeking his counsel. I hope his memory will be a blessing to his family, colleagues, and students.

Jack N. Rakove

Contents

The Federalist

by Alexander Hamilton, James Madison, and John Jay

THE ESSENTIAL ESSAYS

PART ONE

Introduction:
The Federalist in Context

On October 27, 1787, the *Independent Journal* of New York City published the first essay of *The Federalist*. Americans had already begun a
spirited debate over the new Federal Constitution that the distinguished members of the Federal Convention had proposed only six
weeks earlier. The Anti-Federalist opponents of the Constitution
quickly identified the dangers it posed to the authority of the states
and the liberties of their citizens. Its Federalist supporters promptly
replied that only its speedy adoption would preserve the Union and
the prosperity and security of its people. A few leading statements of
the rival positions had appeared in the press, but no one had yet
begun to offer a systematic exposition of the Constitution.

That was the agenda that the writer who signed himself "Publius"
set in the first essay of *The Federalist*. Publius was the pen name chosen by Alexander Hamilton, who first conceived the project, and
shared by his two coauthors, John Jay and James Madison. Together,
they ultimately wrote eighty-five essays in defense of the Constitution.
Hamilton was not only the organizer of the project, but by far its leading contributor. Exhaustive modern scholarship credits him with fifty-
one essays, Madison with twenty-nine, and Jay (owing to poor health)
with only five.[1]

Hamilton opened that first essay by reminding his immediate audience, "The People of the State of New-York," of their remarkable
opportunity and responsibility:

1

It has been frequently remarked, that it seems to have been reserved to the people of this country, by their conduct and example, to decide the important question, whether societies of men are really capable or not, of establishing good government from reflection and choice, or whether they are forever destined to depend, for their political constitutions, on accident and force.

Here Hamilton echoed the concluding paragraph of John Adams's influential pamphlet, *Thoughts on Government,* which had summoned the revolutionaries of 1776 to begin writing new republican constitutions for the states. Then, too, Adams had exulted at being "sent into life at a time when the great lawgivers of antiquity would have wished to have lived." Like Adams, Hamilton believed that Americans enjoyed an opportunity known to few peoples in history. But over the intervening decade, the understanding of this opportunity had evolved in significant ways. For Adams, constitution-making was primarily a work for "lawgivers"—exceptional thinkers who could deliberate for the whole society. In 1776, there was no clear concept of allowing society itself to approve (or ratify) a constitution once the lawgivers had acted. By 1787, however, it was evident that a true republican constitution had to be both framed by a special deliberative body *and* then ratified by the people at large. For Hamilton, "reflection and choice" were thus required of both the drafters of the text and the people, or at least the relatively large pool of free white adult males entitled to elect delegates to the state ratification conventions.

In writing *The Federalist,* Hamilton and Madison enjoyed the great advantage of having participated in every phase of the movement for constitutional reform. Both had supported the revision of the Articles of Confederation, the original federal constitution, since serving together in the Continental Congress in the early 1780s. Both had been present at the Annapolis Convention of September 1786, where a dozen commissioners from five states issued the call for a general convention to gather in May 1787. Both took an active part in the deliberations at Philadelphia, although Hamilton's role was sharply circumscribed when his two New York colleagues went home in early July, leaving their state no longer legally represented. Now both expected to play commanding roles in overcoming potential Anti-Federalist majorities in their home states of New York and Virginia. And in the years to come, as their common purposes of the 1780s gave way to the partisan disputes of the 1790s, the two men fashioned rival interpretations of the Constitution whose adoption they once championed.[2]

All of these factors help to explain the commanding authority that *The Federalist* enjoys in modern interpretations of the Constitution. Its essays can be read for multiple purposes: as evidence of the concerns that prevailed at Philadelphia; as illustrations of the best arguments to be made for ratification; and for insight into the political philosophies of the two main authors. But the breadth of their project sets *The Federalist* apart from everything else published during the ratification debates. No rival text on either side of the question examined the Constitution so carefully, or made the case for strengthening the federal Union so powerfully. Together, the exceptional stature of the authors and the extent of their commentary place *The Federalist* in a category by itself.

For these reasons, we typically read *The Federalist* as the one American work that unequivocally belongs in the great canon of Western political theory—a work we can compare, with some caution, to the writings of Thomas Hobbes, John Locke, Montesquieu, or other luminaries. But locating *The Federalist* in its proper historical context requires understanding the nature of the political choice on which Americans were reflecting in 1787 and 1788.

THE ROAD TO PHILADELPHIA

The Continental Congress began preparing the Articles of Confederation in June 1776, as part of its final decision to declare independence from Britain. Disputes over the apportionment of representation and expenses among the states, and the control of western lands, delayed completion of the Articles until November 1777.[3] Its ratification was further delayed after a bloc of "landless" states with limited western boundaries insisted that Congress should have jurisdiction over the trans-Appalachian west, which other states claimed on the basis of their original royal charters. By the time the Articles took effect on March 1, 1781, many leaders believed that this first national constitution already required amendment. Under the Articles, Congress lacked independent sources of revenue. To raise the resources required to wage war, it had to rely on the states to carry out the recommendations and requisitions it regularly sent them. Although the states worked hard to comply, the demands of the war frequently outran their capacity to do so. To a newcomer to Congress like James Madison, its inability to compel the states to do their duty exposed a capital defect in the design of the Confederation. To Alexander Hamilton, who spent most of the war as aide-de-camp to General George Washington, the weakness of the Union was compounded by his countrymen's failure to recognize that a modern state and its army required a modern system of taxation, banking, and public finance.[4]

Any amendment to the Articles, however, required the consent of all thirteen state legislatures, and this proved impossible to achieve. The first proposed amendment, to allow Congress to collect an impost (or duty) on imported goods, was lost when it was rejected by the small state of Rhode Island. After American independence was finally recognized in April 1783 by the Treaty of Paris, Congress proposed other amendments requesting independent sources of revenue and authority to regulate foreign commerce. But these met the same fate. By 1786 it seemed evident that the rule of unanimity would doom any amendment. Congress itself had sunk so low in the public esteem that any amendment it proposed would be tainted at the source.

In January 1786, the Virginia legislature sought to break this impasse by calling for a general convention to discuss vesting Congress with authority to regulate commerce. The initial response gave cause for optimism: Eight states appointed deputies to go to the meeting at Annapolis. When the appointed time came in September, however, only a dozen commissioners from five states appeared, too few to act. Yet the commissioners present were a respectable lot. In addition to Madison and Hamilton, they included John Dickinson, the leading drafter of the Confederation; Edmund Randolph, soon to be elected governor of Virginia; and Abraham Clark, a veteran leader from New Jersey. Seizing on a clause in the commission of the New Jersey delegates, the Annapolis Convention called for a general convention to revise the Confederation to meet at Philadelphia in May.[5] Madison returned to Virginia and set out to initiate this process by convincing the state legislature to issue a formal invitation to the other states. Congress hesitantly added its own endorsement in February 1787, although doing so meant that it was approving a procedure unknown to the Articles of Confederation. The outbreak of Shays' Rebellion in Massachusetts, a protest by overtaxed and debt-burdened farmers against the state's conservative policies of taxation, added new urgency to the meeting. By early spring every state but intractable Rhode Island had appointed delegates.

Agreement that a convention should meet, however, did not establish any consensus on what it would do once assembled. By the winter of 1787, three sets of issues were converging in the thinking of leaders like Madison, Hamilton, and John Jay (then serving as secretary for foreign affairs) to shape the general agenda for the Convention.

The first and most obvious involved the familiar criticisms of the Confederation. Without its own sources of revenue, Congress could barely support a national government. It could not maintain adequate troops on the frontier, where land cessions from the states had led to the establishment of a national domain above the Ohio River that it wished to open for settlement. Without authority to regulate commerce, it could not restrict the flood of British goods into American harbors, to the detriment of American merchants and artisans, or pressure Britain to open valuable West Indian markets to American ships. Without a clear basis for the supremacy of national acts, it could not compel the states to abide by key provisions of the Treaty of Paris, thereby losing diplomatic leverage to induce Britain to surrender its posts along the northern frontier, as the treaty obliged it to do. Under such an "imbecile" form of union, how much longer could Congress survive as a working government?

But the Union faced a second set of threats. Even if Congress had the resources to carry out its basic responsibilities, it was becoming an open question whether Americans shared enough interests in common to remain a single nation. With the war over and independence secure, each state could regard itself as a sovereign, autonomous polity. Moreover, there was reason to fear that the Union could devolve into two or three regional confederacies. This was especially the case when Secretary Jay's willingness to yield American rights to navigate the Mississippi River in exchange for a commercial treaty with Spain produced a stark sectional cleavage in Congress. The eight northernmost states strongly favored securing a treaty, but to the five states from Maryland southward, it seemed far more important to further the expansion of American settlement in the trans-Appalachian interior. This division added new urgency to the cause of constitutional reform, because it implied that the Union could collapse sooner rather than later if the ills afflicting Congress went untreated.

Beyond these national issues, however, some leaders felt that the Convention should also address the character of republican government within the states. By 1780, all the states but Connecticut and Rhode Island had adopted new constitutions of government, firmly grounded in republican principles. But the performance of these new governments during the war and after, coupled with popular dissatisfaction with their decisions and policies, raised troubling questions about both the stability of institutions and the political virtue of their citizens. One could blame the state constitutions for making government too responsive to the people, or the people for demanding too much of their representatives, or representatives for acting too hastily and unthinkingly. But wherever blame fell (and there was plenty to go around), to someone like Madison it seemed evident that the project of constitutional reform should address the problems of the state governments as well as Congress.[6]

The experience of the states was relevant in one other respect. Under the Articles, the first federal government was highly anomalous. As a unicameral deliberative assembly, it resembled a legislature, but its principal tasks of conducting war and diplomacy made it seem more like an executive body. Congress had created both executive departments and a small judiciary (for admiralty matters), but these operated as subordinate agencies lacking independent constitutional status. Many observers believed that the Union had to be reconstituted as a normal government in the full sense of the received doctrine of separation of powers, with a bicameral legislature, and independent executive and judicial departments. The closest examples of what such a government should look like were to be found in the states. And this meant that the occasion for reforming the national government in 1787 could draw a host of lessons from the republican constitutions of government the states had established since 1776.

THE AUTHORS

No one was better prepared to draw these lessons than the three coauthors of *The Federalist*. Together, their experiences touched on all of the issues and problems just described, and in ways that complemented each other almost perfectly.[7]

Alexander Hamilton, the youngest, was born on January 11, 1757, on the island of Nevis in the West Indies, the out-of-wedlock son of Rachel Faucett, the estranged wife of John Michael Levine, and James Hamilton, who abandoned Rachel before her death in 1768 left Hamilton an orphan. In 1772 he made his way to New York, where he enrolled at King's College (now Columbia University). There he published his first political work, a pamphlet defending the First Continental Congress of 1774 against loyalist attacks. In 1776, he joined the Continental Army as a captain of artillery, and in 1777 became aide-de-camp to its commander, George Washington. The relation was close but sometimes strained, and a spat between the two men in 1781 spurred Hamilton to request a combat assignment that allowed him to lead the final assault at Yorktown, the siege that effectively delivered victory to the Americans. After leaving the army, Hamilton served in the Continental Congress in 1782 and 1783, where he supported the controversial efforts of Superintendent of Finance Robert Morris to secure permanent revenues for Congress. Hamilton then pursued a profitable legal practice in New York City. His entrance into the city's elite was boosted by his marriage in 1780 to Elizabeth Schuyler, daughter of General Philip Schuyler, the scion of one of the state's most prominent families. In 1784 Hamilton successfully argued the case of *Rutgers v. Waddington,* often cited as one of the key decisions that laid a foundation for the emerging practice of *judicial review* — the doctrine that would enable courts to overturn legislative acts that violate constitutional norms.

Three themes dominated Hamilton's approach to politics. The first, which has fascinated his biographers, was his deep personal ambition and self-conscious desire for fame and glory.[8] That ambition was manifest not only in his bravery in battle, but also in his distinctive understanding of the importance of the executive, the one branch of government where personal ambition could shine with the greatest luster. The second theme was rooted in his wartime experience. Like so many of his fellow officers, Hamilton was angered by the joint failure of Congress and the states to keep the Continental Army adequately manned and supplied. In their view, the war had repeatedly demonstrated that a federal system that divided responsibility between the Union and the states exposed the army to as great a risk from inefficient government as from the maneuvers of the enemy. What distinguished Hamilton from his fellow officers was not any difference in attitude in this respect, but rather his interest in the mysteries of public finance, a subject he took some care to study even during the war.

To study public finance in the eighteenth century meant observing the workings of the British state — the very government Americans had just repudiated. Many Americans regarded the institutions and practices that Britain had developed since 1689 to finance war in Europe and its empire overseas as political anathema. These innovations, including the creation of a substantial public debt, had enabled the ministers of the crown to use the techniques of political influence and patronage to control Parliament, thereby sapping the great principle of parliamentary supremacy that the Glorious Revolution of 1688–1689 had supposedly established. Most Americans saw the rise of executive power in Britain since 1689, and the modern state it managed, as ominous developments.[9]

Hamilton, however, viewed these developments sympathetically and wanted to understand how they worked. Although he was as familiar as anyone with the principles of republican government that Americans had espoused since 1776, his own interests and priorities lay elsewhere. Hamilton was less a constitutionalist than a state-builder. He was less concerned, that is, with achieving the desired balance among institutions of government in order to preserve the rights of citizens than with ensuring that those institutions could protect the nation against whatever challenges it faced. Those challenges, he believed, were more likely to come from enemies abroad than would-be tyrants at home. Hamilton was perhaps the one political leader of his generation who secretly agreed with the famous couplet of Alexander Pope:

> For forms of government let fools contest,
> That which is best administered is best.

Administration was synonymous with execution, and Hamilton's grasp of the essential importance and advantages of executive power also distinguished him from his contemporaries.

It certainly distinguished him from James Madison, whose ideas of executive power remained tentative even as he prepared for the Federal Convention—and who strongly opposed Hamilton's efforts to consolidate the authority of the executive branch after 1789. Nor did the contrasts between the two men stop there. Hamilton's driven ambition reflected, in part, his checkered background; he was the "bastard brat of a Scots pedlar," as John Adams famously declared. The Madison family also claimed humble origins—the immigrant founder was a ship's carpenter—but Hamilton's coauthor was the eldest son of the largest landowner in Orange County, Virginia. He was born six years before Hamilton, on March 16, 1751, and educated at the College of New Jersey (now Princeton University), where he took his degree in 1771 and then stayed on to study ancient Hebrew and Greek. Back home after 1772, Madison fretted about his health, his lack of vocation, and his rustic isolation. But then the outbreak of the Revolution gave him a political vocation, just as it steered Hamilton into the army. Madison was soon drawn into politics, first as a delegate to the provincial convention that wrote the state constitution and to the new state assembly, then as a member of the governor's advisory council. In 1780 he began three and a half years of uninterrupted service in the Continental Congress, returning home only when the term-limits provision of the Articles of Confederation forced him to do so. He was quickly elected to the state legislature, where he became the dominant figure.[10]

Madison's approach to politics had different emphases from Hamilton's. As a member of Congress in the early 1780s, he was intent on giving Congress every power it needed to direct the war effectively, even recommending that Congress be allowed to use armed force against recalcitrant states. Yet he also protected Virginia's key interests, especially on the sensitive issue of the cession of its western land claims to Congress. As a state legislator, he struggled to persuade his colleagues to give Congress the support it deserved, yet he also grappled with the parochial loyalties and interests that usually mark state politics. Privately, Madison judged the failings of the assemblymen as harshly as Hamilton and his fellow officers would have done. But rather than transfer decisive power to the executive, as Hamilton preferred, Madison hoped to improve the quality of legislative deliberation at every level of government.

It was this absorption in the processes of deliberation and lawmaking that turned his attention to the problem of constitutional design. In the republican governments to which Americans were dedicated, he realized, the legislature would "necessarily predominate"; but if left unchecked, it would also attempt to draw "all power into its impetuous vortex."[11] The challenge of republican constitutionalism, Madison came to think, was to encourage legislatures to act more responsibly and less impetuously, while also enabling the weaker departments of the executive and judiciary to withstand legislative "encroachments."

Madison's constitutional concerns also reflected his dual career as congressman and state lawmaker. Like Hamilton, his experiences convinced him that the principal challenge was to correct the imbalance between the Union and the states in favor of the national government. Yet unlike the immigrant Hamilton, who made New York his home as a matter of convenience, Madison's loyalty to Virginia was born and bred in the bone. However much he wanted to strengthen the Union at the expense of the states, he understood that much of the daily business of government would remain a responsibility of the latter. And this sensitivity to the residual authority of the states was compounded by his pained awareness that the security and prosperity of his native region depended on its ability to control the law of slavery. Madison detested slavery on moral grounds, but like his southern countrymen, he could not imagine how their region could survive without it.[12]

To a modern reader, Madison's fatalist toleration of slavery is a terrible blot on his otherwise liberal convictions, but it should not obscure one other crucial facet of his political philosophy. From his youth, Madison was passionately committed to the principle of freedom of conscience, and this in turn evolved into a strikingly modern, even libertarian emphasis on the importance of protecting individual and minority rights against domination by the community. In the eighteenth century, this was still a novel conception. In the Anglo-American tradition, the more orthodox view was that the problem of rights was to protect the entire community—the people at large—against the potential tyranny of the monarchy. But in a republic, Madison realized, the great problem henceforth would be to protect individuals and minorities against the popular majorities who would be the real sources of power.[13]

John Jay, the oldest of the three contributors, was descended from one of the groups that had experienced the worst of the religious persecutions that wracked Europe after the Reformation. His ancestors were Huguenots, French Protestants who had been slaughtered by the thousands during the civil wars of the sixteenth century. Like Hamilton, Jay was a graduate of King's College and a New York City lawyer, but his road to revolution differed from that of his two younger collaborators. For Hamilton and Madison, the choice in 1774 was easy: They were young men, and everyone around them was supporting "the common cause" of resistance against the despotic acts of crown and Parliament. But Jay had entered resistance politics earlier, at a time when the logic and the stakes of defying Britain were less apparent.

Jay in fact was one of a key group of moderate leaders from the middle states (New York, Pennsylvania, New Jersey, Delaware, and Maryland). These men were not ideologues like Samuel Adams of Massachusetts or Richard Henry Lee of Virginia, who chanted the principles of Anglo-American liberty almost as a mantra, and who found unusual personal fulfillment in political life itself. Rather, they were men of affairs and business who knew how to weigh risks and balance potential benefits and losses. As a delegate to the First and Second Continental Congresses, Jay resisted independence until the British ministry's refusal to negotiate seriously with the colonies left no alternative. He was also a major author of the New York State Constitution of 1777, a more avowedly conservative document than most of the other charters drafted the previous year.

After serving as president of Congress in 1779, Jay accepted a commission as minister to Spain. This proved a frustrating and discouraging assignment. But Congress also added Jay to its peace commission, whose other active members were Benjamin Franklin and John Adams. In the negotiations that began in earnest in 1782, Jay took a leading role in persuading Franklin, the senior diplomat, that the American commissioners had to negotiate independently with Britain and not play the docile partner to their ally, France.

Following his return to America in 1784, Congress made Jay its secretary for foreign affairs. Here his handling of the negotiations over the Mississippi River arguably contributed to the urgency of constitutional reform by exacerbating sectional tensions within Congress, but his experience was noteworthy in another respect. The experience of watching Congress supervise foreign affairs convinced Jay that the national government would operate far more effectively if its various powers were divided among different institutions, rather than concentrated in a unicameral Congress. Yet even as the states were appointing their delegations to the Federal Convention, Jay doubted that the meeting would prove a success. "I do not promise much further immediate Good from the measure," he wrote John Adams in February, "than that it will tend to approximate the public Mind to the Changes which ought to take place."[14]

THE FEDERAL CONVENTION

Madison had his doubts, too, but he was intent on making sure that the Convention succeeded. One key step was to persuade a reluctant George Washington that his charismatic, dignified presence was essential.[15] But Madison's preparations for Philadelphia went further. In effect, this was the great occasion for which he had been readying himself since 1780. As a veteran legislator and leading advocate of constitutional reform, he understood the advantages to be gained by attempting to set an agenda for the Convention's deliberations. A year earlier, he had begun a systematic course of reading in the history of other confederacies, relying on several trunks of books that Thomas Jefferson had sent him from Paris. Now, back in Congress in early 1787, Madison drew on both this material and his own experience to frame that agenda.[16]

Madison's program began by recognizing that any federal system based on the voluntary compliance of the states with national measures was inherently defective. That was the lesson taught by the experience of the past decade, but that could also be confirmed by considering the divergent interests of the states, the likelihood that state-based politicians would advance their own ambitions by opposing national measures, and the mutual suspicions that states would naturally harbor about each other. It followed that the Union had to be allowed to act directly upon the American people—not the states—by enacting, executing, and adjudicating its own laws. This in turn required reconstituting the Union as a government in the full sense of the term, with distinct and independent legislative, executive, and judicial branches.[17]

In conceiving how these national institutions would be constructed, Madison pondered the defects of the state constitutions written since independence. In his view, these governments suffered from two major flaws. First, their legislatures were enacting too many unwise laws, some in response to the clamor of their constituents, some infringing the just rights of different groups of citizens, and many that merited more careful deliberation and drafting. More thought had to be given to the problem of preventing unwise and unjust legislation. Second, legislatures were consolidating their power over the two subordinate branches of the executive and judiciary, which were actually responsible for ensuring that laws were carried out effectively and justly. Ways had to be found, Madison concluded, to enable these "weaker" departments to resist the "encroachments" of the legislature.

The experience of the states thus provided an experimental laboratory from which to draw lessons about the design of national institutions. But Madison further believed that the reconstitution of the Union could also provide solutions for problems of internal governance within the states. In his view, the new Congress should be armed with a *negative* (or veto) over state legislation. Such a power would prevent the states from adopting measures that sought to obstruct national acts. But it would also enable the national government to intervene within the states to thwart unjust laws violating the essential rights and interests of minorities.[18]

Madison's strategy for Philadelphia had one other critical element. A Congress that would make law for the American people had to be bicameral, and in apportioning seats in *both* houses, Madison firmly believed, a rule based on population and perhaps wealth had to replace the one state, one vote rule under which the Continental Congress had operated since 1774. Any rule that allowed the states to retain an equal vote even in one house would be fundamentally unjust. Madison knew that the small states would resist such a change, but they would ultimately have to yield, he believed, if the more populous states banded together.

These ideas shaped the plan that the Virginia delegates drafted while they waited for a quorum of the other delegations to be reached, as it finally was, two weeks late.[19] On May 29, Governor Edmund Randolph opened the deliberations by reading the Virginia Plan, which the Convention debated over the next fortnight. The demand for proportional representation in both houses quickly became the great sticking point. A few delegates, led by John Dickinson of Delaware, suggested deferring any discussion of representation until agreement was reached on the powers the national government should exercise. But Madison and his allies insisted that representation had to be resolved first because the large states would be unwilling to grant the national government significant powers if the small states retained their unjust advantage.

In mid-June, the small states counterattacked with the New Jersey Plan, giving fewer powers to a unicameral Congress in which the states would retain their equal vote. Hamilton responded with his famous speech of June 18, introducing his own plan, which, by design or not, made the Virginia Plan seem moderate in comparison. (Or as Hamilton supposedly said, next to the Articles of Confederation the Virginia Plan was *pork still, with a little change of the sauce.*) Speaking in a distinctly unrepublican idiom, Hamilton praised the key roles of the House of Lords and the monarchy in preserving the British constitution, and then went on to list the five key "principles necessary for the support of Government," which he described as

I   Interest to Support it
II Opinion of Utility & necessity
III Habitual sense of obligation
IV Force
V   Influence

This was the analysis of a cold realist, assessing the habits, attitudes, and mechanisms of maintaining loyalty to government.[20]

The next day, Madison drew on his pre-Convention analyses of the "vices of the political system of the U. States" to explain why the New Jersey Plan would be completely inadequate to the exigencies of the Union. After he spoke, the Convention promptly rejected the New Jersey Plan. But the delegates now confronted the stalemate over representation that threatened to bring the meeting to a halt. Over the next four weeks, the large-state bloc tried to argue the small states into submission, insisting that rules of proportional representation had to apply to both houses. Following arguments laid down by Madison, they told the small states that they had nothing to fear, because the interests of the more populous states were so divergent that their representatives could never coalesce to dominate the government. But the small-state leaders held their ground, replying that they could never accept a rule that left them at the mercy of the large states. At the same time, the delegates wrestled with the equally vexing question of deciding whether the southern states should be allowed to count their slaves in the allocation of seats in the House of Representatives.

This question proved easier to compromise than the allocation of votes in the Senate. Although northern delegates were *morally* offended by the idea of counting slaves who could never be regarded as citizens in any sense of the term, they grudgingly agreed that the contribution that slaves made to the national economy and the minority status of the South provided an adequate *political* justification for the eventual rule of counting slaves as three-fifths of free persons. But the problem of representing states as states was not amenable to compromise. In the climactic vote of July 16, the small states carried the day, securing equal representation of the states in the Senate, but by the narrowest margin possible: five states to four, with Massachusetts, a large state, divided (and therefore effectively losing its vote).

This result stunned the large-state leaders. Previously the small states had occasionally threatened to bolt the Convention if they did not get their way; now some of the large-state delegates indicated they were not prepared to go on. Within a day or two, however, passions cooled enough for debate to proceed. One early casualty of the decision of July 16 was Madison's pet scheme for a congressional negative on state laws, replaced by an initially weak version of the provision that eventually evolved into the Supremacy Clause of the Constitution.

In late July the delegates shifted their attention to an issue they had previously considered only briefly: the election of the executive. Here the framers were genuinely puzzled to imagine how a strong executive—the "monarchical" branch of government—could be safely reconstituted on republican principles. The more the delegates discussed the alternative modes of election—by the people, the Congress, or an independent body of electors—the more perplexed they grew. Election by the people seemed a doubtful method, not because the framers feared the people would be swayed by demagogues, but rather because it was difficult to imagine how the voters could ever make an effective choice among a number of provincial candidates in a highly decentralized polity like the United States. Election by Congress would solve that problem, because its members would have the best information about suitable candidates. But if one wished to make the executive independent of Congress, the president would have to be elected for a single lengthy term. Many delegates, including Hamilton, strongly believed that the promise of reelection would work to inspire the best ambitions in officeholders; others worried that giving the president a lengthy term would turn the presidency into a proto-type for monarchy. The objection to vesting the choice in a set of elec-tors was that no one had a good idea who these electors would be. On balance, congressional election for a single term of seven years seemed the least problematic choice, but the delegates' agreement on this point was tenuous.

In late July, the Convention took a ten-day recess while a committee of detail converted the resolutions adopted thus far into a working draft of a constitution. The remaining six weeks of deliberation (August 6–September 17) produced critical decisions in three main areas.

First, the Convention replaced the open-ended grant of legislative authority in the Virginia Plan with a set of specific enumerated pow-ers, buttressed by a clause enabling Congress to "make all laws which shall be necessary and proper for carrying into Execution the foregoing Powers." These powers included a general authority over taxation and interstate and foreign commerce, the two defects in the Confederation repeatedly discussed since 1780, as well as extensive powers over war-making. It is possible that the broad statement of legislative power in the Virginia Plan had been meant to serve only as a placeholder pend-ing resolution of the dispute over representation, but in any case, the enumeration of specific legislative powers in Article I made explicit the new understanding that a constitution was itself a mechanism whereby a sovereign people granted to government the authority to undertake certain tasks and duties in their behalf. The act of delegat-ing power had become a means of limiting it as well.

Second, the delegates gradually developed a new and powerful con-ception of the supremacy of national law, and in the process recog-nized that the judiciary would henceforth play a major role in policing the boundary separating the jurisdictions of the national and state governments. The first statement of this theory, initially endorsed in mid-July, had been a weak one. But in August the Convention strengthened it so that in its final version it declared that

> This Constitution, and the Laws of the United States which shall be made in Pursuance thereof; and all Treaties made, or which shall be made, under the Authority of the United States, shall be the supreme Law of the Land; and the Judges in every State shall be bound thereby, any Thing in the Constitution or Laws of any State to the Contrary notwithstanding.

State judges were explicitly bound to enforce federal law; national judges were implicitly expected to do so. And to ensure the legal supremacy of the Constitution, the framers devised a special scheme of ratification by popularly elected conventions, so that its authority could be said to rest on a direct grant from the sovereign people.

Third, in late August and early September, a reaction set in against earlier decisions that seemed to make the Senate the most powerful institution in the new government, and the presidency emerged as the net beneficiary of this reaction. The source of this shift remains unclear. In part it may have reflected the large states' lingering resentment of the equal state vote; in part, too, it may have reflected doubts that a body elected by the state legislatures would be as independent as hoped. Whatever the reason, these key decisions seemingly strengthened the executive at the expense of the Senate. The power to make treaties and to appoint judges, ambassadors, and other major officials, which had previously been lodged in the Senate alone, was now given to the president, acting with the advice and consent of the Senate.

Meanwhile, after the Convention had again deadlocked over the mode of presidential election, the same committee revived the idea of an appointment by special electors, with the Senate making the final choice should the electors fail to reach a majority. The president would serve for four years, and be eligible for reelection—exactly the incentive to good behavior that Hamilton desired. What was objectionable about this proposal was not the use of electors but the role of the Senate. Many delegates doubted that the electors, meeting in their separate states, would ever produce a majority, which was what made a scheme of contingent election necessary. But if that power was vested in the Senate, as the committee proposed, how would the president act with the independence the framers desired? It took three days of debate for the framers to stumble on a solution, placing the final power of election in the House of Representatives, voting by states. This preserved the political compromise in which the large states would have the advantage in the electoral stage, because each state would have the same number of electors as its representatives and senators combined, but they would lose that advantage whenever a contingent election proved necessary.

The acceptance of this formula reveals an important shift in the mood of the Convention. In July, the narrow decision giving each state an equal vote in the Senate had been a victory for one side and a defeat for the other. Now the balance struck between proportional representation in the House and equal state representation in the Senate could be regarded as a compromise to be replicated in the election of the president. A mutual sense of having compromised on these and other matters bound virtually all of the forty-two delegates still present as the Convention prepared to adjourn in mid-September. Nearly four months of deliberation had forged a commitment to support the completed Constitution, regardless of the defeats the delegates had incurred and the doubts they still harbored on particular points. Only three delegates refused to add their signatures to the final text: George Mason and Edmund Randolph of Virginia, and Elbridge Gerry of Massachusetts.

Madison, the leading architect of the Convention, was at first less than enthused about its results. Writing to Jefferson shortly before the Convention adjourned, he ventured to "hazard an opinion" that the Constitution "will neither effectually *answer* its *national object* nor prevent the local *mischiefs* which every where *excite disgusts* ag[ain]st the *state governments.*" Six weeks later, Madison explained this harsh judgment by providing Jefferson with an elaborate defense of his proposed negative on state laws, incorporating many of the ideas about the factious nature of republican politics that would reappear in *Federalist* 10 a month later. It is clear from this letter that Madison found the Constitution inadequate in one critical respect: The national government would still lack the power to prevent the states from enacting unwise and unjust legislation that would threaten both the supremacy of national law and the just rights of individuals and minorities within the states.[21]

Hamilton, too, wrote an equally revealing memorandum shortly after the Convention, a set of "Conjectures about the New Constitution." Its title notwithstanding, this was no analysis of the merits of the Constitution, but rather a candid political assessment of the prospects for ratification. "The present appearances and all other circumstances considered," Hamilton predicted, "the probability seems to be on the side of its adoption," but "there will be nothing astonishing in the Contrary" result coming to pass. Should the Constitution be ratified, Hamilton further observed, General Washington would likely be the first president, and that controlling political fact might "enable the government to acquire more consistency than the Constitution seems to promise for so great a Country." Then the national government might in turn gain decisive advantages over the states, even perhaps to the point of "dividing the larger states into smaller districts," and thereby weakening the competitive rivalry between them. Otherwise, Hamilton bleakly observed, the "contests about the boundaries of power" in the federal system might lead to "a dissolution of the Union. This after all seems to be the most likely result."[22]

Thus neither of the two leading authors of *The Federalist* left Philadelphia convinced that the Constitution would prove adequate to the exigencies of the Union, much less cure all the vices of the American political system. But neither did they have the luxury of pursuing any course other than wholesale support for its ratification. Politics being the art of the possible, they understood that the Federalist forces they expected to command would have to proceed as if there was no alternative to a prompt and unequivocal ratification. In joining together as Publius, they would have to make the best case possible for ratification; but in doing so, they could also look for ways and opportunities to place their own ideas before the American public.

THE ANTI-FEDERALIST CRITIQUE
OF THE CONSTITUTION

Delegates from twelve states signed the completed Constitution on September 17, 1787. Hamilton signed alone for New York, which had not been legally represented since the departure in July of his colleagues John Lansing and Robert Yates.[23] Also conspicuous by its absence was Rhode Island, which had not even sent a delegation. But its absence had a liberating effect. A state that refused to attend the Convention was unlikely to approve its proceedings, and that in turn demonstrated the need to circumvent the rule that amendments to the Confederation receive approval from all thirteen states. Moreover, the wisdom of asking the state legislatures to judge a Constitution that would impose new limits on their authority also seemed doubtful.

Rather than abide by these rules, the Convention thus proposed that the Constitution would be adopted when approved by popularly elected conventions in nine states. Expediency alone might have persuaded the framers to adopt this scheme. But this proposal rested on deeper considerations. Appealing to the direct authority of the people offered one way to answer the predictable charge that the Convention had acted improperly, even illegally, by scrapping the Articles of Confederation entirely and adopting a wholly new Constitution. If the people were the ultimate source of all authority, a direct expression of their will would supersede the existing authority of the Confederation, the state legislatures, and even the state constitutions. Equally important, grounding the Constitution in a direct expression of popular sovereignty would provide a legal foundation for the binding authority that the Supremacy Clause claimed.

The judgment the people could express would be powerful, but in one critical sense, also limited: The only action the state conventions could take was to approve or reject the Constitution in its entirety, not adopt some articles while balking at others. Nor could they suspend their decision while waiting for future amendments, because that would open the Constitution to a potentially endless process of revision as unmediated amendments made their way from state to state. In effect, the people, through their delegates, could speak with a loud voice, but their delegates could utter only one of two words: "aye" or "nay."[24]

The same restrictions, however, did not apply to the popular debate that would precede the state conventions. Here Americans were free to say whatever they wanted: to contrast the promise of vigorous national government with the "imbecility" of the Continental Congress, or to identify all those ominous provisions that seemed designed to consolidate all real power in a distant national capital while the more responsive governments of the states were left to wither away. It took a few days for copies of the Constitution to appear in the press, but a vigorous debate soon began, not only in newspapers and pamphlets, but also in the taverns, coffeehouses, public squares, churches, and everywhere else citizens exchanged their views.

In this debate, the Anti-Federalist opponents of the Constitution were at an initial disadvantage. The press tended to favor ratification, and Anti-Federalists complained that their views were not given the attention they deserved.[25] Anti-Federalists also suffered from having to counter the prestige of the Convention. Federalists repeatedly cited the presence of Benjamin Franklin and George Washington at Philadelphia as proof of the Convention's benevolent motives. By contrast, the handful of delegates who supported the Anti-Federalist cause—most notably George Mason of Virginia, Luther Martin of Maryland, and Elbridge Gerry of Massachusetts—found themselves subjected to abuse for lacking the good sense to go along with their more numerous colleagues. Anti-Federalists suffered other disadvantages. Criticism of the Constitution could easily be equated with support for the Articles of Confederation, which few wished to offer. Perhaps most important, the Anti-Federalists' tendency to find calamitous dangers lurking in seemingly reasonable and innocuous clauses of the Constitution made their dire warnings easy to lampoon.

For their part, Federalists would have been happy to rest their defense of the Constitution on the prestige and disciplined engagement of the delegates, and on the manifest contrast between the feeble condition of the Confederation and the vigor the Constitution promised to provide. Why bother to descend to the mundane details of the actual document when one could hold the high ground of generality?

Anti-Federalists would not allow their opponents this luxury. Many of their wilder charges reflected what Richard Hofstadter once called "the paranoid style" in American politics.[26] But others were well grounded in essential tenets of American political ideology, often echoing key ideas that had carried the colonists from resistance to revolution only a decade earlier.[27] And as the best Anti-Federalist writers pushed these ideas forward, Federalists had no choice but to respond by defending the Constitution in its details and on its merits.

The central Anti-Federalist charge was that adoption of the Constitution would lead to the *consolidation* of all effective power in the national government. As far as Anti-Federalists were concerned, *they* were the true federalists for wanting to preserve the autonomy of the states, and the Federalists and Publius had committed rhetorical burglary by appropriating that name for their own ends. In the Anti-Federalist view, the states would either be swallowed by the federal leviathan, or else survive as hollow jurisdictions performing trivial functions. Congress would use its general taxing authority to exhaust all the productive sources of revenue, leaving the states scrambling for funds while trying to collect the least popular taxes. The Necessary and Proper Clause would enable Congress to extend its effective legislative jurisdiction to any object it chose, making the enumeration of powers a merely nominal limitation. The Supremacy Clause would similarly operate to sweep aside any resistance to national law that the states might mount. In the hands of an ambitious, grasping national legislature, these provisions alone would reduce the states to shells of their former authority. And should the states attempt to resist, the national government's command of a "standing army" and its oversight of the state militia would give it a monopoly of coercive power.

To demonstrate how and why the proposed government would exploit these clauses and others, Anti-Federalists evoked fears that had figured prominently in Anglo-American politics since the seventeenth century. Sounding much like the revolutionaries of 1776, they warned that the innate human desire for power would drive officeholders in every branch of the new government to aggrandize their authority, at the expense of the residual authority of the states and the just rights of their citizens. Presidents would either aspire to become potential monarchs or else serve as the tools of an "aristocratic" Senate vested with an improper blend of legislative, executive, and (through the trial of impeachments) judicial powers, and insulated from effective political control through the six-year terms members would serve. The House of Representatives, the one popularly elected branch of government, would forfeit its historic role as the safeguard of the people's rights and interests. Elected from districts far larger than the individual towns and counties that selected state legislators, representatives would lack the sympathy and knowledge required to serve their constituents. Nor would the courts do any better. The Constitution's provisions for trial by jury, a great "bulwark" of civil liberty, seemed especially weak, while a judiciary protected by life tenure would enlarge its own authority by interpreting congressional powers broadly. And the framers' failure to adopt a bill of rights, defining the legitimate boundaries of public authority, meant that the people themselves would never know when the national government was abusing its prescribed powers.

Inspired by assumptions and fears like these, Anti-Federalists viewed the Constitution as an invitation to tyranny, punctuated with loopholes that defied the received wisdom of the age. But this wisdom embraced two deeper beliefs that set a broader framework for debate. Both were associated with the writings of the Baron de Montesquieu, whose major work of political theory, *The Spirit of the Laws* (1748), was enormously popular in both Britain and America.

On the first of these positions—the optimal size of a republic—Montesquieu was perhaps more a synthesizer than an original theorist. Anyone well versed in history—as any learned person would then have been—knew that the record of republican government was a depressing story of brief moments of enthusiasm and glory followed by descents into factious feuding and the eventual restoration of authoritarian rule: monarchy if lucky, tyranny if not. With this record, the republican form of government was thought to be always fragile, tenuous, and prone to decay. For republics to survive at all, they were best confined to small, homogeneous communities—certainly no larger than any one of the American states, and arguably smaller than most of them—whose citizens would share similar interests and a strong measure of civic virtue, which meant a willingness to subordinate private interest to public good. For citizens to acquire that virtue, and to participate intelligently in politics, they had to possess sufficient property, because without the independence that property made possible, they would only become the slavish tools of others. A republican citizen should be independent in mind, because he had to deliberate about the public good, but feel a deep loyalty to the community, including a willingness to bear arms in its defense rather than rely on mercenaries who could be as easily paid to subvert a government as to protect it.

Montesquieu's discussion of republican governments in *The Spirit of the Laws* served as an authoritative summary of these views, but his analysis of the other key position—the separation of powers—was more original. In Book 11, Montesquieu described a form of "moderate government" that would make the protection of "political liberty" its basic end. The only example of such a government in the modern world was Britain, which Montesquieu analyzed in chapter 6, "Of the constitution of England." He opened this discussion by redefining the idea of separation of powers, a concept that had first appeared in seventeenth-century England, but in a more primitive form. In his *Two Treatises of Government* (1689), for example, John Locke, the great English philosopher and political radical, had described three forms of power: legislative, ministerial (executive), and federative (relating to foreign affairs), collapsing judicial power into the executive.[28] Writing a half-century later, Montesquieu introduced the modern concept of the judiciary as a third, distinct department of government. "There can be no liberty," he warned, whenever any two forms of power (legislative, executive, judicial) were "united in the same person, or the same body of magistrates."[29] A well-constructed government "whose end is liberty" would maintain this essential separation.

Montesquieu's pronouncements loomed large in two critical respects. First, Americans had ardently identified themselves as republicans since 1776, when they began replacing their defunct colonial governments with new constitutions written in conformity with republican principles. Some states were small enough to meet his criteria for the extent of the republic, but it would take a leap of the imagination to agree that a republican government could operate over the large terrain that the settled United States already occupied, much less the greater expanse it would control as the population surged across the Appalachians. Countries that large were fit material for kingdoms or empires—but not republics.

Second, the state constitutions also subscribed to Montesquieu's general doctrine of separated powers. Not only had they recognized the judiciary as a distinct department, they also incorporated Montesquieu-like statements of the principle of separation in the declarations of rights that accompanied many of the new constitutions. The classic version appeared as Article XXX of the Massachusetts Declaration of Rights of

1780: "In the government of this Commonwealth, the legislative department shall never exercise the executive and judicial powers, or either of
them: The executive shall never exercise the legislative and judicial
powers, or either of them: The judicial shall never exercise the legislative and executive powers, or either of them: to the end it may be a government of laws and not of men."[30] The proposed Federal Constitution
violated this principle in several respects, but nowhere more so than in
the design of the Senate, which seemed to possess all three forms of
power. At Philadelphia, the Senate had become the particular object of
suspicion for George Mason, the non-signer from Virginia who had also
been the principal author of his state's constitution; and Mason's objections to the Constitution became a point of departure for the larger Anti-
Federalist critique.[31]

These two principles militated against the Constitution by raising
fundamental objections to the very notion of a national republic and
the specific institutions it would comprise. Privately, Federalists wondered why an authority like Montesquieu should still command deference. He was, after all, a nobleman of the old regime, however
enlightened his principles, and large swaths of *The Spirit of the Laws*
examined obscure historical events and the customs of other societies.
But he remained an authority to reckon with, the more so because his
ideas had been celebrated by the first constitutionalists of 1776. They
provided a theoretical foundation for the more pointed criticisms that
Anti-Federalist writers offered.

THE FEDERALIST RESPONSE AND THE RESPONSE OF *THE FEDERALIST*

The Anti-Federalist challenge to the Constitution thus worked at several levels. Some of it was couched in the wild charges that Madison
denounced in *Federalist* 46 as "more like the incoherent dreams of a
delirious jealousy, or the misjudged exaggerations of a counterfeit
zeal, than like the sober apprehensions of genuine patriotism." Other
charges, however, identified provisions that did raise genuine questions about the tenor of the new government, such as the adequacy
of its scale of representation, the concentration of power in the Senate,
or the omission of a bill of rights. Moreover, one delegate to the Convention, Luther Martin of Maryland, worked hard to puncture the
aura surrounding the framers by publishing a candid account of the
proceedings, even though doing so violated the delegates' pledge to

maintain the secrecy of their deliberations.[32] The Anti-Federalists had reason to complain that they were waging an uphill battle for attention, but their best writers raised objections trenchant enough to merit a serious response.

As Anti-Federalist criticisms mounted, Federalist writers were thus compelled to answer their opponents' better arguments. Federalists could not rely indefinitely on the prestige of Washington and Franklin, the earnest labors of the Convention, or rosy predictions of future prosperity. By far the most important Federalist response was the public speech that James Wilson gave on October 6, 1787, before an enthusiastic crowd outside Independence Hall in Philadelphia, where the Constitution had been written. The speech became controversial because Wilson defended the omission of a bill of rights on grounds that quickly proved vulnerable to criticism.[33] To provide protection for specific rights might actually be dangerous, Wilson warned, if such statements were wrongly interpreted to mean that some power to regulate the exercise of those rights had in fact been granted. Anti-Federalists were quick to note that the Constitution did indeed explicitly protect a few rights: Did that mean that a power to infringe those rights had not been granted? But equally important, Wilson's speech became a lightning rod of opposition because it appeared authoritative: Wilson had represented Pennsylvania at the Convention, and was the acknowledged leader of Pennsylvania Federalists as they prepared for the ratification convention that would meet in November. There, Federalists held a commanding majority and soon ratified the Constitution by a 2–1 margin.

Far different was the situation that Hamilton faced in neighboring New York. The New York legislature did not meet until January 1788, and it ultimately set late April for the election of delegates to the convention that would not gather at Poughkeepsie until June.[34] In conceiving the project of *The Federalist* in October, Hamilton could not have predicted the dates of either the elections or the convention. Nor did he have a reliable sense of public opinion outside New York City, where the Constitution seemed popular. But Hamilton did know that the Constitution would face vigorous opposition from Governor George Clinton and his supporters. That opposition went beyond abstract fears about the danger of a strong national government. Before 1783, Clinton had been a strong advocate of effective national government. With the state's capital, New York City, occupied by the British from 1776 until the war's end, he could take no other course. But disputes involving the state's eastern and western boundaries had soured New York's relations with Congress, in the process alienating Clinton's affections. Moreover, New York was one state that stood to benefit from the lack of national control over foreign and interstate commerce. British imports unloaded at its great harbor of New York City could be sold in a tristate area, enabling the state to collect customs duties from consumers in New Jersey and Connecticut as well as New York. As a matter of public policy, New York could afford to cast a cool, calculating eye on central authority.

Hamilton had these considerations in mind as he recruited Jay and Madison to join him as Publius. For one of the most striking features of *The Federalist* is that it presents itself first as a sustained brief for the value of the Union and only later as a comprehensive exposition of the Constitution. *The Federalist,* in other words, is both an argument about the necessity of national government in general, and a defense of the particular form of national government proposed by the framers at Philadelphia. The first thirty-six essays of Publius say virtually nothing about the actual institutions the Constitution would create, although in two distinct series of essays—24–29, devoted to issues of defense, and 30–36, devoted to taxation—Hamilton goes to some lengths to justify particular powers that government would exercise. Only with Madison's transitional essay, *Federalist* 37, did Publius shift attention to the work of the Convention and the details of the Constitution—and that essay first appeared on January 11, 1788. By then, five states had ratified the Constitution (Delaware, Georgia, New Jersey, Pennsylvania, and Connecticut) and a sixth convention, in Massachusetts, was getting under way.

How much care and foresight went into planning the division of authorial labor is not clear, but the results suggest a logic to the allocation of duties. Of the first thirty-six essays, Madison wrote only five (including the celebrated Tenth essay, and three essays summarizing the lessons he had drawn from a course of reading on the history of ancient and modern confederacies), and Jay four, before illness knocked him out of the rotation. Thus it was Hamilton, who perhaps had the most advanced conception of the uses to which the powers of the national government could be put, who wrote most of the essays defending the concept of a potent Union. With *Federalist* 37, however, Madison came to the fore, writing all but three of the next twenty-seven essays, which were devoted to examining the legislative powers of Congress, the balance of authority between the Union and the states, the critical discussion of the separation of powers in essays 47–51, and the political capacities and qualifications of the two houses of Congress. Since the mid-1780s, a fascination with the nature of legislative power and the need to improve its exercise had been the engine driving Madison's constitutional thinking, so it was fitting that the bulk of his essays as Publius addressed these concerns. With *Federalist* 64—a discussion of the treaty power and Jay's last contribution—the focus shifted to the executive and judicial branches, and so it was again appropriate that Hamilton wrote all the remaining essays. His understanding of the executive power was more sophisticated and less equivocal than Madison's, and as a leading member of the New York bar, he had already argued one of the key cases that scholars identify as a foundation for the emerging doctrine of judicial review.

In designing their rhetorical strategy, the authors directed their appeal to the moderate spectrum of public opinion: those who were inclined to support the Constitution but were troubled by some of the objections to its ratification, or those who were inclined to oppose it but might be open to persuasion if their objections were answered. There was no need to preach to either the "predetermined patron" of the Constitution or its "predetermined adversary," as Madison called them in *Federalist* 37. These moderate readers had to be willing not only to suspend their own opinions in the interest of hearing reasoned arguments, but also to recognize the real problems the country faced and the real difficulties the Convention had encountered in its deliberations. The appeal to moderation, however, did not preclude Publius from speaking as a partisan for one side, nor did it require respecting Anti-Federalist positions that deserved only disdain.

Moderation also meant balancing respect for received wisdom with openness to the possibility of innovation. In the best-known passages of *The Federalist,* this especially meant finding ways to deal with "the celebrated Montesquieu," the "great man" and "oracle" whose authority was regularly invoked to insist on the necessity of small republics and a rigid separation of powers. In *Federalist* 10, the text that scholars now regard as the classic statement of the general theory of the Constitution, Madison challenged Montesquieu's basic teaching about the size of republics. The liberty that Montesquieu wanted to secure, Madison argued, would be better protected in an extended republic embracing diverse interests than in a smaller society where a majority bent on injustice and misrule could more easily coalesce. In *Federalist* 47, Madison similarly tried to co-opt or neutralize Montesquieu's dictum about the separation of powers. If one asked how the Americans had actually applied their understanding of Montesquieu to the state constitutions, Madison argued, it would be seen that they nowhere adhered to the rigid division that a pure theory of separation would require.

The need to refute, qualify, or co-opt Montesquieu illustrates an important dimension of political argument. In any polity, there are always received sources of wisdom or standard ideas whose authority appears to be deeply entrenched, even axiomatic. Proponents of innovation will always have to discover some way to bend that authority to their ends; if they cannot adapt or co-opt it, they will have to explain why it is less relevant than it seems, or in the most extreme case, to prove why it is wrong. But those who truly are proponents of innovation, like the framers and Federalists of 1787–88, are also likely to have found new modes of reasoning and new ideas of their own. And being innovators, proud of their work, they will be eager to explain the sources of their creativity, to boast of how they have improved upon the wisdom of their predecessors. That impulse will beat all the more strongly among those who contrast new knowledge wrung from experience with purely theoretical writings. The purpose of neutralizing Montesquieu was to clear a space where creative political thinking could take place.

This confidence that creative political thinking could take place, that stock beliefs and authorities could be challenged, exposed a critical difference between the two sides. For Anti-Federalists, the science of politics comprised a fixed body of axioms and principles, tested and confirmed by the lessons of history. That science had produced pointed conclusions about the danger of innovation in government and the value of adhering to first principles. The powerful and the well-born were always looking for ways to aggrandize their power at the expense of the larger society; departures from settled ways of conducting affairs offered them opportunities to pursue their insidious ambitions.

By contrast, for Federalists in general and the authors of *The Federalist* in particular, the science of politics had become a science in the modern sense: a body of knowledge capable of improvement through the use of reason, deliberation, and experiment. There were lessons to be learned and applied from the experience of self-government. Modern generations had knowledge of politics unknown to the philosophers of classical antiquity and medieval Europe. The experience of creating written constitutions itself was an American invention, without known antecedents in history. So was the very definition of a constitution that Americans now used: a document embodying supreme law, adopted at a particular moment, through a process of deliberation. Or again, representation was regarded as a modern practice, unknown to the ancients, and poorly understood and often ineffective in the European societies where it functioned. There were new phenomena under the political sun, and to seek to improve institutions and perfect modes of governance was an honorable, not a treacherous, calling.

To say that Federalists and Publius saw themselves as advocating progress in politics is not to deny the conservative and even reactionary elements in their thought. From the vantage point of 1776, many of the innovations of the Constitution could be described as steps back from some of the ideals and enthusiasms of the first state constitutions. The proposed presidency represented a far more substantial form of executive power than any of the governorships of the states—even the relatively potent offices established in New York in 1777 and Massachusetts in 1780. The idea of an independent judiciary enforcing constitutional norms against the people's duly elected representatives would also have been regarded as suspect and problematic in 1776. Both aspects of the new Constitution can be accurately described as reactions against the general idea of legislative supremacy that had prevailed in 1776.

Yet the framers and Federalists were neither counterrevolutionaries nor reactionaries. They saw their task as one of preserving the American experiment in federalism, republicanism, and constitutionalism not from its sins but from its shortcomings. The content of their ideas may have changed, but not their commitment to the principle of republican government.

The challenge that the authors of *The Federalist* faced, then, was to reconcile the shifts in the balance of power between the nation and the states and between the legislature and the weaker departments of the executive and judiciary to the fundamental principles of republican government. Part of that explanation took place at the level of deep principle, most notably in the defense of the idea of an extended republic in *Federalist* 9 and 10 or the new approach to the separation of powers in *Federalist* 47–51. But the task of explanation also involved describing and justifying an array of particular provisions. Proving that a large republic was possible in theory was only a prelude to the more important task of explaining how it would safely operate in practice. That was where the heavy work of justifying the Constitution would really take place: not in the grand theory but in the prosaic details.

READING *THE FEDERALIST*

Publius cannot be read quite as we read Machiavelli or Hobbes or Locke. Even when we recall that *The Prince, Leviathan,* and the *Two Treatises* were responses to specific events—the crisis of the Florentine republic in the early sixteenth century, the English civil war of the 1640s, the Stuart lurch toward absolutism in the 1680s—we treat these works as exercises in political *philosophy,* imparting lessons or identifying problems of political morality and civic obligation that transcend any given historical moment. By contrast, *The Federalist* is irrevocably tied to the document whose adoption it urges. Although it, too, contains judgments that transcend its original context, we read it primarily for the evidence and insight it provides into the original intentions of the framers of the Constitution and the original understandings of its ratifiers. At bottom, it is sometimes suggested, *The Federalist* is best understood as a campaign document—perhaps even as propaganda.

Propaganda, however, is a loaded term. In its proper meaning, it describes the various techniques that modern governments have deployed to mobilize the uncritical support of their populations. Propaganda plays crudely on the emotions. It evokes stirring symbols of home and hearth, family and fatherland, workplace and battlefield, and crude caricatures of the enemy within and without: the secret subversive, the disloyal alien, the inhuman invader. Propaganda is a term that we routinely apply to the terrible dictatorships of Hitler and Mussolini, Stalin and Mao, as well as the campaigns that democratic governments in Britain and the United States launched to muster popular support for the two world wars of the twentieth century and the Cold War that followed.

The Federalist cannot be described as propaganda in this sense. It does not play crudely upon the emotions, or manipulate symbols in suggestive or simplistic ways. Quite the opposite: Publius repeatedly warns its readers of the danger that the human propensity to be ruled by passions poses to the rule of reason in government. *The Federalist* instead asks readers to weigh its arguments seriously, recalling always that the task of creating a constitution is an exercise in "reflection and choice." (It would be a strange kind of propaganda indeed that relied as much on nuance and complexity as the best *Federalist* essays in fact do.) *The Federalist* is simply one form of political speech, aimed, like all political speech, to persuade readers and listeners to support its positions. Read in this way, the difference between *The Federalist* and the great works of political philosophy diminishes. Their authors probably cared little about how later generations would read their works. Machiavelli, Hobbes, and Locke were as urgently concerned with persuading their first intended readers as were Hamilton and Madison.

But modern readers have several obvious advantages over the first readers. For one thing, we know who the authors were, and how the ideas expressed in their essays correspond to opinions they voiced at Philadelphia, in their correspondence, or even after the Constitution was ratified and the two leading authors faced off on opposite sides of the political-constitutional disputes of the 1790s. We can ask what is the difference between public and private speech; which is more authoritative or revealing—and why? Does it matter, for example, that Madison's famous argument that an extended national republic will provide greater security for individual rights does not explain how citizens will henceforth be protected against the potential abuse of their rights by the states—a subject he discussed at some length in a private letter to Jefferson written only four weeks before *Federalist* 10? Or again, what does it say about "the authority of Publius" that the first time it was cited in congressional debate—as early as June 1789—the author of the relevant essay, Hamilton, let it be known that he had since *"changed his mind"* on the matter in dispute (the power of the president to remove subordinate officials)?[35]

That, at least, is how a historian would read this text: by correlating it with other texts by the same authors, looking carefully at the context within which they were writing (including the objections they sought to answer), recognizing that it was a work of persuasion rather than philosophy (even if that distinction can be overdrawn), and recalling that its authors had a right to change their own minds as well as the minds of those they sought to persuade.

But the modern reader who still wishes to read *The Federalist* as political philosophy also has an advantage over its original audience. They had to read the essays as they individually appeared, and were probably neither able nor willing to go back and forth between the separate installments—at least before the two bound volumes of the McLean edition appeared in the spring of 1788. They could not ask, as we might, whether Madison used the closing paragraphs of *Federalist* 51 to restate the argument of *Federalist* 10 in order to imply that the whole Anti-Federalist emphasis on the separation of powers was misplaced. Indeed, it is an open question whether any of the original readers of *Federalist* 51 could have even understood Madison's allusion to his earlier essay. The modern reader thus has the luxury of reading the essays as an integrated whole, looking for links and connections that original readers never noticed. Or again, because modern readers have reliable knowledge of which author wrote each essay, they can ask whether the separate voices of Hamilton and Madison give Publius the "split personality" that one distinguished commentator detected.[36]

Of course, later readings of *The Federalist* are also affected by the intellectual biases and priorities of their own day. Before the Civil War, the most frequently cited essays of *The Federalist* were those that dealt with the concurrent powers of the Union and the states, a subject Hamilton treated with special care in essays 30–36, devoted to questions of revenue.[37] Those issues are far less urgent today, and interest in those essays has accordingly declined. Nineteenth-century readers displayed no interest at all in *Federalist* 10, the interpretation of which has spawned an entire cottage industry of commentary since its "discovery" in the early twentieth century.[38] Some essays surge into fashion when they touch on subjects that bear on a current dispute. *Federalist* 65 and 66, for example, enjoyed brief spikes of popularity during the impeachment inquiries directed against Richard Nixon in 1974 and Bill Clinton in 1998, as seasoned scholars, intrepid journalists, and untutored congressmen tried to decipher the meaning of that obscure phrase, "high crimes and misdemeanors."

The fact that the interpretation of the Constitution remains an ongoing source of controversy, more than two centuries after its ratification, offers another reason why modern readers repeatedly turn to *The Federalist,* especially when questions arise about the basic design of the national government and the federal system. Even though the persistence of these controversies demonstrates that true and final meanings can rarely if ever be ascribed to the contested clauses of the Constitution, the ambition (or delusion) also persists that an appeal to the original understandings of 1787–88 will somehow provide the answers that our contemporary disputes require. That belief, reinforced by the rhetorical advantages of being able to enlist history on one's own side, naturally leads lawyers, jurists, politicians, and polemicists to recur to the records of 1787–88. And when they do, they repeatedly discover that *The Federalist* is the most lucid, comprehensive, and accessible source we have.

The concluding judgment that Gordon Wood rendered on the political theory of the entire revolutionary generation seems apt here: "It was not political theory in the grand manner, but it was political theory worthy of a prominent place in the history of Western thought."[39]

Amid the frenetic conditions of the ratification campaign of 1787–88, Hamilton and Madison could not labor over their essays with quite the same care that the great political thinkers of early modern Europe devoted to their great works. There were deadlines to meet, and other business to which they had to attend. That they wrote with such insight and perspicuity under these conditions is a tribute to the amount of thought they had already given to the matter at hand, and the inspiration they took from the immediate political project *The Federalist* was conceived to pursue.

NOTES

[1] For further discussion, see Douglass Adair, "The Authorship of the Disputed Federalist Papers," *William and Mary Quarterly*, 3rd ser., 1 (1944): 97–122, 235–64; Frederick Mosteller and David L. Wallace, *Applied Bayesian and Classical Inference: The Case of the Federalist Papers* (New York: Verlag, 1984).

[2] Two excellent essays on the essential political ideas of the two men are Gerald Stourzh, *Alexander Hamilton and the Idea of Republican Government* (Stanford, Calif.: Stanford University Press, 1970); and Lance Banning, *The Sacred Fire of Liberty: James Madison and the Founding of the Federal Republic* (Ithaca, N.Y.: Cornell University Press, 1995).

[3] For the drafting and ratification of the Confederation, see Jack N. Rakove, *The Beginnings of National Politics: An Interpretive History of the Continental Congress* (New York: Alfred A. Knopf, 1979).

[4] For two early examples of Madison's criticisms, see his letters to Thomas Jefferson, March 27, 1780, and May 1, 1782, in Jack N. Rakove, ed., *James Madison: Writings* (New York: Library of America, 1999). Hamilton's views were similarly expressed in a treatise-length letter to the New York congressional delegate, James Duane, Sept. 3, 1780, in Harold C. Syrett and Jacob Cooke, eds., *The Papers of Alexander Hamilton* (New York: Columbia University Press, 1961–1979), II: 400–18.

[5] The commissioners' report, drafted by Hamilton, can be found in ibid., III: 686–90.

[6] The most important study of constitution-making in the states is Gordon S. Wood, *The Creation of the American Republic, 1776–1787* (Chapel Hill: University of North Carolina Press, 1969); also see Willi Paul Adams, *The First American Constitutions: Republican Ideology and the Making of the State Constitutions in the Revolutionary Era*, trans. Rita and Robert Kember, expanded edition (Lanham, Md.: Rowman & Littlefield, 2001). Major studies of the impact of the Revolution on individual states include Edward Countryman, *A People in Revolution: The American Revolution and Political Society in New York, 1760–1790* (Baltimore and London: The Johns Hopkins University Press, 1981); Ronald Hoffman, *A Spirit of Dissension: Economics, Politics, and the Revolution in Maryland* (Baltimore and London: The Johns Hopkins University Press, 1973); and Richard Buel, *Dear Liberty: Connecticut's Mobilization for the Revolutionary War* (Middletown, Conn.: Wesleyan University Press, 1980).

[7] For an intriguing portrait of the three men, see Richard B. Morris, *Witnesses at the Creation: Hamilton, Madison, Jay, and the Constitution* (New York: Holt, Rinehart, and Winston, 1985).

[8] Leading studies of Hamilton include John C. Miller, *Alexander Hamilton: Portrait in Paradox* (New York: Harper and Brothers, 1959); Stourzh, *Hamilton and the Idea of*

Republican Government; and Karl-Friedrich Walling, *Republican Empire: Alexander Hamilton on War and Free Government* (Lawrence: University Press of Kansas, 1999).

[9] On these themes, see John Brewer, *The Sinews of Power: War, Money, and the English State, 1688–1783* (New York: Alfred A. Knopf, 1988); and Bernard Bailyn, *The Origins of American Politics* (New York: Alfred A. Knopf, 1968).

[10] For Madison's early career, see Jack N. Rakove, *James Madison and the Creation of the American Republic,* 2nd ed. (New York: Longman, 2001), 1–48; and Ralph Ketcham, *James Madison: A Biography* (Charlottesville: University Press of Virginia, 1971), 1–173.

[11] This was the great theme he introduced in *Federalist* 48, but he used similar language at the Federal Convention, notably in his speech of July 21, 1787, reprinted in Max Farrand, ed., *The Records of the Federal Convention of 1787* (New Haven, Conn.: Yale University Press, 1966), II: 74.

[12] The best discussion of Madison's attitude toward slavery is Drew McCoy, *The Last of the Fathers: James Madison and the Republican Legacy* (New York: Cambridge University Press, 1989).

[13] I discuss this aspect of Madison's approach to rights at greater length in Jack N. Rakove, *Original Meanings: Politics and Ideas in the Making of the Constitution* (New York: Alfred A. Knopf, 1996), 330–36; and in *Declaring Rights: A Brief History with Documents* (Boston: Bedford/St. Martin's, 1997), 99–107.

[14] John Jay to John Adams, February 21, 1787, Adams Family Papers, microfilm reel 368, Massachusetts Historical Society.

[15] Madison's collaboration with Washington is ably examined in Stuart E. Leibiger, *Founding Friendship: George Washington, James Madison, and the Creation of the American Republic* (Charlottesville: University Press of Virginia, 1999).

[16] For further discussion of Madison's preparations, see Rakove, *Original Meanings,* 42–56; and Banning, *The Sacred Fire of Liberty.*

[17] Key documents include Madison's memorandum on the "Vices of the Political System of the U. States" [April 1787], and his letter to George Washington, April 16, 1787, in Rakove, *James Madison: Writings,* 69–85.

[18] On this point, see especially Charles Hobson, "The Negative on State Laws: James Madison, the Constitution, and the Crisis of Republican Government," *William and Mary Quarterly,* 3rd ser., 36 (1979): 215–35. For a broader discussion of Madison's agenda for the Convention, see Rakove, *Original Meanings,* 46–56.

[19] The following account of the Convention draws extensively on the analysis in Rakove, *Original Meanings,* 57–93. For a fast-paced narrative of the debates at Philadelphia, see Carol Berkin, *A Brilliant Solution: Inventing the American Constitution* (New York: Harcourt Brace, 2002).

[20] Farrand, ed., *Records,* I: 282–93 (Madison's notes), 304–11 (Hamilton's outline).

[21] Madison to Jefferson, Sept. 6 and Oct. 24, 1787, in *Madison: Writings,* 136, 146–52.

[22] Syrett and Cooke, eds., *Papers of Hamilton,* IV: 275–77.

[23] See the public letter of Robert Yates and John Lansing to Governor Clinton, January 14, 1788, in Herbert Storing, ed., *The Complete Anti-Federalist* (Chicago and London: University of Chicago Press, 1987), II: 15–18.

[24] For further discussion of this critical point, see Rakove, *Original Meanings,* 94–130.

[25] John K. Alexander, *The Selling of the Constitutional Convention: A History of News Coverage* (Madison, Wisc.: Madison House, 1990).

[26] See the title essay in Richard Hofstadter, *The Paranoid Style in American Politics, and Other Essays* (New York: Alfred A. Knopf, 1965).

[27] See Bernard Bailyn, *The Ideological Origins of the American Revolution,* enlarged ed. (Cambridge, Mass.: Harvard University Press, 1992); and the seminal early essay of Cecilia Kenyon, "Men of Little Faith: The Anti-Federalists on the Nature of Representative Government," *William and Mary Quarterly,* 3rd ser., 12 (1955): 3–43. For sympathetic accounts of Anti-Federalist ideas, see Storing, *The Complete Anti-Federalist,*

I, *What the Anti-Federalists Were For;* Jackson Turner Main, *The Anti-Federalists: Critics of the Constitution, 1781–1788* (Chapel Hill: University of North Carolina Press, 1961); and Saul Cornell, *The Other Founders: Anti-Federalism and the Dissenting Tradition in America, 1788–1828* (Chapel Hill: University of North Carolina Press, 1999).

[28] John Locke, *Two Treatises of Government,* ed. Peter Laslett (Cambridge, England: Cambridge University Press, 1960, 1988), 364–66. For a more complete discussion, see M. J. C. Vile, *Constitutionalism and the Separation of Powers,* 2nd ed. (Indianapolis: Liberty Fund, 1998).

[29] For the relevant passages, see Philip Kurland and Ralph Lerner, eds., *The Founders' Constitution* (Chicago and London: University of Chicago Press, 1987), I: 624–28. Montesquieu's account of the judicial power in England neglects perhaps the most important development of the eighteenth century: the establishment of the principle that judges would serve during good behavior, rather than at the pleasure of the crown, provided by the Settlement Act of 1701. Instead, Montesquieu treats judicial power as equivalent to the decision-making power of juries.

[30] Kurland and Lerner, eds., *Founders' Constitution,* I: 13–14.

[31] George Mason, "Objections to the Constitution of Government Formed by the Convention," in Storing, ed., *The Complete Anti-Federalist,* II: 11.

[32] Luther Martin, *The Genuine Information Delivered to the Legislature of the State of Maryland Relative to the Proceedings of the General Convention Lately Held at Philadelphia* (Baltimore, 1788), ibid., II: 19–79.

[33] The speech is reprinted in John P. Kaminski and Gaspare J. Saladino, eds., *The Documentary History of the Ratification of the Constitution* (Madison: State Historical Society of Wisconsin, 1976–), II: 337–44.

[34] The definitive study of ratification in New York is Linda Grant De Pauw, *The Eleventh Pillar: New York State and the Federal Constitution* (Ithaca, N.Y.: Cornell University Press, 1966).

[35] This occurred the first time Congress had to debate the meaning of the Constitution, the so-called removal debate of June 1789, which involved asking whether the Senate had to consent to the removal of an officer as well as his appointment, as Hamilton had suggested would be the case in *Federalist 77.* The anecdote is related in a letter from William Loughton Smith to Edward Rutledge, June 21, 1789, *South Carolina Historical Magazine,* 69 (1969): 8.

[36] Alpheus T. Mason, "The Federalist—A Split Personality," *American Historical Review,* 57 (1952): 625–43.

[37] Jack N. Rakove, "Early Uses of *The Federalist,*" in Charles R. Kesler, ed., *Saving the Republic:* The Federalist Papers *and the American Founding* (New York: Free Press, 1987), 240–43; Ira C. Lupu, "Time, the Supreme Court, and *The Federalist,*" *George Washington Law Review,* 66 (1998): 1324.

[38] On the modern discovery of this essay, see Douglass Adair, "The Tenth Federalist Revisited," *William and Mary Quarterly,* 3rd ser., 8 (1951): 48–67; and Paul Bourke, "The Pluralist Reading of James Madison's Tenth *Federalist,*" *Perspectives in American History,* 9 (1975): 271–95.

[39] Wood, *Creation of the American Republic,* 615.

PART TWO

The Documents: *The Federalist*

[HAMILTON]

Federalist 1

Introduction, October 27, 1787

Hamilton uses the first essay to describe the ideal perspective from which readers should view both the Constitution and Publius himself, as one of its avowed supporters. While casting some aspersions on the real motives of the Constitution's opponents, Hamilton cautions his audience to assume that advocates on both sides will share a comparable measure of interests, passions, prejudices, and ambitions. But concerned citizens should rest their decision on something else: "the evidence of truth" and "a judicious estimate of our true interests." The deeper problem that Hamilton raises is whether citizens and leaders will bring to the high act of debating the Constitution the same attitudes that shape their response to ordinary political decisions, or whether they are capable of occupying a higher ground in this vital debate. Hamilton thus introduces a theme that Publius will repeatedly explore: the interplay between the narrow calculations of self-interest that shape our daily conduct, and the broader considerations of "true interest" and "public good" that should govern public affairs. The challenge is to accept that passion and interest are forces to be reckoned with, but then to demonstrate that ways can be found to reason about politics and governance, both by checking the damage that passion may inflict and by finding ways to make true deliberation possible. That challenge must be faced in designing a constitution and securing its ratification, and in the ordinary conduct of government.

To the People of the State of New York.
After an unequivocal experience of the inefficacy of the subsisting Foederal Government, you are called upon to deliberate on a new Constitution for the United States of America. The subject speaks its own importance; comprehending in its consequences, nothing less than the existence of the UNION, the safety and welfare of the parts of which it is composed, the fate of an empire, in many respects, the most interesting in the world. It has been frequently remarked, that it seems to have been reserved to the people of this country, by their conduct and example, to decide the important question, whether societies of men are really capable or not, of establishing good government from reflection and choice, or whether they are forever destined to depend, for their political constitutions, on accident and force. If there be any truth in the remark, the crisis, at which we are arrived, may with propriety be regarded as the æra in which that decision is to be made; and a wrong election of the part we shall act, may, in this view, deserve to be considered as the general misfortune of mankind.

This idea will add the inducements of philanthropy to those of patriotism to heighten the solicitude, which all considerate and good men must feel for the event. Happy will it be if our choice should be directed by a judicious estimate of our true interests, unperplexed and unbiassed by considerations not connected with the public good. But this is a thing more ardently to be wished, than seriously to be expected. The plan offered to our deliberations, affects too many particular interests, innovates upon too many local institutions, not to involve in its discussion a variety of objects foreign to its merits, and of views, passions and prejudices little favourable to the discovery of truth.

Among the most formidable of the obstacles which the new Constitution will have to encounter, may readily be distinguished the obvious interest of a certain class of men in every State to resist all changes which may hazard a diminution of the power, emolument[1] and consequence of the offices they hold under the State-establishments—and the perverted ambition of another class of men, who will either hope to aggrandise themselves by the confusions of their country, or will flatter themselves with fairer prospects of elevation from the subdivi-

---

[1] *emolument:* compensation or other privileges and benefits of office.

sion of the empire into several partial confederacies, than from its union under one government.

It is not, however, my design to dwell upon observations of this nature. I am well aware that it would be disingenuous to resolve indiscriminately the opposition of any set of men (merely because their situations might subject them to suspicion) into interested or ambitious views: Candour will oblige us to admit, that even such men may be actuated by upright intentions; and it cannot be doubted that much of the opposition which has made its appearance, or may hereafter make its appearance, will spring from sources, blameless at least, if not respectable, the honest errors of minds led astray by preconceived jealousies and fears. So numerous indeed and so powerful are the causes, which serve to give a false bias to the judgment, that we upon many occasions, see wise and good men on the wrong as well as on the right side of questions, of the first magnitude to society. This circumstance, if duly attended to, would furnish a lesson of moderation to those, who are ever so much persuaded of their being in the right, in any controversy. And a further reason for caution, in this respect, might be drawn from the reflection, that we are not always sure, that those who advocate the truth are influenced by purer principles than their antagonists. Ambition, avarice, personal animosity, party opposition, and many other motives, not more laudable than these, are apt to operate as well upon those who support as upon those who oppose the right side of a question. Were there not even these inducements to moderation, nothing could be more illjudged than that intolerant spirit, which has, at all times, characterised political parties. For, in politics as in religion, it is equally absurd to aim at making proselytes by fire and sword. Heresies in either can rarely be cured by persecution.

And yet however just these sentiments will be allowed to be, we have already sufficient indications, that it will happen in this as in all former cases of great national discussion. A torrent of angry and malignant passions will be let loose. To judge from the conduct of the opposite parties, we shall be led to conclude, that they will mutually hope to evince the justness of their opinions, and to increase the number of their converts by the loudness of their declamations, and by the bitterness of their invectives. An enlightened zeal for the energy and efficiency of government will be stigmatized, as the off-spring of a temper fond of despotic power and hostile to the principles of liberty. An overscrupulous jealousy of danger to the rights of the people, which is more commonly the fault of the head than of the heart, will be represented as mere pretence and artifice; the bait for popularity at the expence of public good. It will be forgotten, on the one hand, that jealousy is the usual concomitant of violent love, and that the noble enthusiasm of liberty is too apt to be infected with a spirit of narrow and illiberal distrust. On the other hand, it will be equally forgotten, that the vigour of government is essential to the security of liberty; that, in the contemplation of a sound and well informed judgment, their interest can never be separated; and that a dangerous ambition more often lurks behind the specious mask of zeal for the rights of the people, than under the forbidding appearance of zeal for the firmness and efficiency of government. History will teach us, that the former has been found a much more certain road to the introduction of despotism, than the latter, and that of those men who have overturned the liberties of republics the greatest number have begun their career, by paying an obsequious court to the people, commencing Demagogues and ending Tyrants.

In the course of the preceeding observations I have had an eye, my Fellow Citizens, to putting you upon your guard against all attempts, from whatever quarter, to influence your decision in a matter of the utmost moment to your welfare by any impressions other than those which may result from the evidence of truth. You will, no doubt, at the same time, have collected from the general scope of them that they proceed from a source not unfriendly to the new Constitution. Yes, my Countrymen, I own to you, that, after having given it an attentive consideration, I am clearly of opinion, it is your interest to adopt it. I am convinced, that this is the safest course for your liberty, your dignity, and your happiness. I effect not reserves, which I do not feel. I will not amuse you with an appearance of deliberation, when I have decided. I frankly acknowledge to you my convictions, and I will freely lay before you the reasons on which they are founded. The consciousness of good intentions disdains ambiguity. I shall not however multiply professions on this head. My motives must remain in the depository of my own breast: My arguments will be open to all, and may be judged of by all. They shall at least be offered in a spirit, which will not disgrace the cause of truth.

I propose in a series of papers to discuss the following interesting particulars—*The utility of the* UNION *to your political prosperity—The insufficiency of the present Confederation to preserve that Union—The necessity of a government at least equally energetic with the one proposed to the attainment of this object—The conformity of the proposed constitution to the true principles of republican government—Its analogy to your own state constitution—and lastly, The additional security, which its adoption will afford to the preservation of that species of government, to liberty and to property.*

In the progress of this discussion I shall endeavour to give a satisfactory answer to all the objections which shall have made their appearance that may seem to have any claim to your attention.

It may perhaps be thought superfluous to offer arguments to prove the utility of the UNION, a point, no doubt, deeply engraved on the hearts of the great body of the people in every state, and one, which it may be imagined has no adversaries. But the fact is, that we already hear it whispered in the private circles of those who oppose the new constitution, that the Thirteen States are of too great extent for any general system, and that we must of necessity resort to separate confederacies of distinct portions of the whole.* This doctrine will, in all probability, be gradually propagated, till it has votaries enough to countenance an open avowal of it. For nothing can be more evident, to those who are able to take an enlarged view of the subject, than the alternative of an adoption of the new Constitution, or a dismemberment of the Union. It will therefore be of use to begin by examining the advantages of that Union, the certain evils and the probable dangers, to which every State will be exposed from its dissolution. This shall accordingly constitute the subject of my next address.

PUBLIUS.

* The same idea, tracing the arguments to their consequences, is held out in several of the later publications against the New Constitution.

[HAMILTON]

Federalist 6

Concerning Dangers from War between the States, November 14, 1787

Following Hamilton's opening essay, the next four numbers of The Federalist *were written by John Jay, the secretary for foreign affairs under the Confederation. His principal theme was the necessity of union for the effective conduct of foreign relations. If the Union broke down into separate regional confederacies, Jay warned, foreign nations would take advantage of disunity to meddle in American affairs.*

With Federalist 6, *however, Hamilton identified a fresh set of dangers that would arise from disunion or the creation of separate confederacies: potential clashes between the states. Americans should not think that they were immune to the ambitions that plagued the monarchies and empires of the Old World, with their endless wars over land, commerce, or dynastic rivalries. Nor should they think they could avoid the conflicts that other republics had known throughout history, or assume that "perpetual peace" would be the natural condition of the states if they were disunited. By challenging these optimistic assumptions, Hamilton demonstrates why he is often regarded as a founder of the "realist" tradition in American thinking about national security, a tradition that assumes that the struggle for power and advantage is the natural condition of all states, and that even republics have to be mindful of the dangers that ensue.*

To the People of the State of New York.
The three last numbers of this Paper have been dedicated to an enumeration of the dangers to which we should be exposed, in a state of disunion, from the arms and arts of foreign nations. I shall now proceed to delineate dangers of a different, and, perhaps, still more alarming kind, those which will in all probability flow from dissentions between the States themselves, and from domestic factions and convulsions. These have been already in some instances slightly anticipated, but they deserve a more particular and more full investigation.

A man must be far gone in Utopian speculations who can seriously doubt, that if these States should either be wholly disunited, or only united in partial confederacies, the subdivisions into which they might be thrown would have frequent and violent contests with each other. To presume a want of motives for such contests, as an argument against their existence, would be to forget that men are ambitious, vindictive and rapacious. To look for a continuation of harmony between a number of independent unconnected sovereignties, situated in the same neighbourhood, would be to disregard the uniform course of human events, and to set at defiance the accumulated experience of ages.

The causes of hostility among nations are innumerable. There are some which have a general and almost constant operation upon the collective bodies of society: Of this description are the love of power or the desire of preeminence and dominion—the jealousy of power, or the desire of equality and safety. There are others which have a more circumscribed, though an equally operative influence, within their spheres: Such are the rivalships and competitions of commerce between commercial nations. And there are others, not less numerous than either of the former, which take their origin intirely in private passions; in the attachments, enmities, interests, hopes and fears of leading individuals in the communities of which they are members. Men of this class, whether the favourites of a king or of a people, have in too many instances abused the confidence they possessed; and assuming the pretext of some public motive, have not scrupled to sacrifice the national tranquility to personal advantage, or personal gratification.

The celebrated Pericles, in compliance with the resentments of a prostitute,* at the expence of much of the blood and treasure of his countrymen, attacked, vanquished and destroyed, the city of the *Samnians*. The same man, stimulated by private pique against the *Megarensians,*† another nation of Greece, or to avoid a prosecution with which he was threatened as an accomplice in a supposed theft of the statuary *Phidias,*‡ or to get rid of the accusations prepared to be brought against him for dissipating the funds of the State in the purchase of popularity,§ or from a combination of all these causes, was the primitive author of that famous and fatal war, distinguished in the Grecian annals by the name of the *Pelopponesian* war; which, after various vicissitudes, intermissions and renewals, terminated in the ruin of the Athenian commonwealth.

The ambitious Cardinal, who was Prime Minister to Henry VIIIth. permitting his vanity to aspire to the Tripple-Crown,** entertained hopes of succeeding in the acquisition of that splendid prize by the influence of the Emperor Charles Vth. To secure the favour and interest of this enterprising and powerful Monarch, he precipitated England into a war with France, contrary to the plainest dictates of Policy, and at the hazard of the safety and independence, as well of the Kingdom over which he presided by his councils, as of Europe in general. For if there ever was a Sovereign who bid fair to realise the project of universal monarchy it was the Emperor Charles Vth, of whose intrigues Wolsey was at once the instrument and the dupe.

The influence which the bigottry of one female,†† the petulancies of another,‡‡ and the cabals of a third,§§ had in the co[n]temporary

* ASPASIA, vide PLUTARCH'S life of Pericles.
† —Idem.
‡ —Idem. Phidias was supposed to have stolen some public gold with the connivance of Pericles for the embelishment of the statue of Minerva.
§ Idem.
** Worn by the Popes.
†† Madame De Maintenon.
‡‡ Dutchess of Marlborough.
§§ Madame De Pompadoure.

policy, ferments and pacifications of a considerable part of Europe are topics that have been too often descanted upon not to be generally known.[2]

To multiply examples of the agency of personal considerations in the production of great national events, either foreign or domestic, according to their direction would be an unnecessary waste of time. Those who have but a superficial acquaintance with the sources from which they are to be drawn will themselves recollect a variety of instances; and those who have a tolerable knowledge of human nature will not stand in need of such lights, to form their opinion either of the reality or extent of that agency. Perhaps however a reference, tending to illustrate the general principle, may with propriety be made to a case which has lately happened among ourselves. If SHAYS had not been a *desperate debtor* it is much to be doubted whether Massachusetts would have been plunged into a civil war.[3]

But notwithstanding the concurring testimony of experience, in this particular, there are still to be found visionary, or designing men, who stand ready to advocate the paradox of perpetual peace between the States, though dismembered and alienated from each other. The genius of republics (say they) is pacific; the spirit of commerce has a tendency to soften the manners of men and to extinguish those inflammable humours which have so often kindled into wars. Commercial republics, like ours, will never be disposed to waste themselves in

[2]The references to persons and events from both antiquity and modern history that Hamilton makes in the preceding three paragraphs indicate the extent to which he expected informed readers to be able to apply lessons of history to the debate over the Constitution. In the eighteenth century, history was regarded as a laboratory of human experience from which useful lessons could be drawn and applied to contemporary affairs. "The ambitious Cardinal" to whom Hamilton refers in the preceding paragraph was Thomas Wolsey, who died a natural death in 1530 shortly before he was due to be executed for treason against his master, King Henry VIII. Charles V was the greatest monarch of early sixteenth-century Europe, governing numerous kingdoms and jurisdictions as both head of the Hapsburg dynasty and Holy Roman Emperor. The three prominent women cited in this paragraph all played prominent roles in recent European politics. Madame de Maintenon had been secretly married to the great French monarch Louis XIV in 1684, and helped persuade him to pursue the bloody persecution of the French Protestants (Huguenots). The Duchess of Marlborough, wife of the great British general (and ancestor of the famous prime minister Winston Churchill), was an influential adviser to Queen Anne from 1702 to 1710. Madame de Pompadour, the longtime mistress of Louis XV, was thought to exercise even greater influence over the affairs of France. Hamilton, it might be noted, also fell under the influence of a calculating woman in the 1790s, when he entered into an affair with Maria Reynolds.

[3]The reference is to Captain Daniel Shays, the Revolutionary War veteran who led an uprising of debtor farmers in western Massachusetts during the fall of 1786 and early winter of 1786–87.

ruinous contentions with each other. They will be governed by mutual interest, and will cultivate a spirit of mutual amity and concord.

Is it not (we may ask these projectors in politics) the true interest of all nations to cultivate the same benevolent and philosophic spirit? If this be their true interest, have they in fact pursued it? Has it not, on the contrary, invariably been found, that momentary passions and immediate interests have a more active and imperious controul over human conduct than general or remote considerations of policy, utility or justice? Have republics in practice been less addicted to war than monarchies? Are not the former administered by *men* as well as the latter? Are there not aversions, predilections, rivalships and desires of unjust acquisition that affect nations as well as kings? Are not popular assemblies frequently subject to the impulses of rage, resentment, jealousy, avarice, and of other irregular and violent propensities? Is it not well known that their determinations are often governed by a few individuals, in whom they place confidence, and are of course liable to be tinctured by the passions and views of those individuals? Has commerce hitherto done any thing more than change the objects of war? Is not the love of wealth as domineering and enterprising a passion as that of power or glory? Have there not been as many wars founded upon commercial motives, since that has become the prevailing system of nations, as were before occasioned b[y] the cupidity of territory or dominion? Has not the spirit of commerce in many instances administered new incentives to the appetite both for the one and for the other? Let experience the least fallible guide of human opinions be appealed to for an answer to these inquiries.

Sparta, Athens, Rome and Carthage were all Republics; two of them, Athens and Carthage, of the commercial kind. Yet were they as often engaged in wars, offensive and defensive, as the neighbouring Monarchies of the same times. Sparta was little better than a well regulated camp; and Rome was never sated of carnage and conquest.

Carthage, though a commercial Republic, was the aggressor in the very war that ended in her destruction. Hannibal had carried her arms into the heart of Italy and to the gates of Rome, before Scipio, in turn, gave him an overthrow in the territories of Carthage and made a conquest of the Commonwealth.

Venice in latter times figured more than once in wars of ambition; 'till becoming an object of terror to the other Italian States, Pope Julius the Second found means to accomplish that formidable league,*

---

*The League of Cambray, comprehending the Emperor, the King of France, the King of Arragon, and most of the Italian Princes and States.

which gave a deadly blow to the power and pride of this haughty Republic.

The Provinces of Holland, 'till they were overwhelmed in debts and taxes, took a leading and conspicuous part in the wars of Europe. They had furious contests with England for the dominion of the sea; and were among the most persevering and most implacable of the opponents of Lewis XIV.

In the government of Britain the representatives of the people compose one branch of the national legislature. Commerce has been for ages the predominant pursuit of that country. Few nations, nevertheless, have been more frequently engaged in war; and the wars, in which that kingdom has been engaged, have in numerous instances proceeded from the people.

There have been, if I may so express it, almost as many popular as royal wars. The cries of the nation and the importunities of their representatives have, upon various occasions, dragged their monarchs into war, or continued them in it contrary to their inclinations, and, sometimes, contrary to the real interests of the State. In that memorable struggle for superiority, between the rival Houses of *Austria* and *Bourbon* which so long kept Europe in a flame, it is well known that the antipathies of the English against the French, seconding the ambition, or rather the avarice of a favourite leader,* protracted the war beyond the limits marked out by sound policy and for a considerable time in opposition to the views of the Court.

The wars of these two last mentioned nations have in a great measure grown out of commercial considerations—The desire of supplanting and the fear of being supplanted either in particular branches of traffic or in the general advantages of trade and navigation; and sometimes even the more culpable desire of sharing in the commerce of other nations, without their consent.

The last war but two between Britain and Spain sprang from the attempts of the English merchants, to prosecute an illicit trade with the Spanish main. These unjustifiable practices on their part produced severities on the part of the Spaniards, towards the subjects of Great Britain, which were not more justifiable; because they exceeded the bounds of a just retaliation, and were chargeable with inhumanity and cruelty. Many of the English who were taken on the Spanish coasts were sent to dig in the mines of Potosi; and by the usual progress of a spirit of resentment, the innocent were after a while confounded with

* The Duke of Marlborough.

the guilty in indiscriminate punishment. The complaints of the merchants kindled a violent flame throughout the nation, which soon after broke out in the house of commons, and was communicated from that body to the ministry. Letters of reprisal were granted and a war ensued, which in its consequences overthrew all the alliances that but twenty years before had been formed, with sanguine expectations of the most beneficial fruits.

From this summary of what has taken place in other countries, whose situations have borne the nearest resemblance to our own, what reason can we have to confide in those reveries, which would seduce us into an expectation of peace and cordiality between the members of the present confederacy, in a state of separation? Have we not already seen enough of the fallacy and extravagance of those idle theories which have amused us with promises of an exemption from the imperfections, weaknesses and evils incident to society in every shape? Is it not time to awake from the deceitful dream of a golden age, and to adopt as a practical maxim for the direction of our political conduct, that we, as well as the other inhabitants of the globe, are yet remote from the happy empire of perfect wisdom and perfect virtue?

Let the point of extreme depression to which our national dignity and credit have sunk—let the inconveniences felt every where from a lax and ill administration of government—let the revolt of a part of the State of North-Carolina—the late menacing disturbances in Pennsylvania and the actual insurrections and rebellions in Massachusetts declare!

So far is the general sense of mankind from corresponding with the tenets of those, who endeavour to lull asleep our apprehensions of discord and hostility between the States, in the event of disunion, that it has from long observation of the progress of society become a sort of axiom in politics, that vicinity, or nearness of situation, constitutes nations natural enemies. An intelligent writer expresses himself on this subject to this effect—"NEIGHBOURING NATIONS (says he) are naturally ENEMIES of each other, unless their common weakness forces them to league in a CONFEDERATE REPUBLIC, and their constitution prevents the differences that neighbourhood occasions, extinguishing that secret jealousy, which disposes all States to aggrandise themselves at the expence of their neighbours."* This passage, at the same time points out the EVIL and suggests the REMEDY.

PUBLIUS.

---

*Vide Principes des Negotiations par L'Abbe de Mably.

Federalist 9

The Utility of the Union as a Safeguard against Domestic Faction and Insurrection, November 21, 1787

In this essay, Hamilton introduces the theme that Madison will pursue in greater detail in the Tenth Federalist: *the well-documented vulnerability of republican governments to destructive factional conflict. While suggesting that the conclusions drawn from this history have been carried too far, Hamilton concedes that the problem is real enough to merit attention. He then concentrates his analysis on the advantages of linking individual republics — like the American states — into a confederation whose common resources might be used to counteract the danger of factious outbreaks within its individual members. In developing this point, Hamilton illustrates the Federalists' general confidence in the American capacity to make "improvements" in the "science of politics." At the same time, he ingeniously demonstrates that the authority whom the opponents of the Constitution like to invoke, Montesquieu, can also be deployed on behalf of its ratification.*

To the People of the State of New York.

A Firm Union will be of the utmost moment to the peace and liberty of the States as a barrier against domestic faction and insurrection. It is impossible to read the history of the petty Republics of Greece and Italy, without feeling sensations of horror and disgust at the distractions with which they were continually agitated, and at the rapid succession of revolutions, by which they were kept in a state of perpetual vibration, between the extremes of tyranny and anarchy. If they exhibit occasional calms, these only serve as short-lived contrasts to the furious storms that are to succeed. If now and then intervals of felicity open themselves to view, we behold them with a mixture of regret arising from the reflection that the pleasing scenes before us are soon to be overwhelmed by the tempestuous waves of sedition and party-rage. If momentary rays of glory break forth from the gloom, while they dazzle us with a transient and fleeting brilliancy, they at the same time admonish us to lament that the vices of government should pervert the direction and tarnish the lustre of those bright talents and exalted indowments, for which the favoured soils, that produced them, have been so justly celebrated.

From the disorders that disfigure the annals of those republics, the advocates of despotism have drawn arguments, not only against the forms of republican government, but against the very principles of civil liberty. They have decried all free government, as inconsistent with the order of society, and have indulged themselves in malicious exultation over its friends and partizans. Happily for mankind, stupendous fabrics reared on the basis of liberty, which have flourished for ages, have in a few glorious instances refuted their gloomy sophisms. And, I trust, America will be the broad and solid foundation of other edifices not less magnificent, which will be equally permanent monuments of their errors.

But it is not to be denied that the portraits, they have sketched of republican government, were too just copies of the originals from which they were taken. If it had been found impracticable, to have devised models of a more perfect structure, the enlightened friends to liberty would have been obliged to abandon the cause of that species of government as indefensible. The science of politics, however, like most other sciences has received great improvement. The efficacy of various principles is now well understood, which were either not known at all, or imperfectly known to the ancients. The regular distribution of power into distinct departments—the introduction of legislative ballances and checks—the institution of courts composed of judges, holding their offices during good behaviour—the representation of the people in the legislature by deputies of their own election—these are either wholly new discoveries or have made their principal progress towards perfection in modern times. They are means, and powerful means, by which the excellencies of republican government may be retained and its imperfections lessened or avoided. To this catalogue of circumstances, that tend to the amelioration of popular systems of civil government, I shall venture, however novel it may appear to some, to add one more on a principle, which has been made the foundation of an objection to the New Constitution, I mean the ENLARGEMENT of the ORBIT within which such systems are to revolve either in respect to the dimensions of a single State, or to the consolidation of several smaller States into one great confederacy. The latter is that which immediately concerns the object under consideration. It will however be of use to examine the principle in its application to a single State which shall be attended to in another place.

The utility of a confederacy, as well to suppress faction and to guard the internal tranquillity of States, as to increase their external force and security, is in reality not a new idea. It has been practiced upon in different countries and ages, and has received the sanction of the most applauded writers, on the subjects of politics. The opponents of the PLAN proposed have with great assiduity cited and circulated the observations of Montesquieu on the necessity of a contracted territory for a republican government. But they seem not to have been apprised of the sentiments of that great man expressed in another part of his work, nor to have adverted to the consequences of the principle to which they subscribe, with such ready acquiescence.

When Montesquieu recommends a small extent for republics, the standards he had in view were of dimensions, far short of the limits of almost every one of these States. Neither Virginia, Massachusetts, Pennsylvania, New-York, North-Carolina, nor Georgia, can by any means be compared with the models, from which he reasoned and to which the terms of his description apply. If we therefore take his ideas on this point, as the criterion of truth, we shall be driven to the alternative, either of taking refuge at once in the arms of monarchy, or of spliting ourselves into an infinity of little jealous, clashing, tumultuous commonwealths, the wretched nurseries of unceasing discord and the miserable objects of universal pity or contempt. Some of the writers, who have come forward on the other side of the question, seem to have been aware of the dilemma; and have even been bold enough to hint at the division of the larger States, as a desirable thing. Such an infatuated policy, such a desperate expedient, might, by the multiplication of petty offices, answer the views of men, who possess not qualifications to extend their influence beyond the narrow circles of personal intrigue, but it could never promote the greatness or happiness of the people of America.

Referring the examination of the principle itself to another place, as has been already mentioned, it will be sufficient to remark here, that in the sense of the author who has been most emphatically quoted upon the occasion, it would only dictate a reduction of the SIZE of the more considerable MEMBERS of the Union; but would not militate against their being all comprehended in one Confederate Government. And this is the true question, in the discussion of which we are at present interested.

So far are the suggestions of Montesquieu from standing in opposition to a general Union of the States, that he explicitly treats of a CONFEDERATE REPUBLIC as the expedient for extending the sphere of popular government and reconciling the advantages of monarchy with those of republicanism.

"It is very probable (says he*) that mankind would have been obliged, at length, to live constantly under the government of a SINGLE PERSON, had they not contrived a kind of constitution, that has all the internal advantages of a republican, together with the external force of a monarchial government. I mean a CONFEDERATE REPUBLIC.

"This form of Government is a Convention, by which several smaller *States* agree to become members of a larger *one,* which they intend to form. It is a kind of assemblage of societies, that constitute a new one, capable of encreasing by means of new associations, till they arrive to such a degree of power as to be able to provide for the security of the united body.

"A republic of this kind, able to withstand an external force, may support itself without any internal corruption. The form of this society prevents all manner of inconveniencies.

"If a single member should attempt to usurp the supreme authority, he could not be supposed to have an equal authority and credit, in all the confederate states. Were he to have too great influence over one, this would alarm the rest. Were he to subdue a part, that which would still remain free might oppose him with forces, independent of those which he had usurped, and overpower him before he could be settled in his usurpation.

"Should a popular insurrection happen, in one of the confederate States, the others are able to quell it. Should abuses creep into one part, they are reformed by those that remain sound. The State may be destroyed on one side, and not on the other; the confederacy may be dissolved, and the confederates preserve their sovereignty.

"As this government is composed of small republics it enjoys the internal happiness of each, and with respect to its external situation it is possessed, by means of the association of all the advantages of large monarchies."

I have thought it proper to quote at length these interesting passages, because they contain a luminous abrigement of the principal arguments in favour of the Union, and must effectually remove the false impressions, which a misapplication of other parts of the work was calculated to produce. They have at the same time an intimate connection with the more immediate design of this Paper; which is to illustrate the tendency of the Union to repress domestic faction and insurrection.

* *Spirit of Laws, Vol. I. Book IX. Chap. I.*

A distinction, more subtle than accurate has been raised between a *confederacy* and a *consolidation* of the States. The essential characteristic of the first is said to be, the restriction of its authority to the members in their collective capacities, without reaching to the individuals of whom they are composed. It is contended that the national council ought to have no concern with any object of internal administration. An exact equality of suffrage between the members has also been insisted upon as a leading feature of a Confederate Government. These positions are in the main arbitary; they are supported neither by principle nor precedent. It has indeed happened that governments of this kind have generally operated in the manner, which the distinction, taken notice of, supposes to be inherent in their nature—but there have been in most of them extensive exceptions to the practice, which serve to prove as far as example will go, that there is no absolute rule on the subject. And it will be clearly shewn, in the course of this investigation, that as far as the principle contended for has prevailed, it has been the cause of incurable disorder and imbecility in the government.

The definition of a *Confederate Republic* seems simply to be, an "assemblage of societies" or an association of two or more States into one State. The extent, modifications and objects of the Foederal authority are mere matters of discretion. So long as the separate organisation of the members be not abolished, so long as it exists by a constitutional necessity for local purposes, though it should be in perfect subordination to the general authority of the Union, it would still be, in fact and in theory, an association of States, or a confederacy. The proposed Constitution, so far from implying an abolition of the State Governments, makes them constituent parts of the national sovereignty by allowing them a direct representation in the Senate, and leaves in their possession certain exclusive and very important portions of sovereign power. This fully corresponds, in every rational import of the terms, with the idea of a Foederal Government.

In the Lycian confederacy, which consisted of twenty three CITIES or republics, the largest were intitled to *three* votes in the COMMON COUNCIL, those of the middle class to *two* and the smallest to *one*. The COMMON COUNCIL had the appointment of all the judges and magistrates of the respective CITIES. This was certainly the most delicate species of interference in their internal administration; for if there be any thing, that seems exclusively appropriated to the local jurisdictions, it is the appointment of their own officers. Yet Montesquieu, speaking of this association, says "Were I to give a model of an excellent confederate republic, it would be that of Lycia." Thus we perceive that the distinctions insisted upon were not within the contemplation of this enlightened civilian, and we shall be led to conclude that they are the novel refinements of an erroneous theory.

PUBLIUS.

[MADISON]

Federalist 10

The Same Subject Continued, November 22, 1787

Along with the Declaration of Independence of 1776 and Abraham Lincoln's Gettysburg Address of 1863, this essay is one of the trinity of classic statements of American political theory. Its prestige and authority are, however, very much a twentieth-century phenomenon. In 1913, the influential Progressive Era historian Charles A. Beard cited Federalist 10 *as evidence of the primacy of economic interests in the adoption of the Constitution. Other social scientists were calling attention to the importance that Madison attached to factions—redefined as voluntarily constituted interest groups—as the basic elements defining the structure of politics in a modern pluralist society. A generation later, however, the historian Douglass Adair reoriented the interpretation of* Federalist 10 *by locating it firmly within the intellectual context of the eighteenth century rather than the political preoccupations of the twentieth. Madison's essay was properly understood, Adair argued, as a response to the familiar Enlightenment argument that republican governments could safely operate only in small, relatively homogeneous societies, where the citizens shared common interests and a distinctive sense of civic virtue that enabled them to subordinate private interest to public good. If these conditions did not exist, republics would repeatedly fall prey to internal conflict, with one faction struggling to dominate another.*

Numerous scholars have since viewed Madison's argument within this context, while trying to refine its nuances and implications. One major point of controversy has been the relative importance of the two major advantages that Madison ascribes to an extended republic: the difficulty that factions in the larger society will face in coalescing for improper purposes, and the possibility that larger electoral districts will work to improve the quality of representation. Another controversy involves the relative strength of the "republican" and "liberal" strands of Madison's essay. Madison seems to reject the republican belief in the necessity of virtuous citizens, and to accept instead the liberal image of autonomous individuals pursuing their interests and passions by the light of a fallible reason. But his belief in the existence of a true public good that the polity should strive to discover seems closer to a republican notion of the importance of community than a liberal conception, which sees public policy as an aggregate of the preferences of citizens.

Madison's argument rests on two key assumptions about the nature of faction. One is his definition of a faction as any group of citizens that pursues ends "adverse to the rights of other citizens, or to the permanent and aggregate interests of the community." By saying that even a majority may be a faction, Madison consciously calls "into question the fundamental principle of republican Government, that the majority who rule in such Governments, are the safest Guardians both of public Good and of private rights."[1] The second key assumption is that faction is unavoidable because it results both from human nature and the diverse interests that a modern civilized society produces. The sources of faction cannot be eliminated; rather, ways must be found to control and even exploit its effects.

To the People of the State of New York.

Among the numerous advantages promised by a well constructed Union, none deserves to be more accurately developed than its tendency to break and control the violence of faction. The friend of popular governments, never finds himself so much alarmed for their character and fate, as when he contemplates their propensity to this dangerous vice. He will not fail therefore to set a due value on any plan which, without violating the principles to which he is attached, provides a proper cure for it. The instability, injustice and confusion introduced into the public councils, have in truth been the mortal diseases under which popular governments have every where perished; as they continue to be the favorite and fruitful topics from which the adversaries to liberty derive their most specious declamations. The valuable improvements made by the American Constitutions on the popular models, both ancient and modern, cannot certainly be too much admired; but it would be an unwarrantable partiality, to contend that they have as

---

[1]See his memorandum on the "Vices of the Political System of the U. States" [April 1787], which is in effect a first draft of *Federalist 10*. Jack N. Rakove, ed., *James Madison: Writings* (New York: Library of America, 1999), 75.

effectually obviated the danger on this side as was wished and expected. Complaints are every where heard from our most considerate and virtuous citizens, equally the friends of public and private faith, and of public and personal liberty; that our governments are too unstable; that the public good is disregarded in the conflicts of rival parties; and that measures are too often decided, not according to the rules of justice, and the rights of the minor party; but by the superior force of an interested and over-bearing majority. However anxiously we may wish that these complaints had no foundation, the evidence of known facts will not permit us to deny that they are in some degree true. It will be found indeed, on a candid review of our situation, that some of the distresses under which we labor, have been erroneously charged on the operation of our governments; but it will be found, at the same time, that other causes will not alone account for many of our heaviest misfortunes; and particularly, for that prevailing and increasing distrust of public engagements, and alarm for private rights, which are echoed from one end of the continent to the other. These must be chiefly, if not wholly, effects of the unsteadiness and injustice, with which a factious spirit has tainted our public administrations.

By a faction I understand a number of citizens, whether amounting to a majority or minority of the whole, who are united and actuated by some common impulse of passion, or of interest, adverse to the rights of other citizens, or to the permanent and aggregate interests of the community.

There are two methods of curing the mischiefs of faction: the one, by removing its causes; the other, by controling its effects.

There are again two methods of removing the causes of faction: the one by destroying the liberty which is essential to its existence; the other, by giving to every citizen the same opinions, the same passions, and the same interests.

It could never be more truly said than of the first remedy, that it is worse than the disease. Liberty is to faction, what air is to fire, an aliment without which it instantly expires. But it could not be a less folly to abolish liberty, which is essential to political life, because it nourishes faction, than it would be to wish the annihilation of air, which is essential to animal life, because it imparts to fire its destructive agency.

The second expedient is as impracticable, as the first would be unwise. As long as the reason of man continues fallible, and he is at liberty to exercise it, different opinions will be formed. As long as the connection subsists between his reason and his self-love, his opinions and his passions will have a reciprocal influence on each other; and the former will be objects to which the latter will attach themselves. The diversity in the faculties of men from which the rights of property originate, is not less an insuperable obstacle to a uniformity of interests. The protection of these faculties is the first object of Government. From the protection of different and unequal faculties of acquiring property, the possession of different degrees and kinds of property immediately results: and from the influence of these on the sentiments and views of the respective proprietors, ensues a division of the society into different interests and parties.

The latent causes of faction are thus sown in the nature of man; and we see them every where brought into different degrees of activity, according to the different circumstances of civil society. A zeal for different opinions concerning religion, concerning Government and many other points, as well of speculation as of practice; an attachment to different leaders ambitiously contending for pre-eminence and power; or to persons of other descriptions whose fortunes have been interesting to the human passions, have in turn divided mankind into parties, inflamed them with mutual animosity, and rendered them much more disposed to vex and oppress each other, than to co-operate for their common good. So strong is this propensity of mankind to fall into mutual animosities, that where no substantial occasion presents itself, the most frivolous and fanciful distinctions have been sufficient to kindle their unfriendly passions, and excite their most violent conflicts. But the most common and durable source of factions, has been the various and unequal distribution of property. Those who hold, and those who are without property, have ever formed distinct interests in society. Those who are creditors, and those who are debtors, fall under a like discrimination. A landed interest, a manufacturing interest, a mercantile interest, a monied interest, with many lesser interests, grow up of necessity in civilized nations, and divide them into different classes, actuated by different sentiments and views. The regulation of these various and interfering interests forms the principal task of modern Legislation, and involves the spirit of party and faction in the necessary and ordinary operations of Government.

No man is allowed to be a judge in his own cause; because his interest would certainly bias his judgment, and, not improbably, corrupt his integrity. With equal, nay with greater reason, a body of men, are unfit to be both judges and parties, at the same time; yet, what are many of the most important acts of legislation, but so many judicial determinations, not indeed concerning the rights of single persons, but concerning the rights of large bodies of citizens; and what are the different classes of legislators, but advocates and parties to the causes which they determine? Is a law proposed concerning private debts? It is a question to which the creditors are parties on one side, and the debtors on the other. Justice ought to hold the balance between them. Yet the parties are and must be themselves the judges; and the most numerous party, or, in other words, the most powerful faction must be expected to prevail. Shall domestic manufactures be encouraged, and in what degree, by restrictions on foreign manufactures? are questions which would be differently decided by the landed and the manufacturing classes; and probably by neither, with a sole regard to justice and the public good. The apportionment of taxes on the various descriptions of property, is an act which seems to require the most exact impartiality; yet, there is perhaps no legislative act in which greater opportunity and temptation are given to a predominant party, to trample on the rules of justice. Every shilling with which they over-burden the inferior number, is a shilling saved to their own pockets.

It is in vain to say, that enlightened statesmen will be able to adjust these clashing interests, and render them all subservient to the public good. Enlightened statesmen will not always be at the helm: Nor, in many cases, can such an adjustment be made at all, without taking into view indirect and remote considerations, which will rarely prevail over the immediate interest which one party may find in disregarding the rights of another, or the good of the whole.

The inference to which we are brought, is, that the *causes* of faction cannot be removed; and that relief is only to be sought in the means of controling its *effects*.

If a faction consists of less than a majority, relief is supplied by the republican principle, which enables the majority to defeat its sinister views by regular vote: It may clog the administration, it may convulse the society; but it will be unable to execute and mask its violence under the forms of the Constitution. When a majority is included in a faction, the form of popular government on the other hand enables it to sacrifice to its ruling passion or interest, both the public good and the rights of other citizens. To secure the public good, and private rights, against the danger of such a faction, and at the same time to preserve the spirit and the form of popular government, is then the great object to which our enquiries are directed: Let me add that it is the great desideratum,[2] by which alone this form of government can

---

[2] *desideratum:* loosely, the great thing to be desired.

be rescued from the opprobrium under which it has so long labored, and be recommended to the esteem and adoption of mankind.

By what means is this object attainable? Evidently by one of two only. Either the existence of the same passion or interest in a majority at the same time, must be prevented; or the majority, having such co-existent passion or interest, must be rendered, by their number and local situation, unable to concert and carry into effect schemes of oppression. If the impulse and the opportunity be suffered to coincide, we well know that neither moral nor religious motives can be relied on as an adequate control. They are not found to be such on the injustice and violence of individuals, and lose their efficacy in proportion to the number combined together; that is, in proportion as their efficacy becomes needful.

From this view of the subject, it may be concluded, that a pure Democracy, by which I mean, a Society, consisting of a small number of citizens, who assemble and administer the Government in person, can admit of no cure for the mischiefs of faction. A common passion or interest will, in almost every case, be felt by a majority of the whole; a communication and concert results from the form of Government itself; and there is nothing to check the inducements to sacrifice the weaker party, or an obnoxious individual. Hence it is, that such Democracies have ever been spectacles of turbulence and contention; have ever been found incompatible with personal security, or the rights of property; and have in general been as short in their lives, as they have been violent in their deaths. Theoretic politicians, who have patronized this species of Government, have erroneously supposed, that by reducing mankind to a perfect equality in their political rights, they would, at the same time, be perfectly equalized and assimilated in their possessions, their opinions, and their passions.

A Republic, by which I mean a Government in which the scheme of representation takes place, opens a different prospect, and promises the cure for which we are seeking. Let us examine the points in which it varies from pure Democracy, and we shall comprehend both the nature of the cure, and the efficacy which it must derive from the Union.

The two great points of difference between a Democracy and a Republic are, first, the delegation of the Government, in the latter, to a small number of citizens elected by the rest: secondly, the greater number of citizens, and greater sphere of country, over which the latter may be extended.

The effect of the first difference is, on the one hand to refine and enlarge the public views, by passing them through the medium of a chosen body of citizens, whose wisdom may best discern the true interest of their country, and whose patriotism and love of justice, will be least likely to sacrifice it to temporary or partial considerations. Under such a regulation, it may well happen that the public voice pronounced by the representatives of the people, will be more consonant to the public good, than if pronounced by the people themselves convened for the purpose. On the other hand, the effect may be inverted. Men of factious tempers, of local prejudices, or of sinister designs, may by intrigue, by corruption or by other means, first obtain the suffrages, and then betray the interests of the people. The question resulting is, whether small or extensive Republics are most favorable to the election of proper guardians of the public weal: and it is clearly decided in favor of the latter by two obvious considerations.

In the first place it is to be remarked that however small the Republic may be, the Representatives must be raised to a certain number, in order to guard against the cabals of a few; and that however large it may be, they must be limited to a certain number, in order to guard against the confusion of a multitude. Hence the number of Representatives in the two cases, not being in proportion to that of the Constituents, and being proportionally greatest in the small Republic, it follows, that if the proportion of fit characters, be not less, in the large than in the small Republic, the former will present a greater option, and consequently a greater probability of a fit choice.

In the next place, as each Representative will be chosen by a greater number of citizens in the large than in the small Republic, it will be more difficult for unworthy candidates to practise with success the vicious arts, by which elections are too often carried; and the suffrages of the people being more free, will be more likely to centre on men who possess the most attractive merit, and the most diffusive and established characters.

It must be confessed, that in this, as in most other cases, there is a mean, on both sides of which inconveniencies will be found to lie. By enlarging too much the number of electors, you render the representative too little acquainted with all their local circumstances and lesser interests; as by reducing it too much, you render him unduly attached to these, and too little fit to comprehend and pursue great and national objects. The Federal Constitution forms a happy combination in this respect; the great and aggregate interests being referred to the national, the local and particular, to the state legislatures.

The other point of difference is, the greater number of citizens and extent of territory which may be brought within the compass of

Republican, than of Democratic Government; and it is this circumstance principally which renders factious combinations less to be
dreaded in the former, than in the latter. The smaller the society, the
fewer probably will be the distinct parties and interests composing it;
the fewer the distinct parties and interests, the more frequently will a
majority be found of the same party; and the smaller the number of
individuals composing a majority, and the smaller the compass within
which they are placed, the more easily will they concert and execute
their plans of oppression. Extend the sphere, and you take in a greater
variety of parties and interests; you make it less probable that a majority of the whole will have a common motive to invade the rights of
other citizens; or if such a common motive exists, it will be more difficult for all who feel it to discover their own strength, and to act in unison with each other. Besides other impediments, it may be remarked,
that where there is a consciousness of unjust or dishonorable purposes, communication is always checked by distrust, in proportion to
the number whose concurrence is necessary.

Hence it clearly appears, that the same advantage, which a Republic
has over a Democracy, in controling the effects of faction, is enjoyed
by a large over a small Republic—is enjoyed by the Union over the
States composing it. Does this advantage consist in the substitution
of Representatives, whose enlightened views and virtuous sentiments
render them superior to local prejudices, and to schemes of injustice?
It will not be denied, that the Representation of the Union will be most
likely to possess these requisite endowments. Does it consist in the
greater security afforded by a greater variety of parties, against the
event of any one party being able to outnumber and oppress the rest?
In an equal degree does the encreased variety of parties, comprised
within the Union, encrease this security. Does it, in fine, consist in
the greater obstacles opposed to the concert and accomplishment of
the secret wishes of an unjust and interested majority? Here, again, the
extent of the Union gives it the most palpable advantage.

The influence of factious leaders may kindle a flame within their
particular States, but will be unable to spread a general conflagration
through the other States: a religious sect, may degenerate into a political faction in a part of the Confederacy; but the variety of sects dis-
persed over the entire face of it, must secure the national Councils
against any danger from that source: a rage for paper money, for an
abolition of debts, for an equal division of property, or for any other
improper or wicked project, will be less apt to pervade the whole body
of the Union, than a particular member of it; in the same proportion as

such a malady is more likely to taint a particular county or district, than an entire State.

In the extent and proper structure of the Union, therefore, we behold a Republican remedy for the diseases most incident to Republican Government. And according to the degree of pleasure and pride, we feel in being Republicans, ought to be our zeal in cherishing the spirit, and supporting the character of Federalists.

PUBLIUS.

[MADISON]

Federalist 14

An Objection Drawn from the Extent of Country Answered, November 30, 1787

Like Federalist *10, this essay defends the project of creating an extended republic by insisting that the stock criticisms directed against republics properly apply only to democracies, where the citizens rule directly. Unlike* Federalist *10, which unfolds through a series of carefully drawn distinctions, here Madison speaks far more directly, reminding Americans of the advantages they already possess in forming a nation. But then Madison closes the essay on a more urgent if flowery note, recalling that the Revolution itself was no less a novelty and a risk than the Constitution appears to be. Like Hamilton in* Federalist *9, he suggests that the study of politics is not confined to time-honored truths and received traditions, but is rather a field open for innovation and improvement.*

To the People of the State of New York.
We have seen the necessity of the union as our bulwark against foreign danger, as the conservator of peace among ourselves, as the guardian of our commerce and other common interests, as the only substitute for those military establishments which have subverted the liberties of the old world; and as the proper antidote for the diseases of faction, which have proved fatal to other popular governments, and of which alarming symptoms have been betrayed by our own. All that remains, within this branch of our enquiries, is to take notice of an objection, that may be drawn from the great extent of country which the union embraces. A few observations on this subject will be the more proper, as it is perceived that the adversaries of the new constitution

are availing themselves of a prevailing prejudice, with regard to the practicable sphere of republican administration, in order to supply by imaginary difficulties, the want of those solid objections, which they endeavor in vain to find.

The error which limits Republican Government to a narrow district, has been unfolded and refuted in preceding papers.[1] I remark here only, that it seems to owe its rise and prevalence, chiefly to the confounding of a republic with a democracy: And applying to the former reasonings drawn from the nature of the latter. The true distinction between these forms was also adverted to on a former occasion.[2] It is, that in a democracy, the people meet and exercise the government in person; in a republic they assemble and administer it by their representatives and agents. A democracy consequently will be confined to a small spot. A republic may be extended over a large region.

To this accidental source of the error may be added the artifice of some celebrated authors, whose writings have had a great share in forming the modern standard of political opinions. Being subjects either of an absolute, or limited monarchy, they have endeavored to heighten the advantages or palliate the evils of those forms; by placing in comparison with them, the vices and defects of the republican, and by citing as specimens of the latter, the turbulent democracies of ancient Greece, and modern Italy. Under the confusion of names, it has been an easy task to transfer to a republic, observations applicable to a democracy only, and among others, the observation that it can never be established but among a small number of people, living within a small compass of territory.

Such a fallacy may have been the less perceived as most of the governments of antiquity were of the democratic species; and even in modern Europe, to which we owe the great principle of representation, no example is seen of a government wholly popular, and founded at the same time wholly on that principle. If Europe has the merit of discovering this great mechanical power in government, by the simple agency of which, the will of the largest political body may be concentred, and its force directed to any object, which the public good requires; America can claim the merit of making the discovery the basis of unmixed and extensive republics. It is only to be lamented, that any of her citizens should wish to deprive her of the additional merit of displaying its full efficacy on the establishment of the comprehensive system now under her consideration.

[1] See Essays 9 and 10.
[2] See Essay 10.

As the natural limit of a democracy is that distance from the central point, which will just permit the most remote citizens to assemble as often as their public functions demand; and will include no greater number than can join in those functions; so the natural limit of a republic is that distance from the center, which will barely allow the representatives of the people to meet as often as may be necessary for the administration of public affairs. Can it be said, that the limits of the United States exceed this distance? It will not be said by those who recollect that the Atlantic coast is the longest side of the union; that during the term of thirteen years, the representatives of the States have been almost continually assembled; and that the members from the most distant States are not chargeable with greater intermissions of attendance, than those from the States in the neighbourhood of Congress.

That we may form a juster estimate with regard to this interesting subject, let us resort to the actual dimensions of the union. The limits as fixed by the treaty of peace are on the east the Atlantic, on the south the latitude of thirty-one degrees, on the west the Mississippi, and on the north an irregular line running in some instances beyond the forty-fifth degree, in others falling as low as the forty-second. The southern shore of Lake Erie lies below that latitude. Computing the distance between the thirty-one and forty-five degrees, it amounts to nine hundred and seventy-three common miles; computing it from thirty-one to forty-two degrees to seven hundred, sixty-four miles and an half. Taking the mean for the distance, the amount will be eight hundred, sixty-eight miles and three-fourths. The mean distance from the Atlantic to the Mississippi does not probably exceed seven hundred and fifty miles. On a comparison of this extent, with that of several countries in Europe, the practicability of rendering our system commensurate to it, appears to be demonstrable. It is not a great deal larger than Germany, where a Diet[3] representing the whole empire is continually assembled; or than Poland before the late dismemberment, where another national Diet was the depository of the supreme power. Passing by France and Spain, we find that in Great Britain, inferior as it may be in size, the representatives of the northern extremity of the island, have as far to travel to the national Council, as will be required of those of the most remote parts of the union.

Favorable as this view of the subject may be, some observations remain which will place it in a light still more satisfactory.

---

[3] *Diet:* a parliamentary assembly.

In the first place it is to be remembered, that the general government is not to be charged with the whole power of making and administering laws. Its jurisdiction is limited to certain enumerated objects, which concern all the members of the republic, but which are not to be attained by the separate provisions of any. The subordinate governments which can extend their care to all those other objects, which can be separately provided for, will retain their due authority and activity. Were it proposed by the plan of the Convention to abolish the governments of the particular States, its adversaries would have some ground for their objection, though it would not be difficult to shew that if they were abolished, the general government would be compelled by the principle of self-preservation, to reinstate them in their proper jurisdiction.

A second observation to be made is, that the immediate object of the Foederal Constitution is to secure the union of the Thirteen Primitive States, which we know to be practicable; and to add to them such other States, as may arise in their own bosoms or in their neighbourhoods, which we cannot doubt to be equally practicable. The arrangements that may be necessary for those angles and fractions of our territory, which lie on our north western frontier, must be left to those whom further discoveries and experience will render more equal to the task.

Let it be remarked in the third place, that the intercourse throughout the union will be daily facilitated by new improvements. Roads will every where be shortened, and kept in better order; accommodations for travellers will be multiplied and meliorated;[4] and interior navigation on our eastern side will be opened throughout, or nearly throughout the whole extent of the Thirteen States. The communication between the western and Atlantic districts, and between different parts of each, will be rendered more and more easy by those numerous canals with which the beneficence of nature has intersected our country, and which art finds it so little difficult to connect and complete.

A fourth and still more important consideration is, that as almost every State will on one side or other, be a frontier, and will thus find in a regard to its safety, an inducement to make some sacrifices for the sake of the general protection; so the States which lie at the greatest distance from the heart of the union, and which of course may partake least of the ordinary circulation of its benefits, will be at the same time immediately contiguous to foreign nations, and will consequently

[4]*meliorated:* improved.

stand on particular occasions, in greatest need of its strength and resources. It may be inconvenient for Georgia or the States forming our western or north eastern borders to send their representatives to the seat of government, but they would find it more so to struggle alone against an invading enemy, or even to support alone the whole expence of those precautions, which may be dictated by the neighbourhood of continual danger. If they should derive less benefit therefore from the union in some respects, than the less distant States, they will derive greater benefit from it in other respects, and thus the proper equilibrium will be maintained throughout.

I submit to you my fellow citizens, these considerations, in full confidence that the good sense which has so often marked your decisions, will allow them their due weight and effect; and that you will never suffer difficulties, however formidable in appearance or however fashionable the error on which they may be founded, to drive you into the gloomy and perilous scene into which the advocates for disunion would conduct you. Hearken not to the unnatural voice which tells you that the people of America, knit together as they are by so many chords of affection, can no longer live together as members of the same family; can no longer continue the mutual guardians of their mutual happiness; can no longer be fellow citizens of one great respectable and flourishing empire. Hearken not to the voice which petulantly tells you that the form of government recommended for your adoption is a novelty in the political world; that it has never yet had a place in the theories of the wildest projectors; that it rashly attempts what it is impossible to accomplish. No my countrymen, shut your ears against this unhallowed language. Shut your hearts against the poison which it conveys; the kindred blood which flows in the veins of American citizens, the mingled blood which they have shed in defence of their sacred rights, consecrate their union, and excite horror at the idea of their becoming aliens, rivals, enemies. And if novelties are to be shunned, believe me the most alarming of all novelties, the most wild of all projects, the most rash of all attempts, is that of rending us in pieces, in order to preserve our liberties and promote our happiness. But why is the experiment of an extended republic to be rejected merely because it may comprise what is new? Is it not the glory of the people of America, that whilst they have paid a decent regard to the opinions of former times and other nations, they have not suffered a blind veneration for antiquity, for custom, or for names, to overrule the suggestions of their own good sense, the knowledge of their own situation, and the lessons of their own experience? To this manly spirit, posterity will be indebted for the possession, and the world for the example of the numerous innovations displayed on the American theatre, in favor of private rights and public happiness. Had no important step been taken by the leaders of the revolution for which a precedent could not be discovered, no government established of which an exact model did not present itself, the people of the United States might, at this moment, have been numbered among the melancholy victims of misguided councils, must at best have been labouring under the weight of some of those forms which have crushed the liberties of the rest of mankind. Happily for America, happily we trust for the whole human race, they pursued a new and more noble course. They accomplished a revolution which has no parallel in the annals of human society: They reared the fabrics of governments which have no model on the face of the globe. They formed the design of a great confederacy, which it is incumbent on their successors to improve and perpetuate. If their works betray imperfections, we wonder at the fewness of them. If they erred most in the structure of the union; this was the work most difficult to be executed; this is the work which has been new modelled by the act of your Convention, and it is that act on which you are now to deliberate and to decide.

PUBLIUS.

[HAMILTON]

Federalist 15

Concerning the Defects of the Present Confederation in Relation to the Principle of Legislation for the States in Their Collective Capacities, December 1, 1787

To Anti-Federalists, the radical evil of the Constitution was that it threatened to transform a Union in which the Continental Congress depended on the compliance of the state governments to carry out its decisions into a genuine national government that would bypass the states and act directly on the population. Once that happened, they warned, the Union would soon grow into a "consolidated" government, exercising every power that mattered while the states literally withered away. For the supporters of the Constitution, as Publius notes in this essay, that same dependence on the states was the "radical vice" of the Confederation. To prove that point, he had to demonstrate that any system of federalism founded on the voluntary compliance of the states with national measures was doomed to failure.

Federalist 15 is customarily attributed to Hamilton, and there is no need to question his authorship. It is worth noting, however, that his analysis of the problem of relying on the free compliance of the states with national measures closely tracks and develops a key item in Madison's pre-Convention memorandum on the "Vices of the Political System of the U. States," leaving one to wonder whether the coauthors might have collaborated on this essay, or at least discussed its contents at some point.

To the People of the State of New York.

In the course of the preceding papers, I have endeavoured, my Fellow Citizens, to place before you in a clear and convincing light, the importance of Union to your political safety and happiness. I have unfolded to you a complication of dangers to which you would be exposed should you permit that sacred knot which binds the people of America together to be severed or dissolved by ambition or by avarice, by jealousy or by misrepresentation. In the sequel of the inquiry, through which I propose to accompany you, the truths intended to be inculcated will receive further confirmation from facts and arguments hitherto unnoticed. If the road, over which you will still have to pass, should in some places appear to you tedious or irksome, you will recollect, that you are in quest of information on a subject the most momentous which can engage the attention of a free people: that the field through which you have to travel is in itself spacious, and that the difficulties of the journey have been unnecessarily increased by the mazes with which sophistry has beset the way. It will be my aim to remove the obstacles to your progress in as compendious a manner, as it can be done, without sacrificing utility to dispatch.

In pursuance of the plan, which I have laid down, for the discussion of the subject, the point next in order to be examined is the "insufficiency of the present confederation to the preservation of the Union." It may perhaps be asked, what need is there of reasoning or proof to illustrate a position, which is not either controverted or doubted; to which the understandings and feelings of all classes of men assent; and which in substance is admitted by the opponents as well as by the friends of the New Constitution? It must in truth be acknowleged that however these may differ in other respects, they in general appear to harmonise in this sentiment at least, that there are material imperfections in our national system, and that something is necessary to be done to rescue us from impending anarchy. The facts that support this opinion are no longer objects of speculation. They have forced

themselves upon the sensibility of the people at large, and have at
length extorted from those, whose mistaken policy has had the principal share in precipitating the extremity, at which we are arrived, a
reluctant confession of the reality of those defects in the scheme of
our Foederal Government, which have been long pointed out and
regretted by the intelligent friends of the Union.

We may indeed with propriety be said to have reached almost the
last stage of national humiliation. There is scarcely any thing that can
wound the pride, or degrade the character of an independent nation,
which we do not experience. Are there engagements to the performance of which we are held by every tie respectable among men?
These are the subjects of constant and unblushing violation. Do we
owe debts to foreigners and to our own citizens contracted in a time of
imminent peril, for the preservation of our political existence? These
remain without any proper or satisfactory provision for their discharge. Have we valuable territories and important posts in the possession of a foreign power, which by express stipulations ought long
since to have been surrendered? These are still retained, to the prejudice of our interests not less than of our rights. Are we in a condition
to resent, or to repel the aggression? We have neither troops nor treasury nor government.* Are we even in a condition to remonstrate with
dignity? The just imputations on our own faith, in respect to the same
treaty, ought first to be removed. Are we entitled by nature and compact to a free participation in the navigation of the Mississippi? Spain
excludes us from it. Is public credit an indispensable resource in time
of public danger? We seem to have abandoned its cause as desperate
and irretrievable. Is commerce of importance to national wealth? Ours
is at the lowest point of declension. Is respectability in the eyes of foreign powers a safeguard against foreign encroachments? The imbecility of our Government even forbids them to treat with us: Our
ambassadors abroad are the mere pageants of mimic sovereignty. Is a
violent and unnatural decrease in the value of land a symptom of
national distress? The price of improved land in most parts of the
country is much lower than can be accounted for by the quantity of
waste land at market, and can only be fully explained by that want of
private and public confidence, which are so alarmingly prevalent
among all ranks and which have a direct tendency to depreciate property of every kind. Is private credit the friend and patron of industry?
That most useful kind which relates to borrowing and lending is re-

---

* I mean for the Union.

duced within the narrowest limits, and this still more from an opinion of insecurity than from the scarcity of money. To shorten an enumeration of particulars which can afford neither pleasure nor instruction it may in general be demanded, what indication is there of national disorder, poverty and insignificance that could befal a community so peculiarly blessed with natural advantages as we are, which does not form a part of the dark catalogue of our public misfortunes?

This is the melancholy situation, to which we have been brought by those very maxims and councils, which would now deter us from adopting the proposed constitution; and which not content with having conducted us to the brink of a precipice, seem resolved to plunge us into the abyss, that awaits us below. Here, my Countrymen, impelled by every motive that ought to influence an enlightened people, let us make a firm stand for our safety, our tranquillity, our dignity, our reputation. Let us at last break the fatal charm which has too long seduced us from the paths of felicity and prosperity.

It is true, as has been before observed, that facts too stubborn to be resisted have produced a species of general assent to the abstract proposition that there exist material defects in our national system; but the usefulness of the concession, on the part of the old adversaries of foederal measures, is destroyed by a strenuous opposition to a remedy, upon the only principles, that can give it a chance of success. While they admit that the Government of the United States is destitute of energy; they contend against conferring upon it those powers which are requisite to supply that energy: They seem still to aim at things repugnant and irreconcilable—at an augmentation of Foederal authority without a diminution of State authority—at sovereignty in the Union and complete independence in the members. They still in fine seem to cherish with blind devotion the political monster of an *imperium in imperio.*[1] This renders a full display of the principal defects of the confederation necessary, in order to shew, that the evils we experience do not proceed from minute or partial imperfections, but from fundamental errors in the structure of the building which cannot be amended otherwise than by an alteration in the first principles and main pillars of the fabric.

The great and radical vice in the construction of the existing Confederation is in the principle of LEGISLATION for STATES or GOVERNMENTS, in their CORPORATE or COLLECTIVE CAPACITIES and as contradistinguished

---

[1] *imperium in imperio:* a state within a state, or more generally, two sovereign authorities within a single jurisdiction; the phrase "*imperium in imperio* is a solecism (or sometimes, as here, a monster) in politics" was commonplace in eighteenth- and nineteenth-century political writing.

from the INDIVIDUALS of whom they consist. Though this principle does not run through all the powers delegated to the Union; yet it pervades and governs those, on which the efficacy of the rest depends. Except as to the rule of apportionment, the United States have an indefinite discretion to make requisitions for men and money; but they have no authority to raise either by regulations extending to the individual citizens of America. The consequence of this is, that though in theory their resolutions concerning those objects are laws, constitutionally binding on the members of the Union, yet in practice they are mere recommendations, which the States observe or disregard at their option.

It is a singular instance of the capriciousness of the human mind, that after all the admonitions we have had from experience on this head, there should still be found men, who object to the New Constitution for deviating from a principle which has been found the bane of the old; and which is in itself evidently incompatible with the idea of GOVERNMENT; a principle in short which if it is to be executed at all must substitute the violent and sanguinary agency of the sword to the mild influence of the Magistracy.

There is nothing absurd or impracticable in the idea of a league or alliance between independent nations, for certain defined purposes precisely stated in a treaty; regulating all the details of time, place, circumstance and quantity; leaving nothing to future discretion; and depending for its execution on the good faith of the parties. Compacts of this kind exist among all civilized nations subject to the usual vicissitudes of peace and war, of observance and non observance, as the interests or passions of the contracting powers dictate. In the early part of the present century, there was an epidemical rage in Europe for this species of compacts; from which the politicians of the times fondly hoped for benefits which were never realised. With a view to establishing the equilibrium of power and the peace of that part of the world, all the resources of negotiation were exhausted, and triple and quadruple alliances were formed; but they were scarcely formed before they were broken, giving an instructive but afflicting lesson to mankind how little dependence is to be placed on treaties which have no other sanction than the obligations of good faith; and which oppose general considerations of peace and justice to the impulse of any immediate interest and passion.

If the particular States in this country are disposed to stand in a similar relation to each other, and to drop the project of a general DISCRETIONARY SUPERINTENDENCE, the scheme would indeed be pernicious, and would entail upon us all the mischiefs that have been enumerated under the first head; but it would have the merit of being at least consistent and practicable. Abandoning all views towards a confederate Government, this would bring us to a simple alliance offensive and defensive; and would place us in a situation to be alternately friends and enemies of each other as our mutual jealousies and rivalships nourished by the intrigues of foreign nations should prescribe to us.

But if we are unwilling to be placed in this perilous situation; if we will still adhere to the design of a national government, or which is the same thing of a superintending power under the direction of a common Council, we must resolve to incorporate into our plan those ingredients which may be considered as forming the characteristic difference between a league and a government; we must extend the authority of the union to the persons of the citizens,—the only proper objects of government.

Government implies the power of making laws. It is essential to the idea of a law, that it be attended with a sanction; or, in other words, a penalty or punishment for disobedience. If there be no penalty annexed to disobedience, the resolutions or commands which pretend to be laws will in fact amount to nothing more than advice or recommendation. This penalty, whatever it may be, can only be inflicted in two ways; by the agency of the Courts and Ministers of Justice, or by military force; by the COERTION of the magistracy, or by the COERTION of arms. The first kind can evidently apply only to men—the last kind must of necessity be employed against bodies politic, or communities or States. It is evident, that there is no process of a court by which their observance of the laws can in the last resort be enforced. Sentences may be denounced against them for violations of their duty; but these sentences can only be carried into execution by the sword. In an association where the general authority is confined to the collective bodies of the communities that compose it, every breach of the laws must involve a state of war, and military execution must become the only instrument of civil obedience. Such a state of things can certainly not deserve the name of government, nor would any prudent man choose to commit his happiness to it.

There was a time when we were told that breaches, by the States, of the regulations of the foederal authority were not to be expected—that a sense of common interest would preside over the conduct of the respective members, and would beget a full compliance with all the constitutional requisitions of the Union. This language at the present day would appear as wild as a great part of what we now hear from the same quarter will be thought, when we shall have received further lessons from that best oracle of wisdom, experience. It at all times betrayed an ignorance of the true springs by which human conduct is actuated, and belied the original inducements to the establishment of civil power. Why has government been instituted at all? Because the passions of men will not conform to the dictates of reason and justice, without constraint. Has it been found that bodies of men act with more rectitude or greater disinterestedness than individuals? The contrary of this has been inferred by all accurate observers of the conduct of mankind; and the inference is founded upon obvious reasons. Regard to reputation has a less active influence, when the infamy of a bad action is to be divided among a number, than when it is to fall singly upon one. A spirit of faction which is apt to mingle its poison in the deliberations of all bodies of men, will often hurry the persons of whom they are composed into improprieties and excesses, for which they would blush in a private capacity.

In addition to all this, there is in the nature of sovereign power an impatience of controul, that disposes those who are invested with the exercise of it, to look with an evil eye upon all external attempts to restrain or direct its operations. From this spirit it happens that in every political association which is formed upon the principle of uniting in a common interest a number of lesser sovereignties, there will be found a kind of excentric tendency in the subordinate or inferior orbs, by the operation of which there will be a perpetual effort in each to fly off from the common center. This tendency is not difficult to be accounted for. It has its origin in the love of power. Power controuled or abridged is almost always the rival and enemy of that power by which it is controuled or abridged. This simple proposition will teach us how little reason there is to expect, that the persons, entrusted with the administration of the affairs of the particular members of a confederacy, will at all times be ready, with perfect good humour, and an unbiassed regard to the public weal, to execute the resolutions or decrees of the general authority. The reverse of this results from the constitution of human nature.

If therefore the measures of the confederacy cannot be executed, without the intervention of the particular administrations, there will be little prospect of their being executed at all. The rulers of the respective members, whether they have a constitutional right to do it or not, will undertake to judge of the propriety of the measures themselves. They will consider the conformity of the thing proposed or required to their immediate interests or aims, the momentary conveniences or inconveniences that would attend its adoption. All this will be done, and in a spirit of interested and suspicious scrutiny, without that knowledge of national circumstances and reasons of state, which is essential to a right judgment, and with that strong predilection in favour of local objects, which can hardly fail to mislead the decision. The same process must be repeated in every member of which the body is constituted; and the execution of the plans, framed by the councils of the whole, will always fluctuate on the discretion of the ill-informed and prejudiced opinion of every part. Those who have been conversant in the proceedings of popular assemblies; who have seen how difficult it often is, when there is no exterior pressure of circumstances, to bring them to harmonious resolutions on important points, will readily conceive how impossible it must be to induce a number of such assemblies, deliberating at a distance from each other, at different times, and under different impressions, long to cooperate in the same views and pursuits.

In our case, the concurrence of thirteen distinct sovereign wills is requisite under the confederation to the complete execution of every important measure, that proceeds from the Union. It has happened as was to have been foreseen. The measures of the Union have not been executed; and the delinquencies of the States have step by step matured themselves to an extreme; which has at length arrested all the wheels of the national government, and brought them to an awful stand. Congress at this time scarcely possess the means of keeping up the forms of administration; 'till the States can have time to agree upon a more substantial substitute for the present shadow of a foederal government. Things did not come to this desperate extremity at once. The causes which have been specified produced at first only unequal and disproportionate degrees of compliance with the requisitions of the Union. The greater deficiencies of some States furnished the pretext of example and the temptation of interest to the complying, or to the least delinquent States. Why should we do more in proportion than those who are embarked with us in the same political voyage? Why should we consent to bear more than our proper share of the common burthen? These were suggestions which human selfishness could not withstand, and which even speculative men, who looked forward to remote consequences, could not, without hesitation, combat. Each State yielding to the persuasive voice of immediate interest and convenience has successively withdrawn its support, 'till the frail and tottering edifice seems ready to fall upon our heads and to crush us beneath its ruins.

PUBLIUS.

Federalist 23

The Necessity of a Government at Least Equally Energetic with the One Proposed, December 18, 1787

Any system of federalism involves dividing power between national and provincial governments. In theory, the requirement of providing security against external enemies offers the strongest case for concentrating power in a national government. But the fear that government might deploy a standing army to strip the people of their basic liberties was deeply rooted in the Anglo-American political tradition. Accordingly, Anti-Federalists argued that the national government should not be able to raise and maintain an army of its own authority. Allowing the states to retain significant control over men and resources would provide a valuable check against tyranny.

With Federalist *23, Hamilton opens a series of essays dedicated to the imperatives of national defense. As in* Federalist *15, Hamilton holds that a system of voluntary state compliance will simply not work. Once one assumes that national defense is a legitimate responsibility of the federal government, it becomes illogical and imprudent to limit its ability to raise and deploy the necessary resources. For Hamilton, this point does not really depend on facts or the evidence of history; rather, it is virtually axiomatic.*

To the People of the State of New York.

The necessity of a Constitution, at least equally energetic with the one proposed, to the preservation of the Union, is the point, at the examination of which we are now arrived.

This enquiry will naturally divide itself into three branches—the objects to be provided for by a Foederal Government—the quantity of power necessary to the accomplishment of those objects—the persons upon whom that power ought to operate. Its distribution and organization will more properly claim our attention under the succeeding head.

The principal purposes to be answered by Union are these—The common defence of the members—the preservation of the public peace as well against internal convulsions as external attacks—the regulation of commerce with other nations and between the States—

the superintendence of our intercourse, political and commercial, with foreign countries.

The authorities essential to the care of the common defence are these—to raise armies—to build and equip fleets—to prescribe rules for the government of both—to direct their operations—to provide for their support. These powers ought to exist without limitation: *Because it is impossible to foresee or define the extent and variety of national exigencies, or the correspondent extent & variety of the means which may be necessary to satisfy them.* The circumstances that endanger the safety of nations are infinite; and for this reason no constitutional shackles can wisely be imposed on the power to which the care of it is committed. This power ought to be co-extensive with all the possible combinations of such circumstances; and ought to be under the direction of the same councils, which are appointed to preside over the common defence.

This is one of those truths, which to a correct and unprejudiced mind, carries its own evidence along with it; and may be obscured, but cannot be made plainer by argument or reasoning. It rests upon axioms as simple as they are universal. The *means* ought to be proportioned to the *end;* the persons, from whose agency the attainment of any *end* is expected, ought to possess the *means* by which it is to be attained.

Whether there ought to be a Foederal Government intrusted with the care of the common defence, is a question in the first instance open to discussion; but the moment it is decided in the affirmative, it will follow, that that government ought to be cloathed with all the powers requisite to the complete execution of its trust. And unless it can be shewn, that the circumstances which may affect the public safety are reducible within certain determinate limits; unless the contrary of this position can be fairly and rationally disputed, it must be admitted, as a necessary consequence, that there can be no limitation of that authority, which is to provide for the defence and protection of the community, in any matter essential to its efficacy; that is, in any matter essential to the *formation, direction* or *support* of the NATIONAL FORCES.

Defective as the present Confederation has been proved to be, this principle appears to have been fully recognized by the framers of it; though they have not made proper or adequate provision for its exercise. Congress have an unlimited discretion to make requisitions of men and money—to govern the army and navy—to direct their operations. As their requisitions were made constitutionally binding upon the States, who are in fact under the most solemn obligations to furnish the supplies required of them, the intention evidently was, that the United States should command whatever resources were by them judged requisite to "the common defence and general welfare." It was presumed that a sense of their true interests, and a regard to the dictates of good faith, would be found sufficient pledges for the punctual performance of the duty of the members to the Foederal Head.

The experiment has, however demonstrated, that this expectation was ill founded and illusory; and the observations made under the last head, will, I imagine, have sufficed to convince the impartial and discerning, that there is an absolute necessity for an entire change in the first principles of the system: That if we are in earnest about giving the Union energy and duration, we must abandon the vain project of legislating upon the States in their collective capacities: We must extend the laws of the Foederal Government to the individual citizens of America: We must discard the fallacious scheme of quotas and requisitions, as equally impracticable and unjust. The result from all this is, that the Union ought to be invested with full power to levy troops; to build and equip fleets, and to raise the revenues, which will be required for the formation and support of an army and navy, in the customary and ordinary modes practiced in other governments.

If the circumstances of our country are such, as to demand a compound instead of a simple, a confederate instead of a sole government, the essential point which will remain to be adjusted, will be to discriminate the OBJECTS, as far as it can be done, which shall appertain to the different provinces or departments of power; allowing to each the most ample authority for fulfilling the objects committed to its charge. Shall the Union be constituted the guardian of the common safety? Are fleets and armies and revenues necessary to this purpose? The government of the Union must be empowered to pass all laws, and to make all regulations which have relation to them. The same must be the case, in respect to commerce, and to every other matter to which its jurisdiction is permitted to extend. Is the administration of justice between the citizens of the same State, the proper department of the local governments? These must possess all the authorities which are connected with this object, and with every other that may be allotted to their particular cognizance and direction. Not to confer in each case a degree of power, commensurate to the end, would be to violate the most obvious rules of prudence and propriety, and improvidently to trust the great interests of the nation to hands, which are disabled from managing them with vigour and success.

Who so likely to make suitable provisions for the public defence, as that body to which the guardianship of the public safety is confided—which, as the center of information, will best understand the extent and urgency of the dangers that threaten—as the representative of the WHOLE will feel itself most deeply interested in the preservation of every part—which, from the responsibility implied in the duty assigned to it, will be most sensibly impressed with the necessity of proper exertions—and which, by the extension of its authority throughout the States, can alone establish uniformity and concert in the plans and measures, by which the common safety is to be secured? Is there not a manifest inconsistency in devolving upon the Foederal Government the care of the general defence, and leaving in the State governments the *effective* powers, by which it is to be provided for? Is not a want of co-operation the infallible consequence of such a system? And will not weakness, disorder, an undue distribution of the burthens and calamities of war, an unnecessary and intolerable increase of expence, be its natural and inevitable concomitants? Have we not had unequivocal experience of its effects in the course of the revolution, which we have just accomplished?

Every view we may take of the subject, as candid enquirers after truth, will serve to convince us, that it is both unwise and dangerous to deny the Foederal Government an unconfined authority, as to all those objects which are intrusted to its management. It will indeed deserve the most vigilant and careful attention of the people, to see that it be modelled in such a manner, as to admit of its being safely vested with the requisite powers. If any plan which has been, or may be offered to our consideration, should not, upon a dispassionate inspection, be found to answer this description, it ought to be rejected. A government, the Constitution of which renders it unfit to be trusted with all the powers, which a free people *ought to delegate to any government,* would be an unsafe and improper depository of the NATIONAL INTERESTS, wherever THESE can with propriety be confided, the co-incident powers may safely accompany them. This is the true result of all just reasoning upon the subject. And the adversaries of the plan, promulgated by the Convention, ought to have confined themselves to showing that the internal structure of the proposed government, was such as to render it unworthy of the confidence of the people. They ought not to have wandered into inflammatory declamations, and unmeaning cavils about the extent of the powers. The POWERS are not too extensive for the OBJECTS of Foederal administration, or in other words, for the management of our NATIONAL INTERESTS; nor can any satisfactory argument be framed to shew that they are chargeable with such an excess. If it be true, as has been insinuated by some of the writers on the other side, that the difficulty arises from the nature of the thing, and that the extent of the country will not permit us to form a government, in which such ample powers can safely be reposed, it would prove that we ought to contract our views, and resort to the expedient of separate Confederacies, which will move within more practicable spheres. For the absurdity must continually stare us in the face of confiding to a government, the direction of the most essential national interests, without daring to trust it with the authorities which are indispensable to their proper and efficient management. Let us not attempt to reconcile contradictions, but firmly embrace a rational alternative.

I trust, however, that the impracticability of one general system cannot be shewn. I am greatly mistaken, if any thing of weight, has yet been advanced of this tendency; and I flatter myself, that the observations which have been made in the course of these papers, have sufficed to place the reverse of that position in as clear a light as any matter still in the womb of time and experience can be susceptible of. This at all events must be evident, that the very difficulty itself drawn from the extent of the country, is the strongest argument in favor of an energetic government; for any other can certainly never preserve the Union of so large an empire. If we embrace the tenets of those, who oppose the adoption of the proposed Constitution, as the standard of our political creed, we cannot fail to verify the gloomy doctrines, which predict the impracticability of a national system, pervading the entire limits of the present Confederacy.

PUBLIUS.

[HAMILTON]

Federalist 32

The Same Subject Continued (Concerning Taxation), January 2, 1788

After completing his discussion of questions of national defense in Federalist *23–29, Hamilton took up the closely related issue of national taxation. Here again he argued that once the national government was charged with pursuing certain essential objects, its authority to raise the necessary resources could not be limited. This, too, he observed in* Federalist *31, was one of those "primary truths" that could be deduced almost axiomatically.*

But the deeper challenge that Hamilton faced was to explain how Americans would henceforth be able to support two distinct governments—one national, one state—each empowered to collect revenue from a people who often seemed reluctant to pay taxes in any form. Anti-Federalists worried that the national government would monopolize the most productive sources of revenue, thereby forcing the states to levy less popular taxes that citizens would resist paying. They also argued that the members of a distant Congress would feel too little "sympathy" for their constituents to know which taxes would burden ordinary Americans least. In reply, Hamilton goes to some lengths to explain that the Constitution will not divest the states of any of their original authority over taxation. On occasion, it might prove "inexpedient" or "inconvenient" for both governments to tax one object, but that would be a problem for political resolution, not a matter of constitutional conflict.

To the People of the State of New York.

Although I am of opinion that there would be no real danger of the consequences, which seem to be apprehended to the State Governments, from a power in the Union to controul them in the levies of money; because I am persuaded that the sense of the people, the extreme hazard of provoking the resentments of the State Governments, and a conviction of the utility and necessity of local administrations, for local purposes, would be a complete barrier against the oppressive use of such a power: Yet I am willing here to allow in its full extent the justness of the reasoning, which requires that the individual States should possess an independent and uncontrolable authority to raise their own revenues for the supply of their own wants. And making this concession I affirm that (with the sole exception of duties on imports and exports) they would under the plan of the Convention retain that authority in the most absolute and unqualified sense; and that an attempt on the part of the national Government to abridge them in the exercise of it would be a violent assumption of power unwarranted by any article or clause of its Constitution.

An intire consolidation of the States into one complete national sovereignty would imply an intire subordination of the parts; and whatever powers might remain in them would be altogether dependent on the general will. But as the plan of the Convention aims only at a partial Union or consolidation, the State Governments would clearly retain all the rights of sovereignty which they before had and which were not by that act *exclusively* delegated to the United States. This exclusive delegation or rather this alienation of State sovereignty would only exist in three cases; where the Constitution in express terms granted an exclusive authority to the Union; where it granted in one instance an authority to the Union and in another prohibited the States from exercising the like authority; and where it granted an authority to the Union, to which a similar authority in the States would be absolutely and totally *contradictory* and *repugnant*. I use these terms to distinguish this last case from another which might appear to resemble it; but which would in fact be essentially different; I mean where the exercise of a concurrent jurisdiction might be productive of occasional interferences in the *policy* of any branch of administration, but would not imply any direct contradiction or repugnancy in point of constitutional authority. These three cases of exclusive jurisdiction in the Foederal Government may be exemplified by the following instances: The last clause but one in the 8th section of the 1st. article provides expressly that Congress shall exercise *"exclusive legislation"* over the district to be appropriated as the seat of government. This answers to the first case. The first clause of the same section impowers Congress *"to lay and collect taxes, duties, imposts and excises"* and the 2d. clause of the 10th. section of the same article declares that *"no State shall* without the consent of Congress, *lay any imposts or duties on imports or exports* except for the purpose of executing its inspection laws."* Hence would result an exclusive power in the Union to lay duties on imports and exports with the particular exception mentioned; but this power is abriged by another clause which declares that no tax or duty shall be laid on articles exported from any State; in consequence of which qualification it now only extends to the *duties on imports*. This answers to the second case. The third will be found in that clause, which declares that Congress shall have power "to establish an UNIFORM RULE of naturalization throughout the United States." This must necessarily be exclusive; because if each State had power to prescribe a DISTINCT RULE there could be no UNI-FORM RULE.

A case which may perhaps be thought to resemble the latter, but which is in fact widely different, affects the question immediately under consideration. I mean the power of imposing taxes on all articles other than exports and imports. This, I contend, is manifestly a con-current and coequal authority in the United States and in the individual States. There is plainly no expression in the granting clause which makes that power *exclusive* in the Union. There is no independent clause or sentence which prohibits the States from exercising it. So far is this from being the case, that a plain and conclusive argument to the contrary is to be deduced from the restraint laid upon the States in relation to duties on imports and exports. This restriction implies an admission, that if it were not inserted the States would possess the power it excludes, and it implies a further admission, that as to all other taxes the authority of the States remains undiminished. In any other view it would be both unnecessary and dangerous; it would be unnecessary because if the grant to the Union of the power of laying such duties implied the exclusion of the States, or even their subordination in this particular there could be no need of such a restriction; it would be dangerous because the introduction of it leads directly to the conclusion which has been mentioned and which if the reasoning of the objectors be just, could not have been intended; I mean that the States in all cases to which the restriction did not apply would have a concurrent power of taxation with the Union. The restriction in question amounts to what lawyers call a NEGATIVE PREGNANT; that is a *negation* of one thing and an *affirmance* of another; a negation of the authority of the States to impose taxes on imports and exports, and an affirmance of their authority to impose them on all other articles. It would be mere sophistry to argue that it was meant to exclude them *absolutely* from the imposition of taxes of the former kind, and to leave them at liberty to lay others *subject to the controul* of the national Legislature. The restraining or prohibitory clause only says, that they shall not *without the consent of Congress* lay such duties; and if we are to understand this in the sense last mentioned, the Constitution would then be made to introduce a formal provision for the sake of a very absurd conclusion; which is that the States *with the consent* of the national Legislature might tax imports and exports; and that they might tax every other article *unless controuled* by the same body. If this was the intention why not leave it in the first instance to what is alleged to be the natural operation of the original clause conferring a general power of taxation upon the Union? It is evident that this could not have been the intention and that it will not bear a construction of the kind.

As to a supposition of repugnancy between the power of taxation in the States and in the Union, it cannot be supported in that sense which would be requisite to work an exclusion of the States. It is indeed possible that a tax might be laid on a particular article by a State which might render it *inexpedient* that thus a further tax should be laid on the same article by the Union; but it would not imply a constitutional inability to impose a further tax. The quantity of the imposition, the expediency or inexpediency of an increase on either side, would be mutually questions of prudence; but there would be involved no direct contradiction of power. The particular policy of the national and of the State systems of finance might now and then not exactly coincide, and might require reciprocal forbearances. It is not however a mere possibility of inconvenience in the exercise of powers, but an immediate constitutional repugnancy, that can by implication alienate and extinguish a pre-existing right of sovereignty.

The necessity of a concurrent jurisdiction in certain cases results from the division of the sovereign power; and the rule that all authorities of which the States are not explicitly divested in favour of the Union remain with them in full vigour, is not only a theoretical consequence of that division, but is clearly admitted by the whole tenor of the instrument which contains the articles of the proposed constitution. We there find that notwithstanding the affirmative grants of general authorities, there has been the most pointed care in those cases where it was deemed improper that the like authorities should reside in the States, to insert negative clauses prohibiting the exercise of them by the States. The tenth section of the first article consists altogether of such provisions. This circumstance is a clear indication of the sense of the Convention, and furnishes a rule of interpretation out of the body of the act which justifies the position I have advanced, and refutes every hypothesis to the contrary.

PUBLIUS.

[HAMILTON]

Federalist 33

The Same Subject Continued, January 2, 1788

In their litany of objections to the Constitution, Anti-Federalists often gave pride of place to two clauses: the provision in Article I authorizing Congress "To make all Laws which shall be necessary and proper for carrying into Execution" its own delegated powers and others "vested" in the national government; and the clause of Article VI declaring that the Constitution and national laws and treaties "shall be the supreme Law of the Land . . . any Thing in the Constitution or Laws of any State to the

Contrary notwithstanding." Together, these two provisions would seem-ingly enable Congress to judge the extent of its own powers and to over-ride any interfering legislation the states might enact. If applied to the enumerated power of taxation, the two clauses would permit Congress to exhaust every source of revenue it coveted, and the states would have no recourse.

Federalist 33 uses the immediate question of taxation to justify the two clauses in question. Hamilton again relies upon the logic of asking what powers and authority are necessary if the ends of government are to be obtained. Once a government is empowered to raise and collect taxes, the authority to "make all laws which shall be necessary and proper" to execute those powers merely gives it the capacity to carry out its responsi-bilities. Similarly, if its authority is legal, its laws must also be supreme or else they would not be laws.

Hamilton blandly reassured his readers that the only laws that so qualified must conform to the Constitution. But who could say what was truly necessary and proper, or when the Constitution had been violated? Here Hamilton offered no firm answer. The people would have to be the final judges of the impropriety of an act of Congress, he implied, while the matter of preventing Congress from exercising an unconstitutional power was left hanging—at least until Hamilton took up the question of judicial review in Federalist 78.

The residue of the argument against the provisions in the constitution, in respect to taxation, is ingrafted upon the following clauses; the last clause of the eighth section of the first article of the plan under con-sideration, authorises the national legislature "to make all laws which shall be *necessary* and *proper,* for carrying into execution *the powers* by that Constitution vested in the government of the United States, or in any department or officer thereof"; and the second clause of the sixth article declares, that "the Constitution and the Laws of the United States made in *pursuance thereof,* and the treaties made by their authority shall be the *supreme law* of the land; any thing in the consti-tution or laws of any State to the contrary notwithstanding."

These two clauses have been the sources of much virulent invec-tive and petulant declamation against the proposed constitution, they have been held up to the people, in all the exaggerated colours of mis-representation, as the pernicious engines by which their local govern-ments were to be destroyed and their liberties exterminated—as the hideous monster whose devouring jaws would spare neither sex nor age, nor high nor low, nor sacred nor profane; and yet strange as it may appear, after all this clamour, to those who may not have happened to contemplate them in the same light, it may be affirmed with perfect confidence, that the constitutional operation of the intended government would be precisely the same, if these clauses were entirely obliterated, as if they were repeated in every article. They are only declaratory of a truth, which would have resulted by necessary and unavoidable implication from the very act of constituting a Foederal Government, and vesting it with certain specified powers. This is so clear a proposition, that moderation itself can scarcely listen to the railings which have been so copiously vented against this part of the plan, without emotions that disturb its equanimity.

What is a power, but the ability or faculty of doing a thing? What is the ability to do a thing but the power of employing the *means* necessary to its execution? What is a LEGISLATIVE power but a power of making LAWS? What are the *means* to execute a LEGISLATIVE power but LAWS? What is the power of laying and collecting taxes but a *legislative power,* or a power of *making laws,* to lay and collect taxes? What are the proper means of executing such a power but *necessary* and *proper* laws?

This simple train of enquiry furnishes us at once with a test by which to judge of the true nature of the clause complained of. It conducts us to this palpable truth, that a power to lay and collect taxes must be a power to pass all laws *necessary* and *proper* for the execution of that power; and what does the unfortunate and calumniated provision in question do more than declare the same truth; to wit, that the national legislature to whom the power of laying and collecting taxes had been previously given, might in the execution of that power pass all laws *necessary* and *proper* to carry it into effect? I have applied these observations thus particularly to the power of taxation, because it is the immediate subject under consideration, and because it is the most important of the authorities proposed to be conferred upon the Union. But the same process will lead to the same result in relation to all other powers declared in the constitution. And it is *expressly* to execute these powers, that the sweeping clause, as it has been affectedly called, authorises the national legislature to pass all *necessary* and *proper* laws. If there is any thing exceptionable, it must be sought for in the specific powers, upon which this general declaration is predicated. The declaration itself, though it may be chargeable with tautology or redundancy, is at least perfectly harmless.

But SUSPICION may ask why then was it introduced? The answer is, that it could only have been done for greater caution, and to guard against all cavilling refinements in those who might hereafter feel a disposition to curtail and evade the legitimate authorities of the Union. The Convention probably foresaw what it has been a principal aim of these papers to inculcate that the danger which most threatens our political welfare, is, that the State Governments will finally sap the foundations of the Union; and might therefore think it necessary, in so cardinal a point, to leave nothing to construction. Whatever may have been the inducement to it, the wisdom of the precaution is evident from the cry which has been raised against it; as that very cry betrays a disposition to question the great and essential truth which it is manifestly the object of that provision to declare.

But it may be again asked, who is to judge of the *necessity* and *propriety* of the laws to be passed for executing the powers of the Union? I answer first that this question arises as well and as fully upon the simple grant of those powers, as upon the declaratory clause: And I answer in the second place, that the national government, like every other, must judge in the first instance of the proper exercise of its powers; and its constituents in the last. If the Foederal Government should overpass the just bounds of its authority, and make a tyrannical use of its powers; the people whose creature it is must appeal to the standard they have formed, and take such measures to redress the injury done to the constitution, as the exigency may suggest and prudence justify. The propriety of a law in a constitutional light, must always be determined by the nature of the powers upon which it is founded. Suppose by some forced constructions of its authority (which indeed cannot easily be imagined) the Foederal Legislature should attempt to vary the law of descent in any State; would it not be evident that in making such an attempt it had exceeded its jurisdiction and infringed upon that of the State? Suppose again that upon the pretence of an interference with its revenues, it should undertake to abrogate a land tax imposed by the authority of a State, would it not be equally evident that this was an invasion of that concurrent jurisdiction in respect to this species of tax which its constitution plainly supposes to exist in the State governments? If there ever should be a doubt on this head the credit of it will be intirely due to those reasoners, who, in the imprudent zeal of their animosity to the plan of the Convention, have laboured to invelope it in a cloud calculated to obscure the plainest and simplest truths.

But it is said, that the laws of the Union are to be the *supreme law* of the land. But what inference can be drawn from this or what would they amount to, if they were not to be supreme? It is evident they would amount to nothing. A LAW by the very meaning of the term includes supremacy. It is a rule which those to whom it is prescribed are bound to observe. This results from every political association. If individuals enter into a state of society the laws of that society must be the supreme regulator of their conduct. If a number of political societies enter into a larger political society, the laws which the latter may enact, pursuant to the powers entrusted to it by its constitution, must necessarily be supreme over those societies, and the individuals of whom they are composed. It would otherwise be a mere treaty, dependent on the good faith of the parties, and not a government; which is only another word for POLITICAL POWER AND SUPREMACY. But it will not follow from this doctrine that acts of the larger society which are *not pursuant* to its constitutional powers but which are invasions of the residuary authorities of the smaller societies will become the supreme law of the land. These will be merely acts of usurpation and will deserve to be treated as such. Hence we perceive that the clause which declares the supremacy of the laws of the Union, like the one we have just before considered, only declares a truth, which flows immediately and necessarily from the institution of a Foederal Government. It will not, I presume, have escaped observation that it *expressly* confines this supremacy to laws made *pursuant to the Constitution;* which I mention merely as an instance of caution in the Convention; since that limitation would have been to be understood though it had not been expressed.

Though a law therefore for laying a tax for the use of the United States would be supreme in its nature, and could not legally be opposed or controuled; yet a law for abrogating or preventing the collection of a tax laid by the authority of a State (unless upon imports and exports) would not be the supreme law of the land, but an usurpation of power not granted by the constitution. As far as an improper accumulation of taxes on the same object might tend to render the collection difficult or precarious, this would be a mutual inconvenience not arising from a superiority or defect of power on either side, but from an injudicious exercise of power by one or the other, in a manner equally disadvantageous to both. It is to be hoped and presumed however that mutual interest would dictate a concert in this respect which would avoid any material inconvenience. The inference from the whole is—that the individual States would, under the proposed constitution, retain an independent and uncontroulable authority to raise revenue to any extent of which they may stand in need by every kind of taxation except duties on imports and exports. It will be shewn in the next paper that this CONCURRENT JURISDICTION in the article of taxation was the only admissible substitute for an intire subordination, in respect to this branch of power, of the State authority to that of the Union.

PUBLIUS.

[HAMILTON]

Federalist 35

The Same Subject Continued, January 5, 1788

With the sole possible exception of Robert Morris, the superintendent of finance under the Confederation between 1781 and 1784, Hamilton was certainly the new republic's keenest student of public finance. Federalist 35 illuminates his abilities in that field in two ways. It opens with a discussion of the reasons it would be unwise to restrict the Union to particular sources of revenue. But Hamilton then introduces a second theme, taking up the standard Anti-Federalist objection that the new Congress will lack "sympathy" with the conditions of its constituents, and therefore subject them to burdensome taxes. Hamilton seizes on this objection to launch into an insightful discussion of the nature of representation. In the process, he explains why it is unreasonable to expect the members of a representative legislature to resemble the larger society too closely. He further explains why it is unlikely and undesirable that complex public measures, such as schemes of taxation, can result from legislative deliberation; rather, they require preparation by expert ministers of state. Reading this essay, it is easy to see why Hamilton would soon play so ambitious a role as the first secretary of the treasury in the new administration of his once and future chief, George Washington.

To the People of the State of New York.

Before we proceed to examine any other objections to an indefinite power of taxation in the Union, I shall make one general remark; which is, that if the jurisdiction of the national government in the article of revenue should be restricted to particular objects, it would naturally occasion an undue proportion of the public burthens to fall upon those objects. Two evils would spring from this source, the oppression of particular branches of industry, and an unequal distribution of the taxes, as well among the several States as among the citizens of the same State.

Suppose, as has been contended for, the foederal power of taxation were to be confined to duties on imports, it is evident that the government, for want of being able to command other resources, would frequently be tempted to extend these duties to an injurious excess. There are persons who imagine that this can never be carried to too great a length; since the higher they are, the more it is alleged they will tend to discourage an extravagant consumption, to produce a favourable balance of trade, and to promote domestic manufactures. But all extremes are pernicious in various ways. Exorbitant duties on imported articles would beget a general spirit of smuggling; which is always prejudicial to the fair trader, and eventually to the revenue itself: They tend to render other classes of the community tributary in an improper degree to the manufacturing classes to whom they give a premature monopoly of the markets: They sometimes force industry out of its more natural channels into others in which it flows with less advantage. And in the last place they oppress the merchant, who is often obliged to pay them himself without any retribution from the consumer. When the demand is equal to the quantity of goods at market, the consumer generally pays the duty; but when the markets happen to be overstocked, a great proportion falls upon the merchant, and sometimes not only exhausts his profits, but breaks in upon his capital. I am apt to think that a division of the duty between the seller and the buyer more often happens than is commonly imagined. It is not always possible to raise the price of a commodity, in exact proportion to every additional imposition laid upon it. The merchant especially, in a country of small commercial capital, is often under a necessity of keeping prices down, in order to a more expeditious sale.

The maxim that the consumer is the payer, is so much oftener true than the reverse of the proposition, that it is far more equitable the duties on imports should go into a common stock, than that they should redound to the exclusive benefit of the importing States. But it is not so generally true as to render it equitable that those duties should form the only national fund. When they are paid by the merchant, they operate as an additional tax upon the importing State; whose citizens pay their proportion of them in the character of consumers. In this view they are productive of inequality among the States; which inequality would be encreased with the encreased extent of the duties. The confinement of the national revenues to this species of imposts, would be attended with inequality, from a different cause between the manufacturing and the non-manufacturing States. The States which can go furthest towards the supply of their own wants, by their own manufactures, will not, according to their numbers or wealth, consume so great a proportion of imported articles, as those States which are not in the same favourable situation; they would not therefore in this mode alone contribute to the public treasury in a ratio to their abilities. To make them do this, it is necessary that recourse be had to excises; the proper objects of which are particular kinds of manufactures. New-York is more deeply interested in these considerations than such of her citizens as contend for limiting the power of the Union to external taxation can be aware of—New-York is an importing State, and is not likely speedily to be to any great extent a manufacturing State. She would of course suffer in a double light from restraining the jurisdiction of the Union to commercial imposts.

So far as these observations tend to inculcate a danger of the import duties being extended to an injurious extreme it may be observed, conformably to a remark made in another part of these papers,[1] that the interest of the revenue itself would be a sufficient guard against such an extreme. I readily admit that this would be the case as long as other resources were open; but if the avenues to them were closed HOPE stimulated by necessity would beget experiments fortified by rigorous precautions and additional penalties; which for a time would have the intended effect, till there had been leisure to con- trive expedients to elude these new precautions. The first success would be apt to inspire false opinions; which it might require a long course of subsequent experience to correct. Necessity, especially in politics, often occasions false hopes, false reasonings and a system of measures, correspondently erroneous. But even if this supposed excess should not be a consequence of the limitation of the foederal power of taxation the inequalities spoken of would still ensue, though not in the same degree, from the other causes that have been noticed. Let us now return to the examination of objections —

One, which if we may judge from the frequency of its repetition seems most to be relied on, is that the house of representatives is not sufficiently numerous for the reception of all the different classes of citizens; in order to combine the interests and feelings of every part of the community, and to produce a due sympathy between the represen- tative body and its constituents. This argument presents itself under a very specious and seducing form; and is well calculated to lay hold of

---

[1] Hamilton is referring to *Federalist* 21, not included in this text.

the prejudices of those to whom it is addressed. But when we come to dissect it with attention it will appear to be made up of nothing but fair sounding words. The object it seems to aim at is in the first place impracticable, and in the sense in which it is contended for is unnecessary. I reserve for another place the discussion of the question which relates to the sufficiency of the representative body in respect to numbers; and shall content myself with examining here the particular use which has been made of a contrary supposition in reference to the immediate subject of our inquiries.

The idea of an actual representation of all classes of the people by persons of each class is altogether visionary. Unless it were expressly provided in the Constitution that each different occupation should send one or more members the thing would never take place in practice. Mechanics and manufacturers will always be inclined with few exceptions to give their votes to merchants in preference to persons of their own professions or trades. Those discerning citizens are well aware that the mechanic and manufacturing arts furnish the materials of mercantile enterprise and industry. Many of them indeed are immediately connected with the operations of commerce. They know that the merchant is their natural patron and friend; and they are aware that however great the confidence they may justly feel in their own good sense, their interests can be more effectually promoted by the merchant than by themselves. They are sensible that their habits in life have not been such as to give them those acquired endowments, without which in a deliberative assembly the greatest natural abilities are for the most part useless; and that the influence and weight and superior acquirements of the merchants render them more equal to a contest with any spirit which might happen to infuse itself into the public councils unfriendly to the manufacturing and trading interests. These considerations and many others that might be mentioned prove, and experience confirms it, that artisans and manufacturers will commonly be disposed to bestow their votes upon merchants and those whom they recommend. We must therefore consider merchants as the natural representatives of all these classes of the community.

With regard to the learned professions, little need be observed; they truly form no distinct interest in society; and according to their situation and talents will be indiscriminately the objects of the confidence and choice of each other and of other parts of the community.

Nothing remains but the landed interest; and this in a political view and particularly in relation to taxes I take to be perfectly united from the wealthiest landlord to the poorest tenant. No tax can be laid on land which will not affect the proprietor of millions of acres as well as the proprietor of a single acre. Every land-holder will therefore have a common interest to keep the taxes on land as low as possible; and common interest may always be reckoned upon as the surest bond of sympathy. But if we even could suppose a distinction of interest between the opulent land-holder and the middling farmer, what reason is there to conclude that the first would stand a better chance of being deputed to the national legislature than the last? If we take fact as our guide and look into our own senate and assembly we shall find that moderate proprietors of land prevail in both; nor is this less the case in the senate which consists of a smaller number than in the Assembly, which is composed of a greater number. Where the qualifications of the electors are the same, whether they have to choose a small or a large number their votes will fall upon those in whom they have most confidence; whether these happen to be men of large fortunes or of moderate property or of no property at all.

It is said to be necessary that all classes of citizens should have some of their own number in the representative body, in order that their feelings and interests may be the better understood and attended to. But we have seen that this will never happen under any arrangement that leaves the votes of the people free. Where this is the case, the representative body, with too few exceptions to have any influence on the spirit of the government, will be composed of land-holders, merchants, and men of the learned professions. But where is the danger that the interests and feelings of the different classes of citizens will not be understood or attended to by these three descriptions of men? Will not the land-holder know and feel whatever will promote or injure the interests of landed property? and will he not from his own interest in that species of property be sufficiently prone to resist every attempt to prejudice or incumber it? Will not the merchant understand and be disposed to cultivate as far as may be proper the interests of the mechanic and manufacturing arts to which his commerce is so nearly allied? Will not the man of the learned profession, who will feel a neutrality to the rivalships between the different branches of industry, be likely to prove an impartial arbiter between them, ready to promote either, so far as it shall appear to him conducive to the general interests of the society?

If we take into the account the momentary humors or dispositions which may happen to prevail in particular parts of the society, and to which a wise administration will never be inattentive, is the man whose situation leads to extensive inquiry and information less likely to be a competent judge of their nature, extent and foundation than one whose observation does not travel beyond the circle of his neighbours and acquaintances? Is it not natural that a man who is a candidate for the favour of the people and who is dependent on the suffrages of his fellow-citizens for the continuance of his public honors should take care to inform himself of their dispositions and inclinations and should be willing to allow them their proper degree of influence upon his conduct? This dependence, and the necessity of being bound himself and his posterity by the laws to which he gives his assent are the true, and they are the strong chords of sympathy between the representatives and the constituent.

There is no part of the administration of government that requires extensive information and a thorough knowledge of the principles of political economy so much as the business of taxation. The man who understands those principles best will be least likely to resort to oppressive expedients, or to sacrifice any particular class of citizens to the procurement of revenue. It might be demonstrated that the most productive system of finance will always be the least burthensome. There can be no doubt that in order to a judicious exercise of the power of taxation it is necessary that the person in whose hands it is should be acquainted with the general genius, habits and modes of thinking of the people at large and with the resources of the country. And this is all that can be reasonably meant by a knowledge of the interests and feelings of the people. In any other sense the proposition has either no meaning, or an absurd one. And in that sense let every considerate citizen judge for himself where the requisite qualification is most likely to be found.

PUBLIUS.

[MADISON]

Federalist 37

Concerning the Difficulties Which the Convention Must Have Experienced in the Formation of a Proper Plan, January 11, 1788

With this essay, the quill of Publius passed from Hamilton to Madison. More important, this essay marked the transition from the discussion of the necessity and advantages of the Union that had preoccupied Publius thus far, to a justification of the specific provisions of the Constitution itself. The plan was to examine the Constitution systematically, department by department, beginning with Congress (Article I), and then moving on to the executive (Article II) and judiciary (Article III).

But first, Madison uses this essay to discuss how one should think about political phenomena in general, or rather to compare the difficulty of political thinking with other forms of knowledge. Much like Federalist *1, this essay is a plea for moderation in political judgment. But moderation is now required not because one should naturally mistrust the rival motives of the opposing sides, but rather because reasonable citizens should appreciate the difficulties inherent in the enterprise of creating a constitution. Those difficulties take many forms: "the novelty of the undertaking"; the challenge of reconciling "the requisite stability and energy in Government" with the principles of republican liberty; and the essential line-drawing activity required to allocate power between the Union and the states and among the several departments of government. But Madison also asks readers to recognize that political phenomena cannot be as distinct as natural ones, that human organs of perception are fallible, and that the ambiguity of language introduces further sources of confusion. Moreover, the framers did not have the luxury of reasoning about the Constitution in philosophical terms; each represented particular interests that shaped his political judgment.*

To the People of the State of New York.

In reviewing the defects of the existing Confederation, and shewing that they cannot be supplied by a Government of less energy than that before the public, several of the most important principles of the latter fell of course under consideration. But as the ultimate object of these papers is to determine clearly and fully the merits of this Constitution, and the expediency of adopting it, our plan cannot be compleated without taking a more critical and thorough survey of the work of the Convention; without examining it on all its sides; comparing it in all its parts, and calculating its probable effects. That this remaining task may be executed under impressions conducive to a just and fair result, some reflections must in this place be indulged, which candor previously suggests. It is a misfortune, inseparable from human affairs, that public measures are rarely investigated with that spirit of moderation which is essential to a just estimate of their real tendency to advance or obstruct the public good; and that this spirit is more apt to be diminished than prompted, by those occasions which require an unusual exercise of it. To those who have been led by experience to attend to this consideration, it could not appear surprising, that the act of the Convention which recommends so many important changes and innovations, which may be viewed in so many lights and relations, and which touches the springs of so many passions and interests, should find or excite dispositions unfriendly both on one side, and on the other, to a fair discussion and accurate judgment of its merits. In some, it has been too evident from their own publications, that they have scanned the proposed Constitution, not only with a predisposition to censure; but with a predetermination to condemn: as the language held by others betrays an opposite predetermination or bias, which must render their opinions also of little moment in the question. In placing however, these different characters on a level, with respect to the weight of their opinions, I wish not to insinuate that there may not be a material difference in the purity of their intentions. It is but just to remark in favor of the latter description, that as our situation is universally admitted to be peculiarly critical, and to require indispensibly, that something should be done for our relief, the predetermined patron of what has been actually done, may have taken his bias from the weight of these considerations, as well as from considerations of a sinister nature. The predetermined adversary on the other hand, can have been governed by no venial motive whatever. The intentions of the first may be upright, as they may on the contrary be culpable. The views of the last cannot be upright, and must be culpable. But the truth is, that these papers are not addressed to persons falling under either of these characters. They solicit the attention of those only, who add to a sincere zeal for the happiness of their country, a temper favorable to a just estimate of the means of promoting it.

Persons of this character will proceed to an examination of the plan submitted by the Convention, not only without a disposition to find or to magnify faults; but will see the propriety of reflecting that a faultless plan was not to be expected. Nor will they barely make allowances for the errors which may be chargeable on the fallibility to which the Convention, as a body of men, were liable; but will keep in mind that they themselves also are but men, and ought not to assume an infallibility in rejudging the fallible opinions of others.

With equal readiness will it be perceived, that besides these inducements to candor, many allowances ought to be made for the difficulties inherent in the very nature of the undertaking referred to the Convention.

The novelty of the undertaking immediately strikes us. It has been shewn in the course of these papers, that the existing Confederation is founded on principles which are fallacious; that we must consequently change this first foundation, and with it, the superstructure resting upon it. It has been shewn, that the other confederacies which could be consulted as precedents, have been viciated by the same erroneous principles, and can therefore furnish no other light than that of beacons, which give warning of the course to be shunned, without pointing out that which ought to be pursued. The most that the convention could do in such a situation, was to avoid the errors suggested by the past experience of other countries, as well as of our own; and to provide a convenient mode of rectifying their own errors, as future experience may unfold them.

Among the difficulties encountered by the Convention, a very important one must have lain, in combining the requisite stability and energy in Government, with the inviolable attention due to liberty, and to the Republican form. Without substantially accomplishing this part of their undertaking, they would have very imperfectly fulfilled the object of their appointment, or the expectation of the public: Yet, that it could not be easily accomplished, will be denied by no one, who is unwilling to betray his ignorance of the subject. Energy in Government is essential to that security against external and internal danger, and to that prompt and salutary execution of the laws, which enter into the very definition of good Government. Stability in Government, is essential to national character, and to the advantages annexed to it, as well as to that repose and confidence in the minds of the people, which are among the chief blessings of civil society. An irregular and mutable legislation, is not more an evil in itself, than it is odious to the people; and it may be pronounced with assurance, that the people of this country, enlightened as they are, with regard to the nature, and interested, as the great body of them are, in the effects of good Government, will never be satisfied, till some remedy be applied to the vicissitudes and uncertainties, which characterize the State administrations. On comparing, however, these valuable ingredients with the vital principles of liberty, we must perceive at once, the difficulty of mingling them together in their due proportions. The genius of Republican liberty, seems to demand on one side, not only that all power should be derived from the people; but, that those entrusted with it should be kept in dependence on the people, by a short duration of their appointments; and, that, even during this short period, the trust should be placed not in a few, but in a number of hands. Stability, on the contrary, requires, that the hands, in which power is lodged, should continue for a length of time, the same. A frequent change of men will result from a frequent return of electors, and a frequent change of measures, from a frequent change of men: whilst energy in Government requires not only a certain duration of power, but the execution of it by a single hand. How far the Convention may have succeeded in this part of their work, will better appear on a more accurate view of it. From the cursory view, here taken, it must clearly appear to have been an arduous part.

Not less arduous must have been the task of marking the proper line of partition, between the authority of the general, and that of the State Governments. Every man will be sensible of this difficulty, in proportion, as he has been accustomed to contemplate and discriminate objects, extensive and complicated in their nature. The faculties of the mind itself have never yet been distinguished and defined, with satisfactory precision, by all the efforts of the most acute and metaphysical Philosophers. Sense, perception, judgment, desire, volition, memory, imagination, are found to be separated by such delicate shades, and minute gradations, that their boundaries have eluded the most subtle investigations, and remain a pregnant source of ingenious disquisition and controversy. The boundaries between the great kingdoms of nature, and still more, between the various provinces, and lesser portions, into which they are subdivided, afford another illustration of the same important truth. The most sagacious and laborious naturalists have never yet succeeded, in tracing with certainty, the line which separates the district of vegetable life from the neighboring region of unorganized matter, or which marks the termination of the former and the commencement of the animal empire. A still greater obscurity lies in the distinctive characters, by which the objects in each of these great departments of nature, have been arranged and assorted. When we pass from the works of nature, in which all the delineations are perfectly accurate, and appear to be otherwise only from the imperfection of the eye which surveys them, to the institutions of man, in which the obscurity arises as well from the object itself, as from the organ by which it is contemplated; we must perceive the necessity of moderating still farther our expectations and hopes from the efforts of human sagacity. Experience has instructed us that no skill in the science of Government has yet been able to discriminate and define, with sufficient certainty, its three great provinces, the Legislative, Executive and Judiciary; or even the privileges and powers of the different Legislative branches. Questions daily occur in the course of practice, which prove the obscurity which reigns in these subjects, and which puzzle the greatest adepts in political science. The experience of ages, with the continued and combined labors of the most enlightened Legislators and jurists, have been equally unsuccessful in delineating the several objects and limits of different codes of laws and different tribunals of justice. The precise extent of the common law, the statute law, the maritime law, the ecclesiastical law, the law of corporations and other local laws and customs, remain still to be clearly and finally established in Great-Britain, where accuracy in such subjects has been more industriously pursued than in any other part of the world. The jurisdiction of her several courts, general and local, of law, of equity, of admiralty, &c. is not less a source of frequent and intricate discussions, sufficiently denoting the indeterminate limits by which they are respectively circumscribed. All new laws, though penned with the greatest technical skill, and passed on the fullest and most mature deliberation, are considered as more or less obscure and equivocal, until their meaning be liquidated and ascertained by a series of particular discussions and adjudications. Besides the obscurity arising from the complexity of objects, and the imperfection of the human faculties, the medium through which the conceptions of men are conveyed to each other, adds a fresh embarrassment. The use of words is to express ideas. Perspicuity therefore requires not only that the ideas should be distinctly formed, but that they should be expressed by words distinctly and exclusively appropriated to them. But no language is so copious as to supply words and phrases for every complex idea, or so correct as not to include many equivocally denoting different ideas. Hence, it must happen, that however accurately objects may be discriminated in themselves, and however accurately the discrimination may be considered, the definition of them may be rendered inaccurate by the inaccuracy of the terms in which it is delivered. And this unavoidable inaccuracy must be greater or less, according to the complexity and novelty of the objects defined. When the Almighty himself condescends to address mankind in their own language, his meaning, luminous as it must be, is rendered dim and doubtful, by the cloudy medium through which it is communicated. Here then are three sources of vague and incorrect definitions; indistinctness of the object, imperfection of the organ of conception, inadequateness of the vehicle of ideas. Any one of these must produce a certain degree of obscurity. The Convention, in delineating the boundary between the Federal and State jurisdictions, must have experienced the full effect of them all.

To the difficulties already mentioned, may be added the interfering pretensions of the larger and smaller States. We cannot err in supposing that the former would contend for a participation in the Government, fully proportioned to their superior wealth and importance; and that the latter would not be less tenacious of the equality at present enjoyed by them. We may well suppose that neither side would entirely yield to the other, and consequently that the struggle could be terminated only by compromise. It is extremely probable also, that after the ratio of representation had been adjusted, this very compromise must have produced a fresh struggle between the same parties, to give such a turn to the organization of the Government, and to the distribution of its powers, as would encrease the importance of the branches, in forming which they had respectively obtained the greatest share of influence. There are features in the Constitution which warrant each of these suppositions; and as far as either of them is well founded, it shews that the Convention must have been compelled to sacrifice theoretical propriety to the force of extraneous considerations.

Nor could it have been the large and small States only which would marshal themselves in opposition to each other on various points. Other combinations, resulting from a difference of local position and policy, must have created additional difficulties. As every State may be divided into different districts, and its citizens into different classes, which give birth to contending interests and local jealousies; so the different parts of the United States are distinguished from each other, by a variety of circumstances, which produce a like effect on a larger scale. And although this variety of interests, for reasons sufficiently explained in a former paper,[1] may have a salutary influence on the administration of the Government when formed; yet every one must be sensible of the contrary influence which must have been experienced in the task of forming it.

Would it be wonderful if under the pressure of all these difficulties, the Convention should have been forced into some deviations from that artificial structure and regular symmetry, which an abstract view of the subject might lead an ingenious theorist to bestow on a Constitution planned in his closet or in his imagination? The real wonder is, that so many difficulties should have been surmounted; and surmounted with a unanimity almost as unprecedented as it must have been unexpected. It is impossible for any man of candor to reflect on this circumstance, without partaking of the astonishment. It is impossible for the man of pious reflection not to perceive in it, a finger of that Almighty hand which has been so frequently and signally extended to our relief in the critical stages of the revolution. We had occasion in a former paper,[2] to take notice of the repeated trials which

[1] *a former paper: Federalist* 10.
[2] *a former paper: Federalist* 20, not included here.

have been unsuccessfully made in the United Netherlands, for reforming the baneful and notorious vices of their Constitution. The history of almost all the great councils and consultations, held among mankind for reconciling their discordant opinions, assuaging their mutual jealousies, and adjusting their respective interests, is a history of factions, contentions, and disappointments; and may be classed among the most dark and degrading pictures which display the infirmities and depravities of the human character. If, in a few scattered instances, a brighter aspect is presented, they serve only as exceptions to admonish us of the general truth; and by their lustre to darken the gloom of the adverse prospect to which they are contrasted. In revolving the causes from which these exceptions result, and applying them to the particular instance before us, we are necessarily led to two important conclusions. The first is, that the Convention must have enjoyed in a very singular degree, an exemption from the pestilential influence of party animosities; the diseases most incident to deliberative bodies, and most apt to contaminate their proceedings. The second conclusion is, that all the deputations composing the Convention, were either satisfactorily accommodated by the final act; or were induced to accede to it, by a deep conviction of the necessity of sacrificing private opinions and partial interests to the public good, and by a despair of seeing this necessity diminished by delays or by new experiments.

PUBLIUS.

[MADISON]

Federalist 39

The Conformity of the Plan to Republican Principles: An Objection in Respect to the Powers of the Convention Examined, January 16, 1788

Madison opens this essay with a deceptively simple question: Can the new government proposed by the Constitution be regarded as "strictly republican"? And he later poses a second, equally straightforward question: Is it also "federal"? If the answer to both questions is no, the debate over the Constitution is over, for Americans are devoted to both republican and federal principles of government. But the answers turn out to be quite intricate. For Madison uses this essay as an applied demonstration of the rules of political analysis laid down in Federalist 37. *To overcome the ambiguity of language, the key terms,* republican *and* federal, *require clear and consistent definitions. To overcome our impulse to simplify, the characteristics of the new government must be described in close and precise detail.*

The definition of a republican government again hinges on distinguishing a republic, based on representation, from a democracy, where the people debate and decide themselves. But the more difficult challenge is to map the contours of federalism, and here Madison asks readers to bear with him as he lays out no fewer than five distinct criteria by which to judge the federal and national aspects of the Constitution. Ideally, had the Convention approved his proposed veto on state laws, Madison could have offered a simpler description of the federal system than the five-pronged model presented here, for then the sovereign supremacy of the national government would have been conclusively established. But having lost that key point, he now understood that the truth of American federalism could be found only in its prosaic and unique details.

To the People of the State of New York.

The last paper having concluded the observations which were meant to introduce a candid survey of the plan of government reported by the Convention, we now proceed to the execution of that part of our undertaking. The first question that offers itself is, whether the general form and aspect of the government be strictly republican? It is evident that no other form would be reconcileable with the genius of the people of America; with the fundamental principles of the revolution; or with that honorable determination, which animates every votary of freedom, to rest all our political experiments on the capacity of mankind for self-government. If the plan of the Convention therefore be found to depart from the republican character, its advocates must abandon it as no longer defensible.

What then are the distinctive characters of the republican form? Were an answer to this question to be sought, not by recurring to principles, but in the application of the term by political writers, to the constitutions of different States, no satisfactory one would ever be found. Holland, in which no particle of the supreme authority is derived from the people, has passed almost universally under the denomination of a republic. The same title has been bestowed on Venice, where absolute power over the great body of the people, is exercised in the most absolute manner, by a small body of hereditary nobles. Poland, which is a mixture of aristocracy and of monarchy in their worst forms, has been dignified with the same appellation. The government of England, which has one republican branch only, combined with a hereditery aristocracy and monarchy, has with equal impropriety been frequently placed on the list of republics. These examples, which are nearly as dissimilar to each other as to a genuine republic, shew the extreme inaccuracy with which the term has been used in political disquisitions.

If we resort for a criterion, to the different principles on which different forms of government are established, we may define a republic to be, or at least may bestow that name on, a government which derives all its powers directly or indirectly from the great body of the people; and is administered by persons holding their offices during pleasure, for a limited period, or during good behaviour. It is *essential* to such a government, that it be derived from the great body of the society, not from an inconsiderable proportion, or a favored class of it; otherwise a handful of tyrannical nobles, exercising their oppressions by a delegation of their powers, might aspire to the rank of republicans, and claim for their government the honorable title of republic. It is *sufficient* for such a government, that the persons administering it be appointed, either directly or indirectly, by the people; and that they hold their appointments by either of the tenures just specified; otherwise every government in the United States, as well as every other popular government that has been or can be well organized or well executed, would be degraded from the republican character. According to the Constitution of every State in the Union, some or other of the officers of government are appointed indirectly only by the people. According to most of them the chief magistrate himself is so appointed. And according to one, this mode of appointment is extended to one of the coordinate branches of the legislature. According to all the Constitutions also, the tenure of the highest offices is extended to a definite period, and in many instances, both within the legislative and executive departments, to a period of years. According to the provisions of most of the constitutions, again, as well as according to the most respectable and received opinions on the subject, the members of the judiciary department are to retain their offices by the firm tenure of good behaviour.

On comparing the Constitution planned by the Convention, with the standard here fixed, we perceive at once that it is in the most rigid sense conformable to it. The House of Representatives, like that of one branch at least of all the State Legislatures, is elected immediately by the great body of the people. The Senate, like the present Congress, and the Senate of Maryland, derives its appointment indirectly from the people. The President is indirectly derived from the choice of the people, according to the example in most of the States. Even the judges, with all other officers of the Union, will, as in the several States, be the choice, though a remote choice, of the people themselves. The duration of the appointments is equally conformable to the republican standard, and to the model of the State Constitutions. The House of Representatives is periodically elective as in all the States: and for the period of two years as in the State of South-Carolina. The Senate is elective for the period of six years; which is but one year more than the period of the Senate of Maryland; and but two more than that of the Senates of New-York and Virginia. The President is to continue in office for the period of four years; as in New-York and Delaware, the chief magistrate is elected for three years, and in South-Carolina for two years. In the other States the election is annual. In several of the States however, no constitutional provision is made for the impeachment of the Chief Magistrate. And in Delaware and Virginia, he is not impeachable till out of office. The President of the United States is impeachable at any time during his continuance in office. The tenure by which the Judges are to hold their places, is, as it unquestionably ought to be, that of good behaviour. The tenure of the ministerial offices generally will be a subject of legal regulation, conformably to the reason of the case, and the example of the State Constitutions.

Could any further proof be required of the republican complextion of this system, the most decisive one might be found in its absolute prohibition of titles of nobility, both under the Federal and the State Governments; and in its express guarantee of the republican form to each of the latter.

But it was not sufficient, say the adversaries of the proposed Constitution, for the Convention to adhere to the republican form. They ought, with equal care, to have preserved the *federal* form, which regards the union as a *confederacy* of sovereign States; instead of which, they have framed a *national* government, which regards the union as a *consolidation* of the States. And it is asked by what authority this bold and radical innovation was undertaken. The handle which has been made of this objection requires, that it should be examined with some precision.

Without enquiring into the accuracy of the distinction on which the objection is founded, it will be necessary to a just estimate of its force, first to ascertain the real character of the government in question; secondly, to enquire how far the Convention were authorised to propose such a government; and thirdly, how far the duty they owed to their country, could supply any defect of regular authority.

First. In order to ascertain the real character of the government it may be considered in relation to the foundation on which it is to be established; to the sources from which its ordinary powers are to be drawn; to the operation of those powers; to the extent of them; and to the authority by which future changes in the government are to be introduced.

On examining the first relation, it appears on one hand that the Constitution is to be founded on the assent and ratification of the people of America, given by deputies elected for the special purpose; but on the other, that this assent and ratification is to be given by the people, not as individuals composing one entire nation; but as composing the distinct and independent States to which they respectively belong. It is to be the assent and ratification of the several States, derived from the supreme authority in each State, the authority of the people themselves. The act therefore establishing the Constitution, will not be a *national* but a *federal* act.

That it will be a federal and not a national act, as these terms are understood by the objectors, the act of the people as forming so many independent States, not as forming one aggregate nation, is obvious from this single consideration that it is to result neither from the decision of a *majority* of the people of the Union, nor from that of a *majority* of the States. It must result from the *unanimous* assent of the several States that are parties to it, differing no other wise from their ordinary assent than in its being expressed, not by the legislative authority, but by that of the people themselves. Were the people regarded in this transaction as forming one nation, the will of the majority of the whole people of the United States, would bind the minority; in the same manner as the majority in each State must bind the minority; and the will of the majority must be determined either by a comparison of the individual votes; or by considering the will of a majority of the States, as evidence of the will of a majority of the people of the United States. Neither of these rules has been adopted. Each State in ratifying the Constitution, is considered as a sovereign body independent of all others, and only to be bound by its own voluntary act. In this relation then the new Constitution will, if established, be a *federal* and not a *national* Constitution.

The next relation is to the sources from which the ordinary powers of government are to be derived. The house of representatives will derive its powers from the people of America, and the people will be represented in the same proportion, and on the same principle, as they are in the Legislature of a particular State. So far the Government is *national* not *federal*. The Senate on the other hand will derive its powers from the States, as political and co-equal societies; and these will be represented on the principle of equality in the Senate, as they now are in the existing Congress. So far the government is *federal,* not *national*. The executive power will be derived from a very compound source. The immediate election of the President is to be made by the States in their political characters. The votes allotted to them, are in a compound ratio, which considers them partly as distinct and co-equal societies; partly as unequal members of the same society. The eventual election, again is to be made by that branch of the Legislature which consists of the national representatives; but in this particular act, they are to be thrown into the form of individual delegations from so many distinct and co-equal bodies politic. From this aspect of the Government, it appears to be of a mixed character presenting at least as many *federal* as *national* features.

The difference between a federal and national Government as it relates to the *operation of the Government* is supposed to consist in this, that in the former, the powers operate on the political bodies composing the confederacy, in their political capacities: In the latter, on the individual citizens, composing the nation, in their individual capacities. On trying the Constitution by this criterion, it falls under the *national,* not the *federal* character; though perhaps not so compleatly, as has been understood. In several cases and particularly in the trial of controversies to which States may be parties, they must be viewed and proceeded against in their collective and political capacities only. So far the national countenance of the Government on this side seems to be disfigured by a few federal features. But this blemish is perhaps unavoidable in any plan; and the operation of the Government on the people in their individual capacities, in its ordinary and most essential proceedings, may on the whole designate it in this relation a *national* Government.

But if the Government be national with regard to the *operation* of its powers, it changes its aspect again when we contemplate it in relation to the *extent* of its powers. The idea of a national Government involves in it, not only an authority over the individual citizens; but an indefinite supremacy over all persons and things, so far as they are objects of lawful Government. Among a people consolidated into one nation, this supremacy is compleatly vested in the national Legislature. Among communities united for particular purposes, it is vested partly in the general, and partly in the municipal Legislatures. In the former case, all local authorities are subordinate to the supreme; and may be controuled, directed or abolished by it at pleasure. In the latter the local or municipal authorities form distinct and independent portions of the supremacy, no more subject within their respective spheres to the general authority, than the general authority is subject to them, within its own sphere. In this relation then the proposed Government cannot be deemed a *national* one; since its jurisdiction extends to certain enumerated objects only, and leaves to the several States a residuary and inviolable sovereignty over all other objects. It is true that in controversies relating to the boundary between the two jurisdictions, the tribunal which is ultimately to decide, is to be established under the general Government. But this does not change the principle of the case. The decision is to be impartially made, according to the rules of the Constitution; and all the usual and most effectual precautions are taken to secure this impartiality. Some such tribunal is clearly essential to prevent an appeal to the sword, and a dissolution of the compact; and that it ought to be established under the general, rather than under the local Governments; or to speak more properly, that it could be safely established under the first alone, is a position not likely to be combated.

If we try the Constitution by its last relation, to the authority by which amendments are to be made, we find it neither wholly *national,* nor wholly *federal.* Were it wholly national, the supreme and ultimate authority would reside in the *majority* of the people of the Union; and this authority would be competent at all times, like that of a majority of every national society, to alter or abolish its established Government. Were it wholly federal on the other hand, the concurrence of each State in the Union would be essential to every alteration that would be binding on all. The mode provided by the plan of the Convention is not founded on either of these principles. In requiring more than a majority, and particularly, in computing the proportion by *States,* not by *citizens,* it departs from the *national,* and advances towards the *federal* character: In rendering the concurrence of less than the whole number of States sufficient, it loses again the *federal,* and partakes of the *national* character.

The proposed Constitution therefore is in strictness neither a national nor a federal constitution; but a composition of both. In its foundation, it is federal, not national; in the sources from which the ordinary powers of the Government are drawn, it is partly federal, and partly national: in the operation of these powers, it is national, not federal: In the extent of them again, it is federal, not national: And finally, in the authoritative mode of introducing amendments, it is neither wholly federal, nor wholly national.

PUBLIUS.

[MADISON]

Federalist 45

A Further Discussion of the Supposed Danger from the Powers of the Union to the State Governments, January 26, 1788

After describing the legislative powers of the new government in Federalist 41–44, Madison devoted the next two essays to comparing the relative power and political advantages of the Union and the states. His obvious purpose was to reassure readers that the danger of "consolidation" repeatedly evoked by Anti-Federalists was implausible. Drawing on his pre-Convention reading in the history of other confederacies, Madison argues that all the evidence suggested that member states were far more likely to encroach on the central authority than the other way around. Moreover, when one fairly compares the respective duties and powers of the two governments, it is far from clear that the national government will have a decisive advantage over the states. However potent the new government may prove, it will still be the states that will conduct most of the business of governance that affects ordinary Americans in their daily lives.

To the People of the State of New York.
Having shewn that no one of the powers transferred to the federal Government is unnecessary or improper, the next question to be considered is whether the whole mass of them will be dangerous to the portion of authority left in the several States.

The adversaries to the plan of the Convention instead of considering in the first place what degree of power was absolutely necessary for the purposes of the federal Government, have exhausted themselves in a secondary enquiry into the possible consequences of the proposed degree of power, to the Governments of the particular States. But if the Union, as has been shewn, be essential, to the security of the people of America against foreign danger; if it be essential to their security against contentions and wars among the different States; if it be essential to guard them against those violent and oppressive factions which embitter the blessings of liberty, and against those military establishments which must gradually poison its very fountain; if, in a word the Union be essential to the happiness of the people of America, is it not preposterous, to urge as an objection to a government without which the objects of the Union cannot be attained, that such a Government may derogate from the importance of the Governments of the individual States? Was then the American revolution effected, was the American confederacy formed, was the precious blood of thousands spilt, and the hard earned substance of millions lavished, not that the people of America should enjoy peace, liberty and safety; but that the Governments of the individual States, that particular municipal establishments, might enjoy a certain extent of power, and be arrayed with certain dignities and attributes of sovereignty? We have heard of the impious doctrine in the old world that the people were made for kings, not kings for the people. Is the same doctrine to be revived in the new, in another shape, that the solid happiness of the people is to be sacrificed to the views of political institutions of a different form? It is too early for politicians to presume on our forgetting that the public good, the real welfare of the great body of the people is the supreme object to be pursued; and that no form of Government whatever, has any other value, than as it may be fitted for the attainment of this object. Were the plan of the Convention adverse to the public happiness, my voice would be, reject the plan. Were the Union itself inconsistent with the public happiness, it would be, abolish the Union. In like manner as far as the sovereignty of the States cannot be reconciled to the happiness of the people, the voice of every good citizen must be, let the former be sacrificed to the latter. How far the sacrifice is necessary, has been shewn. How far the unsacrificed residue will be endangered, is the question before us.

Several important considerations have been touched in the course of these papers, which discountenance the supposition that the operation of the federal Government will by degrees prove fatal to the State Governments. The more I revolve the subject the more fully I am persuaded that the balance is much more likely to be disturbed by the preponderancy of the last than of the first scale.

We have seen in all the examples of antient and modern confederacies, the strongest tendency continually betraying itself in the members to despoil the general Government of its authorities, with a very ineffectual capacity in the latter to defend itself against the encroachments.

Although in most of these examples, the system has been so dissimilar from that under consideration, as greatly to weaken any inference concerning the latter from the fate of the former; yet as the States will retain under the proposed Constitution a very extensive portion of active sovereignty, the inference ought not to be wholly disregarded. In the Achæan league, it is probable that the federal head had a degree and species of power, which gave it a considerable likeness to the government framed by the Convention. The Lycian confederacy, as far as its principles and form are transmitted, must have borne a still greater analogy to it. Yet history does not inform us that either of them ever degenerated or tended to degenerate into one consolidated government. On the contrary, we know that the ruin of one of them proceeded from the incapacity of the federal authority to prevent the dissentions, and finally the disunion of the subordinate authorities. These cases are the more worthy of our attention, as the external causes by which the component parts were pressed together, were much more numerous and powerful than in our case; and consequently, less powerful ligaments within, would be sufficient to bind the members to the head, and to each other.

In the feudal system we have seen a similar propensity exemplified. Notwithstanding the want of proper sympathy in every instance between the local sovereigns and the people, and the sympathy in some instances between the general sovereign and the latter; it usually happened that the local sovereigns prevailed in the rivalship for encroachments. Had no external dangers, enforced internal harmony and subordination; and particularly had the local sovereigns possessed the affections of the people, the great kingdoms in Europe, would at this time consist of as many independent princes as there were formerly feudatory barons.

The State Governments will have the advantage of the federal Government, whether we compare them in respect to the immediate dependence of the one or the other; to the weight of personal influence which each side will possess; to the powers respectively vested in them; to the predilection and probable support of the people; to the disposition and faculty of resisting and frustrating the measures of each other.

The State Governments may be regarded as constituent and essential parts of the federal Government; whilst the latter is nowise essential to the operation or organisation of the former. Without the intervention of the State Legislatures, the President of the United States cannot be elected at all. They must in all cases have a great share in his appointment, and will perhaps in most cases of themselves determine it. The Senate will be elected absolutely and exclusively by the State Legislatures. Even the House of Representatives, though drawn immediately from the people, will be chosen very much under the influence of that class of men, whose influence over the people obtains for themselves an election into the State Legislatures. Thus each of the principal branches of the federal Government will owe its existence more or less to the favor of the State Governments, and must consequently feel a dependence, which is much more likely to beget a disposition too obsequious, than too overbearing towards them. On the other side, the component parts of the State Governments will in no instance be indebted for their appointment to the direct agency of the federal government, and very little if at all, to the local influence of its members.

The number of individuals employed under the Constitution of the United States, will be much smaller, than the number employed under the particular States. There will consequently be less of personal influence on the side of the former, than of the latter. The members of the legislative, executive and judiciary departments of thirteen and more States; the justices of peace, officers of militia, ministerial officers of justice, with all the county corporation and town-officers, for three millions and more of people, intermixed and having particular acquaintance with every class and circle of people, must exceed beyond all proportion, both in number and influence, those of every description who will be employed in the administration of the federal system. Compare the members of the three great departments, of the thirteen States, excluding from the judiciary department the justices of peace, with the members of the corresponding departments of the single Government of the Union; compare the militia officers of three millions of people, with the military and marine officers of any establishment which is within the compass of probability, or I may add, of possibility, and in this view alone, we may pronounce the advantage of the States to be decisive. If the federal Government is to have collectors of revenue, the State Governments will have theirs also. And as those of the former will be principally on the sea-coast, and not very numerous; whilst those of the latter will be spread over the face of the country, and will be very numerous, the advantage in this view also lies on the same side. It is true that the confederacy is to possess, and may exercise, the power of collecting internal as well as external taxes throughout the States: But it is probable that this power will not be resorted to, except for supplemental purposes of revenue; that an option will then be given to the States to supply their quotas by previous collections of their own; and that the eventual collection under the immediate authority of the Union, will generally be made by the officers, and according to the rules, appointed by the several States. Indeed it is extremely probable that in other instances, particularly in the organisation of the judicial power, the officers of the States will be cloathed with the correspondent authority of the Union. Should it happen however that separate collectors of internal revenue should be appointed under the federal Government, the influence of the whole number would not be a comparison with that of the multitude of State officers in the opposite scale. Within every district, to which a federal collector would be allotted, there would not be less than thirty or forty or even more officers of different descriptions and many of them persons of character and weight, whose influence would lie on the side of the State.

The powers delegated by the proposed Constitution to the Federal Government, are few and defined. Those which are to remain in the State Governments are numerous and indefinite. The former will be exercised principally on external objects, as war, peace, negociation, and foreign commerce; with which last the power of taxation will for the most part be connected. The powers reserved to the several States will extend to all the objects, which, in the ordinary course of affairs, concern the lives, liberties and properties of the people; and the internal order, improvement, and prosperity of the State.

The operations of the Federal Government will be most extensive and important in times of war and danger; those of the State Governments, in times of peace and security. As the former periods will probably bear a small proportion to the latter, the State Governments will here enjoy another advantage over the Federal Government. The more adequate indeed the federal powers may be rendered to the national defence, the less frequent will be those scenes of danger which might favour their ascendency over the governments of the particular States.

If the new Constitution be examined with accuracy and candour, it will be found that the change which it proposes, consists much less in the addition of NEW POWERS to the Union, than in the invigoration of its ORIGINAL POWERS. The regulation of commerce, it is true, is a new power; but that seems to be an addition which few oppose, and from which no apprehensions are entertained. The powers relating to war and peace, armies and fleets, treaties and finance, with the other more considerable powers, are all vested in the existing Congress by the articles of Confederation. The proposed change does not enlarge these powers; it only substitutes a more effectual mode of administering them. The change relating to taxation, may be regarded as the most important: And yet the present Congress have as compleat authority to REQUIRE of the States indefinite supplies of money for the common defence and general welfare, as the future Congress will have to require them of individual citizens; and the latter will be no more bound than the States themselves have been, to pay the quotas respectively taxed on them. Had the States complied punctually with the articles of confederation, or could their compliance have been enforced by as peaceable means as may be used with success towards single persons, our past experience is very far from countenancing an opinion that the State Governments would have lost their constitutional powers, and have gradually undergone an entire consolidation. To maintain that such an event would have ensued, would be to say at once, that the existence of the State Governments is incompatible with any system whatever that accomplishes the essential purposes of the Union.

PUBLIUS.

[MADISON]

Federalist 46

The Subject of the Last Paper Resumed with an Examination of the Comparative Means of Influence of the Federal and State Governments, January 29, 1788

Beyond the formal distribution of legal authority between the Union and the states, Madison understood that the balance of power between them would ultimately depend on the political influence and allegiance each would wield and command. In a republic, as Madison reminded Jefferson in October 1788, the "real power lies in the majority of the community"—that is, in the people at large. Where these majorities chose to attach their affections could not be determined merely by looking at the powers given to the nation or the states. It would depend, more fundamentally, on how effectively those powers were used, or which government the people found more attractive.

Here, again, Madison argued that the Union would have to wage an uphill struggle to wrest the affection of the people away from the familiar state governments. Most members of the national government itself would carry their provincial prejudices with them. And should the national government nonetheless manage to launch "ambitious encroachments" on the states, it would only provoke the united opposition of the state governments, which, in the worst-case scenario, would be able to mobilize the militia in defense of their rightful authority.

Madison's emphasis on the relative advantages of the states is noteworthy in several respects. First, it accurately reflected his private assessment of the difficulties the new government would face in surmounting the parochialism of American politics. Second, it indicated how little danger he felt the new government would actually pose to the states. Third, it anticipated the position he would take ten years later, when he and Jefferson respectively drafted the Virginia and Kentucky resolutions in opposition to the policies pursued by the administration of John Adams and his loyal supporters in Congress and the judiciary. Numerous events in the 1790s, beginning with the adoption of Secretary of the Treasury Hamilton's financial program, suggested that the national government might become more powerful than Madison had anticipated. Moreover, by 1798, all three branches of the federal government were firmly controlled by the dominant Federalist party to which Madison and Thomas Jefferson were strongly opposed. As a result, the two leaders seemed to have little choice but to appeal to the state governments to resist what they regarded as the unconstitutional measures of the Alien and Sedition Acts of 1798. A decade earlier, Madison had merely speculated about the unlikely scenario of the states having to mobilize against improper national acts; now that speculation became the basis of his political strategy. In fact, that strategy did not work. Other states refused to join in concerted opposition to the two acts. But the sharply contested election of 1800 vindicated the two Virginians as their Democratic-Republican party carried the presidency and both houses of Congress.

To the People of the State of New York.

Resuming the subject of the last paper, I proceed to enquire whether the Foederal Government or the State Governments will have the advantage with regard to the predilection and support of the people. Notwithstanding the different modes in which they are appointed, we must consider both of them, as substantially dependent on the great body of the citizens of the United States. I assume this position here as it respects the first, reserving the proofs for another place. The Foederal and State Governments are in fact but different agents and trustees of the people, instituted with different powers, and designated for different purposes. The adversaries of the Constitution seem to have lost sight of the people altogether in their reasonings on this subject; and to have viewed these different establishments, not only as mutual rivals and enemies, but as uncontrouled by any common superior in their efforts to usurp the authorities of each other. These gentlemen must here be reminded of their error. They must be told that the ultimate authority, wherever the derivative may be found, resides in the people alone; and that it will not depend merely on the comparative ambition or address of the different governments, whether either, or which of them, will be able to enlarge its sphere of jurisdiction at the expence of the other. Truth no less than decency requires, that the event in every case, should be supposed to depend on the sentiments and sanction of their common constituents.

Many considerations, besides those suggested on a former occasion, seem to place it beyond doubt, that the first and most natural attachment of the people will be to the governments of their respective States. Into the administration of these, a greater number of individuals will expect to rise. From the gift of these a greater number of offices and emoluments will flow. By the superintending care of these, all the more domestic, and personal interests of the people will be regulated and provided for. With the affairs of these, the people will be more familiarly and minutely conversant. And with the members of these, will a greater proportion of the people have the ties of personal acquaintance and friendship, and of family and party attachments; on the side of these therefore the popular bias, may well be expected most strongly to incline.

Experience speaks the same language in this case. The foederal administration, though hitherto very defective, in comparison with what may be hoped under a better system, had during the war, and particularly, whilst the independent fund of paper emissions[1] was in credit, an activity and importance as great as it can well have, in any future circumstances whatever. It was engaged too in a course of measures, which had for their object, the protection of every thing that was dear, and the acquisition of every thing that could be desireable to the people at large. It was nevertheless, invariably found, after the transient enthusiasm for the early Congresses was over, that the attention and attachment of the people were turned anew to their own particular government; that the Foederal Council, was at no time the idol of popular favor; and that opposition to proposed enlargements of its

---

[1] *independent fund of paper emissions:* Madison refers to the various forms of paper currency that the Continental Congress issued before 1780 to pay for the war.

powers and importance, was the side usually taken by the men who wished to build their political consequence on the prepossessions of their fellow citizens.

If therefore, as has been elsewhere remarked, the people should in future become more partial to the foederal than to the State governments, the change can only result, from such manifest and irresistible proofs of a better administration, as will overcome all their antecedent propensities. And in that case, the people ought not surely to be precluded from giving most of their confidence where they may discover it to be most due: But even in that case, the State governments could have little to apprehend, because it is only within a certain sphere, that the federal power can, in the nature of things, be advantageously administered.

The remaining points on which I proposed to compare the foederal and State governments, are the disposition, and the faculty they may respectively possess, to resist and frustrate the measures of each other.

It has been already proved, that the members of the foederal will be more dependent on the members of the State governments, than the latter will be on the former. It has appeared also, that the prepossessions of the people on whom both will depend, will be more on the side of the State governments, than of the Foederal Government. So far as the disposition of each, towards the other, may be influenced by these causes, the State governments must clearly have the advantage. But in a distinct and very important point of view, the advantage will lie on the same side. The prepossessions which the members themselves will carry into the Foederal Government, will generally be favorable to the States; whilst it will rarely happen, that the members of the State governments will carry into the public councils, a bias in favor of the general government. A local spirit will infallibly prevail much more in the members of the Congress, than a national spirit will prevail in the Legislatures of the particular States. Every one knows that a great proportion of the errors committed by the State Legislatures proceeds from the disposition of the members to sacrifice the comprehensive and permanent interest of the State, to the particular and separate views of the counties or districts in which they reside. And if they do not sufficiently enlarge their policy to embrace the collective welfare of their particular State, how can it be imagined, that they will make the aggregate prosperity of the Union, and the dignity and respectability of its government, the objects of their affections and consultations? For the same reason, that the members of the State Legislatures, will be unlikely to attach themselves sufficiently to national objects, the members of the Foederal Legislature will be likely to attach themselves too much to local objects. The States will be to the latter, what counties and towns are to the former. Measures will too often be decided according to their probable effect, not on the national prosperity and happiness, but on the prejudices, interests and pursuits of the governments and people of the individual States. What is the spirit that has in general characterized the proceedings of Congress? A perusal of their journals as well as the candid acknowledgments of such as have had a seat in that assembly, will inform us, that the members have but too frequently displayed the character, rather of partizans of their respective States, than of impartial guardians of a common interest; that whereon one occasion improper sacrifices have been made of local considerations to the aggrandizement of the Foederal Government; the great interests of the nation have suffered on an hundred, from an undue attention to the local prejudices, interests and views of the particular States. I mean not by these reflections to insinuate, that the new Foederal Government will not embrace a more enlarged plan of policy than the existing government may have pursued, much less that its views will be as confined as those of the State Legislatures; but only that it will partake sufficiently of the spirit of both, to be disinclined to invade the rights of the individual States, or the prerogatives of their governments. The motives on the part of the State governments, to augment their prerogatives by defalcations from the Foederal Government, will be overruled by no reciprocal predispositions in the members.

Were it admitted however that the Foederal Government may feel an equal disposition with the State governments to extend its power beyond the due limits, the latter would still have the advantage in the means of defeating such encroachments. If an act of a particular State, though unfriendly to the national government, be generally popular in that State, and should not too grossly violate the oaths of the State officers, it is executed immediately and of course, by means on the spot, and depending on the State alone. The opposition of the Foederal Government, or the interposition of Foederal officers, would but inflame the zeal of all parties on the side of the State, and the evil could not be prevented or repaired, if at all, without the employment of means which must always be resorted to with reluctance and difficulty. On the other hand, should an unwarrantable measure of the Foederal Government be unpopular in particular States, which would seldom fail to be the case, or even a warrantable measure be so, which may sometimes be the case, the means of opposition to it are powerful and at hand. The disquietude of the people, their repugnance and perhaps refusal to co-operate with the officers of the Union, the frowns of the executive magistracy of the State, the embarrassments created by legislative devices, which would often be added on such occasions, would oppose in any State difficulties not to be despised; would form in a large State very serious impediments, and where the sentiments of several adjoining States happened to be in unison, would present obstructions which the Foederal Government would hardly be willing to encounter.

But ambitious encroachments of the Foederal Government, on the authority of the State governments, would not excite the opposition of a single State or of a few States only. They would be signals of general alarm. Every Government would espouse the common cause. A correspondence would be opened. Plans of resistance would be concerted. One spirit would animate and conduct the whole. The same combination in short would result from an apprehension of the foederal, as was produced by the dread of a foreign yoke; and unless the projected innovations should be voluntarily renounced, the same appeal to a trial of force would be made in the one case, as was made in the other. But what degree of madness could ever drive the Foederal Government to such an extremity? In the contest with Great Britain, one part of the empire was employed against the other. The more numerous part invaded the rights of the less numerous part. The attempt was unjust and unwise; but it was in speculation absolutely chimerical.[2] But what would be the contest in the case we are supposing? Who would be the parties? A few representatives of the people, would be opposed to the people themselves; or rather one set of representatives would be contending against thirteen sets of representatives, with the whole body of their common constituents on the side of the latter.

The only refuge left for those who prophecy the downfall of the State Governments, is the visionary supposition that the Foederal Government may previously accumulate a military force for the projects of ambition. The reasonings contained in these papers must have been employed to little purpose indeed, if it could be necessary now to disprove the reality of this danger. That the people and the States should for a sufficient period of time elect an uninterrupted succession of men ready to betray both; that the traitors should throughout this period,

---

[2]*chimerical:* fantastic or inconceivable. Madison suggests that the British government did have some reason to think it could prevail over the American colonists.

uniformly and systematically pursue some fixed plan for the extension of the military establishment; that the governments and the people of the States should silently and patiently behold the gathering storm, and continue to supply the materials, until it should be prepared to burst on their own heads, must appear to every one more like the incoherent dreams of a delirious jealousy, or the misjudged exaggerations of a counterfeit zeal, than like the sober apprehensions of genuine patriotism. Extravagant as the supposition is, let it however be made. Let a regular army, fully equal to the resources of the country be formed; and let it be entirely at the devotion of the Foederal Government; still it would not be going too far to say, that the State Governments with the people on their side would be able to repel the danger. The highest number to which, according to the best computation, a standing army can be carried in any country, does not exceed one hundredth part of the whole number of souls; or one twenty-fifth part of the number able to bear arms. This proportion would not yield in the United States an army of more than twenty-five or thirty thousand men. To these would be opposed a militia amounting to near half a million of citizens with arms in their hands, officered by men chosen from among themselves, fighting for their common liberties, and united and conducted by governments possessing, their affections and confidence. It may well be doubted whether a militia thus circumstanced could ever be conquered by such a proportion of regular troops. Those who are best acquainted with the late successful resistance of this country against the British arms will be most inclined to deny the possibility of it. Besides the advantage of being armed, which the Americans possess over the people of almost every other nation, the existence of subordinate governments to which the people are attached, and by which the militia officers are appointed, forms a barrier against the enterprizes of ambition, more insurmountable than any which a simple government of any form can admit of. Notwithstanding the military establishments in the several kingdoms of Europe, which are carried as far as the public resources will bear, the governments are afraid to trust the people with arms. And it is not certain that with this aid alone, they would not be able to shake off their yokes. But were the people to possess the additional advantages of local governments chosen by themselves, who could collect the national will, and direct the national force; and of officers appointed out of the militia, by these governments and attached both to them and to the militia, it may be affirmed with the greatest assurance, that the throne of every tyranny in Europe would be speedily overturned, in spite of the legions which surround it. Let us not insult the free and gallant citizens of America with the suspicion that they would be less able to defend the rights of which they would be in actual possession, than the debased subjects of arbitrary power would be to rescue theirs from the hands of their oppressors. Let us rather no longer insult them with the supposition, that they can ever reduce themselves to the necessity of making the experiment, by a blind and tame submission to the long train of insidious measures, which must precede and produce it.

The argument under the present head may be put into a very concise form, which appears altogether conclusive. Either the mode in which the Foederal Government is to be constructed will render it sufficiently dependant on the people, or it will not. On the first supposition, it will be restrained by that dependence from forming schemes obnoxious to their constituents. On the other supposition it will not possess the confidence of the people, and its schemes of usurpation will be easily defeated by the State Governments; who will be supported by the people.

On summing up the considerations stated in this and the last paper, they seem to amount to the most convincing evidence, that the powers proposed to be lodged in the Foederal Government, are as little formidable to those reserved to the individual States, as they are indispensibly necessary to accomplish the purposes of the Union; and that all those alarms which have been sounded, of a meditated or consequential annihilation of the State Governments, must, on the most favorable interpretation, be ascribed to the chimerical fears of the authors of them.

PUBLIUS.

[MADISON]

Federalist 47

The Meaning of the Maxim, Which Requires a Separation of the Departments of Power, Examined and Ascertained, January 30, 1788

With this essay, Madison begins a sustained effort to reconcile the innovations of the Constitution with the received doctrine of separation of powers. In its pure form, that doctrine held that there were three distinct forms of power—legislative, executive, and judicial—and that a well-balanced government would keep each of these powers separate from the other two in both its essential functions and its personnel. From the van-

tage point of 1776, the Constitution seemed to violate this understanding in various ways. The executive veto over legislation, for example, seemed to make the president a part of the legislature. If judges exercised the power to review and overturn legislation on constitutional grounds, they could be said to be acting legislatively, too. But the most frequent accusations were directed against the Senate. It was said to violate the doctrine of separation by exercising all three kinds of power: the legislative, which it shared with the House of Representatives; the executive, which it shared with the president by virtue of their joint power over appointments and treaties; and even the judicial, which it would occasionally exercise as a court of impeachment (and which it might use to mask unconstitutional acts of the executive against charges that would be brought by the House of Representatives).

This modified version of the separation of powers that the Constitution created is what we often call "checks and balances." It sought to preserve the balance and equilibrium of the departments of government not by separating them rigidly, but rather by giving each institution peculiar means of self-defense and by varying the modes of their appointment and their tenure in office. In this revised form, separation of powers came to replace the older theory of "mixed government." That theory held that the equilibrium of government required incorporating the three great estates of king, aristocracy, and people within the legislature itself (so that the British Parliament consisted of a House of Commons, a House of Lords, and a crown that could veto legislation). Americans had no king or aristocracy to incorporate, but the idea of balance remained a cardinal principle of constitutionalism.

Federalist 47 opens this discussion of separation of powers by restating the basic concept and examining its proper definition, especially as espoused by "the celebrated Montesquieu" in The Spirit of the Laws *and as exemplified in the practice of the American states. Like Hamilton in* Federalist 9, *Madison seeks to co-opt Montesquieu for his own purposes, by showing that his doctrine is more complicated than Anti-Federalists have appreciated. But rather than rely solely on Montesquieu, Madison also uses empirical evidence from the constitutions of the states themselves to provide a fresh definition of separation of powers that accords with practice as well as theory. Here again he applies the lessons about political reasoning he had first discussed in* Federalist 37.

To the People of the State of New York.

Having reviewed the general form of the proposed government, and the general mass of power allotted to it: I proceed to examine the particular structure of this government, and the distribution of this mass of power among its constituent parts.

One of the principal objections inculcated by the more respectable adversaries to the constitution, is its supposed violation of the political maxim, that the legislative, executive and judiciary departments ought to be separate and distinct. In the structure of the federal government, no regard, it is said, seems to have been paid to this essential precaution in favor of liberty. The several departments of power are distributed and blended in such a manner, as at once to destroy all symmetry and beauty of form; and to expose some of the essential parts of the edifice to the danger of being crushed by the disproportionate weight of other parts.

No political truth is certainly of greater intrinsic value or is stamped with the authority of more enlightened patrons of liberty than that on which the objection is founded. The accumulation of all powers legislative, executive and judiciary in the same hands, whether of one, a few or many, and whether hereditary, self appointed, or elective, may justly be pronounced the very definition of tyranny. Were the federal constitution therefore really chargeable with this accumulation of power or with a mixture of powers having a dangerous tendency to such an accumulation, no further arguments would be necessary to inspire a universal reprobation of the system. I persuade myself however, that it will be made apparent to every one, that the charge cannot be supported, and that the maxim on which it relies, has been totally misconceived and misapplied. In order to form correct ideas on this important subject, it will be proper to investigate the sense, in which the preservation of liberty requires, that the three great departments of power should be separate and distinct.

The oracle who is always consulted and cited on this subject, is the celebrated Montesquieu. If he be not the author of this invaluable precept in the science of politics, he has the merit at least of displaying, and recommending it most effectually to the attention of mankind. Let us endeavour in the first place to ascertain his meaning on this point.

The British constitution was to Montesquieu, what Homer has been to the didactic writers on epic poetry. As the latter have considered the work of the immortal Bard, as the perfect model from which the principles and rules of the epic art were to be drawn, and by which all similar works were to be judged; so this great political critic appears to have viewed the constitution of England, as the standard, or to use his own expression, as the mirrour of political liberty; and to have delivered in the form of elementary truths, the several characteristic principles of that particular system. That we may be sure then not to mistake his meaning in this case, let us recur to the source from which the maxim was drawn.

On the slightest view of the British constitution we must perceive, that the legislative, executive and judiciary departments are by no means totally separate and distinct from each other. The executive magistrate forms an integral part of the legislative authority. He alone has the prerogative of making treaties with foreign sovereigns, which when made have, under certain limitations, the force of legislative acts. All the members of the judiciary department are appointed by him; can be removed by him on the address of the two Houses of Parliament, and form, when he pleases to consult them, one of his constitutional councils. One branch of the legislative department forms also, a great constitutional council to the executive chief; as on another hand, it is the sole depositary of judicial power in cases of impeachment, and is invested with the supreme appellate jurisdiction, in all other cases. The judges again are so far connected with the legislative department, as often to attend and participate in its deliberations, though not admitted to a legislative vote.

From these facts by which Montesquieu was guided it may clearly be inferred, that in saying "there can be no liberty where the legislative and executive powers are united in the same person, or body of magistrates," or "if the power of judging be not separated from the legislative and executive powers," he did not mean that these departments ought to have no *partial agency* in, or no *controul* over the acts of each other. His meaning, as his own words import, and still more conclusively as illustrated by the example in his eye, can amount to no more than this, that where the *whole* power of one department is exercised by the same hands which possess the *whole* power of another department, the fundamental principles of a free constitution, are subverted. This would have been the case in the constitution examined by him, if the King who is the sole executive magistrate, had possessed also the compleat legislative power, or the supreme administration of justice; or if the entire legislative body, had possessed the supreme judiciary, or the supreme executive authority. This however is not among the vices of that constitution. The magistrate in whom the whole executive power resides cannot of himself make a law, though he can put a negative on every law, nor administer justice in person, though he has the appointment of those who do administer it. The judges can exercise no executive prerogative, though they are shoots from the executive stock, nor any legislative function, though they may be advised with by the legislative councils. The entire legislature, can perform no judiciary act, though by the joint act of two of its branches, the judges may be removed from their offices; and though one of its branches is possessed of the judicial power in the last resort. The entire legislature again can exercise no executive preroga- tive, though one of its branches constitutes the supreme executive magistracy; and another, on the empeachment of a third, can try and condemn all the subordinate officers in the executive department.

The reasons on which Montesquieu grounds his maxim are a further demonstration of his meaning. "When the legislative and executive pow- ers are united in the same person or body" says he, "there can be no lib- erty, because apprehensions may arise lest *the same* monarch or senate should *enact* tyrannical laws, to *execute* them in a tyrannical manner." Again "Were the power of judging joined with the legislative, the life and liberty of the subject would be exposed to arbitrary controul, for *the judge* would then be *the legislator.* Were it joined to the executive power, *the judge* might behave with all the violence of *an oppressor.*" Some of these reasons are more fully explained in other passages; but briefly stated as they are here, they sufficiently establish the meaning which we have put on this celebrated maxim of this celebrated author.

If we look into the constitutions of the several states we find that notwithstanding the emphatical, and in some instances, the unqualified terms in which this axiom has been laid down, there is not a single instance in which the several departments of power have been kept absolutely separate and distinct. New-Hampshire, whose constitution was the last formed, seems to have been fully aware of the impossibil- ity and inexpediency of avoiding any mixture whatever of these depart- ments; and has qualified the doctrine by declaring "that the legislative, executive and judiciary powers ought to be kept as separate from, and independent of each other *as the nature of a free government will admit; or as is consistent with that chain of connection, that binds the whole fab- ric of the constitution in one indissoluble bond of unity and amity."* Her constitution accordingly mixes these departments in several respects. The senate which is a branch of the legislative department is also a judicial tribunal for the trial of empeachments. The president who is the head of the executive department, is the presiding member also of the senate; and besides an equal vote in all cases, has a casting vote in case of a tie. The executive head is himself eventually elective every year by the legislative department; and his council is every year chosen by and from the members of the same department. Several of the officers of state are also appointed by the legislature. And the members of the judiciary department are appointed by the executive department.

The constitution of Massachusetts has observed a sufficient though less pointed caution in expressing this fundamental article of liberty. It declares "that the legislative department shall never exercise the executive and judicial powers, or either of them: The executive shall never exercise the legislative and judicial powers, or either of them: The judicial shall never exercise the legislative and executive powers, or either of them." This declaration corresponds precisely with the doctrine of Montesquieu as it has been explained, and is not in a single point violated by the plan of the Convention. It goes no farther than to prohibit any one of the entire departments from exercising the powers of another department. In the very constitution to which it is prefixed, a partial mixture of powers has been admitted. The Executive Magistrate has a qualified negative on the Legislative body; and the Senate, which is a part of the Legislature, is a court of impeachment for members both of the executive and judiciary departments. The members of the judiciary department again are appointable by the executive department, and removeable by the same authority, on the address of the two legislative branches. Lastly, a number of the officers of government are annually appointed by the legislative department. As the appointment to offices, particularly executive offices, is in its nature an executive function, the compilers of the Constitution have in this last point at least, violated the rule established by themselves.

I pass over the constitutions of Rhode-Island and Connecticut, because they were formed prior to the revolution; and even before the principle under examination had become an object of political attention.

The constitution of New-York contains no declaration on this subject; but appears very clearly to have been framed with an eye to the danger of improperly blending the different departments. It gives nevertheless to the executive magistrate a partial controul over the legislative department; and what is more, gives a like controul to the judiciary department, and even blends the executive and judiciary departments in the exercise of this controul. In its council of appointment, members of the legislative are associated with the executive authority in the appointment of officers both executive and judiciary. And its court for the trial of impeachments and correction of errors, is to consist of one branch of the legislature and the principal members of the judiciary department.

The constitution of New-Jersey has blended the different powers of government more than any of the preceding. The governor, who is the executive magistrate, is appointed by the legislature; is chancellor and ordinary or surrogate of the state; is a member of the supreme court of appeals, and president with a casting vote, of one of the legislative branches. The same legislative branch acts again as executive council to the governor, and with him constitutes the court of appeals. The members of the judiciary department are appointed by the legislative department, and removeable by one branch of it, on the impeachment of the other.

According to the constitution of Pennsylvania, the president, who is head of the executive department, is annually elected by a vote in which the legislative department predominates. In conjunction with an executive council, he appoints the members of the judiciary department, and forms a court of impeachments for trial of all officers, judiciary as well as executive. The judges of the supreme court, and justices of the peace, seem also to be removeable by the legislature; and the executive power of pardoning in certain cases to be referred to the same department. The members of the executive council are made EX OFFICIO justices of peace throughout the state.

In Delaware, the chief executive magistrate is annually elected by the legislative department. The speakers of the two legislative branches are vice-presidents in the executive department. The executive chief, with six others, appointed three by each of the legislative branches, constitute the supreme court of appeals: He is joined with the legislative department in the appointment of the other judges. Throughout the states it appears that the members of the legislature may at the same time be justices of the peace. In this state, the members of one branch of it are EX OFFICIO justices of peace; as are also the members of the executive council. The principal officers of the executive department are appointed by the legislative; and one branch of the latter forms a court of impeachments. All officers may be removed on address of the legislature.

Maryland has adopted the maxim in the most unqualified terms; declaring that the legislative, executive and judicial powers of government, ought to be forever separate and distinct from each other. Her constitution, notwithstanding makes the executive magistrate appointable by the legislative department; and the members of the judiciary, by the executive department.

The language of Virginia is still more pointed on this subject. Her constitution declares, "that the legislative, executive and judiciary departments, shall be separate and distinct; so that neither exercise the powers properly belonging to the other; nor shall any person exercise the powers of more than one of them at the same time; except that the justices of the county courts shall be eligible to either house of assembly." Yet we find not only this express exception, with respect to the members of the inferior courts; but that the chief magistrate with his executive council are appointable by the legislature; that two members of the latter are triennially displaced at the pleasure of the legislature; and that all the principal offices, both executive and judiciary, are filled by the same department. The executive prerogative of pardon, also is in one case vested in the legislative department.

The constitution of North-Carolina, which declares, "that the legislative, executive and supreme judicial powers of government, ought to be forever separate and distinct from each other," refers at the same time to the legislative department, the appointment not only of the executive chief, but all the principal officers within both that and the judiciary department.

In South-Carolina, the constitution makes the executive magistracy eligible by the legislative department. It gives to the latter also the appointment of the members of the judiciary department, including even justices of the peace and sheriffs; and the appointment of officers in the executive department, down to captains in the army and navy of the state.

In the constitution of Georgia, where it is declared, "that the legislative, executive and judiciary departments shall be separate and distinct, so that neither exercise the powers properly belonging to the other." We find that the executive department is to be filled by appointments of the legislature; and the executive prerogative of pardon, to be finally exercised by the same authority. Even justices of the peace are to be appointed by the legislature.

In citing these cases in which the legislative, executive and judiciary departments, have not been kept totally separate and distinct, I wish not to be regarded as an advocate for the particular organizations of the several state governments. I am fully aware that among the many excellent principles which they exemplify, they carry strong marks of the haste, and still stronger of the inexperience, under which they were framed. It is but too obvious that in some instances, the fundamental principle under consideration has been violated by too great a mixture, and even an actual consolidation of the different powers; and that in no instance has a competent provision been made for maintaining in practice the separation delineated on paper. What I have wished to evince is, that the charge brought against the proposed constitution, of violating a sacred maxim of free government, is warranted neither by the real meaning annexed to that maxim by its author; nor by the sense in which it has hitherto been understood in America. This interesting subject will be resumed in the ensuing paper.

PUBLIUS.

[MADISON]

Federalist 48

The Same Subject Continued with a View to the Means of Giving Efficacy in Practice to That Maxim, February 1, 1788

The declarations of rights that accompanied the first state constitutions often included articles affirming the basic concept of separated powers. But Madison had come to believe that such statements — or, for that matter, declarations of rights themselves — were only "parchment barriers" unless supported by effective mechanisms of enforcement. If the goal of separation was to protect the liberty of citizens by preserving each department in the exercise of its proper functions, then the challenge was to identify where encroachments were most likely to arise. In the Anglo-American tradition, the legislature had been the body that historically required protection against the crown and its minions. In 1776, Americans had accordingly looked backward and treated the unchecked power of the executive as the great danger. But experience and logic now suggested another conclusion. In a republic, the chief threat would come from the legislature itself, and an effective theory of separation would have to take that into account. Madison thus uses Federalist *48 to explain why the legislature is the most dangerous institution in a republican government. His explanation combines an appreciation of the political advantages that the legislature enjoys over the other branches with a recognition that its very power to make rules will enable it to encroach on the executive and judiciary through "complicated and indirect measures."*

To the People of the State of New York.
It was shewn in the last paper, that the political apothegm[1] there examined, does not require that the legislative, executive and judi-

[1] *apothegm:* maxim.

ciary departments should be wholly unconnected with each other. I shall undertake in the next place, to shew that unless these departments be so far connected and blended, as to give to each a constitutional controul over the others, the degree of separation which the maxim requires as essential to a free government, can never in practice, be duly maintained.

It is agreed on all sides, that the powers properly belonging to one of the departments, ought not to be directly and compleatly administered by either of the other departments. It is equally evident, that neither of them ought to possess directly or indirectly, an overruling influence over the others in the administration of their respective powers. It will not be denied, that power is of an encroaching nature, and that it ought to be effectually restrained from passing the limits assigned to it. After discriminating therefore in theory, the several classes of power, as they may in their nature be legislative, executive, or judiciary; the next and most difficult task, is to provide some practical security for each against the invasion of the others. What this security ought to be, is the great problem to be solved.

Will it be sufficient to mark with precision the boundaries of these departments in the Constitution of the government, and to trust to these parchment barriers against the encroaching spirit of power? This is the security which appears to have been principally relied on by the compilers of most of the American Constitutions. But experience assures us, that the efficacy of the provision has been greatly over-rated; and that some more adequate defence is indispensibly necessary for the more feeble, against the more powerful members of the government. The legislative department is every where extending the sphere of its activity, and drawing all power into its impetuous vortex.

The founders of our republics have so much merit for the wisdom which they have displayed, that no task can be less pleasing than that of pointing out the errors into which they have fallen. A respect for truth however obliges us to remark, that they seem never for a moment to have turned their eyes from the danger to liberty from the overgrown and all-grasping prerogative of an hereditary magistrate, supported and fortified by an hereditary branch of the legislative authority. They seem never to have recollected the danger from legislative usurpations; which by assembling all power in the same hands, must lead to the same tyranny as is threatened by executive usurpations.

In a government, where numerous and extensive prerogatives are placed in the hands of a hereditary monarch, the executive department is very justly regarded as the source of danger, and watched with all the jealousy which a zeal for liberty ought to inspire. In a democracy, where a multitude of people exercise in person the legislative functions, and are continually exposed by their incapacity for regular deliberation and concerted measures, to the ambitious intrigues of their executive magistrates, tyranny may well be apprehended on some favorable emergency, to start up in the same quarter. But in a representative republic, where the executive magistracy is carefully limited both in the extent and the duration of its power; and where the legislative power is exercised by an assembly, which is inspired by a supposed influence over the people with an intrepid confidence in its own strength; which is sufficiently numerous to feel all the passions which actuate a multitude; yet not so numerous as to be incapable of pursuing the objects of its passions, by means which reason prescribes; it is against the enterprising ambition of this department, that the people ought to indulge all their jealousy and exhaust all their precautions.

The legislative department derives a superiority in our governments from other circumstances. Its constitutional powers being at once more extensive and less susceptible of precise limits, it can with the greater facility, mask under complicated and indirect measures, the encroachments which it makes on the co-ordinate departments. It is not unfrequently a question of real-nicety in legislative bodies, whether the operation of a particular measure, will, or will not extend beyond the legislative sphere. On the other side, the executive power being restrained within a narrower compass, and being more simple in its nature; and the judiciary being described by land marks, still less uncertain, projects of usurpation by either of these departments, would immediately betray and defeat themselves. Nor is this all: As the legislative department alone has access to the pockets of the people, and has in some Constitutions full discretion, and in all, a prevailing influence over the pecuniary rewards of those who fill the other departments, a dependence is thus created in the latter, which gives still greater facility to encroachments of the former.

I have appealed to our own experience for the truth of what I advance on this subject. Were it necessary to verify this experience by particular proofs, they might be multiplied without end. I might find a witness in every citizen who has shared in, or been attentive to, the course of public administrations. I might collect vouchers in abundance from the records and archieves of every State in the Union. But as a more concise and at the same time, equally satisfactory evidence,

I will refer to the example of two States, attested by two unexceptionable authorities.

The first example is that of Virginia, a State which, as we have seen, has expressly declared in its Constitution, that the three great departments ought not to be intermixed. The authority in support of it is Mr. Jefferson, who, besides his other advantages for remarking the operation of the government, was himself the chief magistrate of it. In order to convey fully the ideas with which his experience had impressed him on this subject, it will be necessary to quote a passage of some length from his very interesting "Notes on the State of Virginia." (P. 195.) "All the powers of government, legislative, executive and judiciary, result to the legislative body. The concentrating these in the same hands is precisely the definition of despotic government. It will be no alleviation that these powers will be exercised by a plurality of hands, and not by a single one, 173 despots would surely be as oppressive as one. Let those who doubt it turn their eyes on the republic of Venice. As little will it avail us that they are chosen by ourselves. An *elective despotism,* was not the government we fought for; but one which should not only be founded on free principles, but in which the powers of government should be so divided and balanced among several bodies of magistracy, as that no one could transcend their legal limits, without being effectually checked and restrained by the others. For this reason that Convention which passed the ordinance of government, laid its foundation on this basis, that the legislative, executive and judiciary departments should be separate and distinct, so that no person should exercise the powers of more than one of them at the same time. *But no barrier was provided between these several powers.* The judiciary and executive members were left dependent on the legislative for their subsistence in office, and some of them for their continuance in it. If therefore the Legislature assumes executive and judiciary powers, no opposition is likely to be made; nor if made can it be effectual; because in that case, they may put their proceeding into the form of an act of Assembly, which will render them obligatory on the other branches. They have accordingly *in many* instances *decided rights* which should have been left to *judiciary controversy;* and *the direction of the executive during the whole time of their session, is becoming habitual and familiar."*

The other State which I shall take for an example, is Pennsylvania; and the other authority the council of censors which assembled in the years 1783 and 1784. A part of the duty of this body, as marked out by the Constitution was, "to enquire whether the Constitution had been preserved inviolate in every part; and whether the legislative and executive branches of government had performed their duty as guardians of the people, or assumed to themselves, or exercised other or greater powers than they are entitled to by the Constitution." In the execution of this trust, the council were necessarily led to a comparison, of both the legislative and executive proceedings, with the constitutional powers of these departments; and from the facts enumerated, and to the truth of most of which, both sides in the council subscribed, it appears that the Constitution had been flagrantly violated by the Legislature in a variety of important instances.

A great number of laws had been passed violating without any apparent necessity, the rule requiring that all bills of a public nature, shall be previously printed for the consideration of the people; altho' this is one of the precautions chiefly relied on by the Constitution, against improper acts of the Legislature.

The constitutional trial by jury had been violated; and powers assumed, which had not been delegated by the Constitution.

Executive powers had been usurped.

The salaries of the Judges, which the Constitution expressly requires to be fixed, had been occasionally varied; and cases belonging to the judiciary department, frequently drawn within legislative cognizance and determination.

Those who wish to see the several particulars falling under each of these heads, may consult the Journals of the council which are in print. Some of them, it will be found may be imputable to peculiar circumstances connected with the war: But the greater part of them may be considered as the spontaneous shoots of an ill-constituted government.

It appears also, that the executive department had not been innocent of frequent breaches of the Constitution. There are three observations however, which ought to be made on this head. *First.* A great proportion of the instances, were either immediately produced by the necessities of the war, or recommended by Congress or the Commander in Chief. *Secondly.* In most of the other instances, they conformed either to the declared or the known sentiments of the legislative department. *Thirdly.* The executive department of Pennsylvania is distinguished from that of the other States, by the number of members composing it. In this respect it has as much affinity to a legislative assembly, as to an executive council. And being at once exempt from the restraint of an individual responsibility for the acts of the body, and deriving confidence from mutual example and joint influence; unauthorized measures would of course be more freely hazarded, than where the executive department is administered by a single hand or by a few hands.

The conclusion which I am warranted in drawing from these observations is, that a mere demarkation on parchment of the constitutional limits of the several departments, is not a sufficient guard against those encroachments which lead to a tyrannical concentration of all the powers of government in the same hands.

PUBLIUS.

[MADISON]

Federalist 49 and 50

The Same Subject Continued with the Same View, February 2, 1788
The Same Subject Continued with the Same View, February 5, 1788

At first glance, these two essays seem to digress from the discussion of separation of powers that Madison began in Federalist *47. Here Madison takes as his point of departure a passage from Thomas Jefferson's* Notes on the State of Virginia, *which proposed that apparent violations by one department of the constitutional powers and duties of another department might be resolved by calling a popularly elected convention to consider correcting the violation or even reforming the constitution. But the proposed federal Constitution contained no such provision. Why, then, should Madison go out of his way to discuss it?*

The answer to that question must involve Madison's reasons for challenging the great theoretical advantage of Jefferson's proposal: that it would allow the sovereign people themselves to resolve constitutional disputes. In these two essays, Madison goes to great lengths to explain why such appeals to the people are ill advised, not only for the immediate purpose of preserving a proper separation of powers, but also for the long-term stability of the Constitution. By demonstrating that the people cannot be expected to maintain the equilibrium of a constitution, Madison clears a path for explaining why the necessary separation must be provided by the actual design of institutions within the government itself. But read carefully, these two essays also offer a revealing insight into Madison's deeper reservations about popular government. He seems to imply that the only time public opinion can be safely invoked for constitutional purposes is at the initial formation of the regime. On virtually every other occasion, the risks will far outweigh the theoretical benefits.

Federalist 49

To the People of the State of New York.

The author of the "Notes on the state of Virginia," quoted in the last paper, has subjoined to that valuable work, the draught of a constitution which had been prepared in order to be laid before a convention expected to be called in 1783 by the legislature, for the establishment of a constitution for that commonwealth. The plan, like every thing from the same pen, marks a turn of thinking original, comprehensive and accurate; and is the more worthy of attention, as it equally displays a fervent attachment to republican government, and an enlightened view of the dangerous propensities against which it ought to be guarded. One of the precautions which he proposes, and on which he appears ultimately to rely as a palladium[1] to the weaker departments of power, against the invasions of the stronger, is perhaps altogether his own, and as it immediately relates to the subject of our present enquiry, ought not to be overlooked.

His proposition is, "that whenever any two of the three branches of government shall concur in opinion, each by the voices of two thirds of their whole number, that a convention is necessary for altering the constitution or *correcting breaches of it,* a convention shall be called for the purpose."

As the people are the only legitimate fountain of power, and it is from them that the constitutional charter, under which the several branches of government hold their power, is derived; it seems strictly consonant to the republican theory, to recur to the same original authority, not only whenever it may be necessary to enlarge, diminish, or new-model the powers of government; but also whenever any one of the departments may commit encroachments on the chartered authorities of the others. The several departments being perfectly co-ordinate by the terms of their common commission, neither of them, it is evident, can pretend to an exclusive or superior right of settling the boundaries between their respective powers; and how are the encroachments of the stronger to be prevented, or the wrongs of the weaker to be redressed, without an appeal to the people themselves; who, as the grantors of the commission, can alone declare its true meaning and enforce its observance?

There is certainly great force in this reasoning, and it must be allowed to prove, that a constitutional road to the decision of the

---

[1] *palladium:* safeguard. In American political writing of this era, such institutions as trial by jury, freedom of the press, or a well-armed militia were often described as a "palladium of liberty," that is, something essential to its preservation.

people, ought to be marked out, and kept open, for certain great and extraordinary occasions. But there appear to be insuperable objections against the proposed recurrence to the people, as a provision in all cases for keeping the several departments of power within their constitutional limits.

In the first place, the provision does not reach the case of a combination of two of the departments against a third. If the legislative authority, which possesses so many means of operating on the motives of the other departments, should be able to gain to its interest either of the others, or even one-third of its members, the remaining department could derive no advantage from this remedial provision. I do not dwell however on this objection, because it may be thought to lie rather against the modification of the principle, than against the principle itself.

In the next place, it may be considered as an objection inherent in the principle, that as every appeal to the people would carry an implication of some defect in the government, frequent appeals would in great measure deprive the government of that veneration, which time bestows on every thing, and without which perhaps the wisest and freest governments would not possess the requisite stability. If it be true that all governments rest on opinion, it is no less true that the strength of opinion in each individual, and its practical influence on his conduct, depend much on the number which he supposes to have entertained the same opinion. The reason of man, like man himself is timid and cautious, when left alone; and acquires firmness and confidence, in proportion to the number with which it is associated. When the examples, which fortify opinion, are *antient* as well as *numerous,* they are known to have a double effect. In a nation of philosophers, this consideration ought to be disregarded. A reverence for the laws, would be sufficiently inculcated by the voice of an enlightened reason. But a nation of philosophers is as little to be expected as the philosophical race of kings wished for by Plato. And in every other nation, the most rational government will not find it a superfluous advantage, to have the prejudices of the community on its side.

The danger of disturbing the public tranquility by interesting too strongly the public passions, is a still more serious objection against a frequent reference of constitutional questions, to the decision of the whole society. Notwithstanding the success which has attended the revisions of our established forms of government, and which does so much honour to the virtue and intelligence of the people of America, it must be confessed, that the experiments are of too ticklish a nature to be unnecessarily multiplied. We are to recollect that all the existing constitutions were formed in the midst of a danger which repressed the passions most unfriendly to order and concord; of an enthusiastic confidence of the people in their patriotic leaders, which stifled the ordinary diversity of opinions on great national questions; of a universal ardor for new and opposite forms, produced by a universal resentment and indignation against the antient government; and whilst no spirit of party, connected with the changes to be made, or the abuses to be reformed, could mingle its leven in the operation. The future situations in which we must expect to be usually placed, do not present any equivalent security against the danger which is apprehended.

But the greatest objection of all is, that the decisions which would probably result from such appeals, would not answer the purpose of maintaining the constitutional equilibrium of the government. We have seen that the tendency of republican governments is to an aggrandizement of the legislative, at the expence of the other departments. The appeals to the people therefore would usually be made by the executive and judiciary departments. But whether made by one side or the other, would each side enjoy equal advantages on the trial? Let us view their different situations. The members of the executive and judiciary departments, are few in number, and can be personally known to a small part only of the people. The latter by the mode of their appointment, as well as, by the nature and permanency of it, are too far removed from the people to share much in their prepossessions. The former are generally the objects of jealousy: And their administration is always liable to be discoloured and rendered unpopular. The members of the legislative department, on the other hand, are numerous. They are distributed and dwell among the people at large. Their connections of blood, of friendship and of acquaintance, embrace a great proportion of the most influencial part of the society. The nature of their public trust implies a personal influence among the people, and that they are more immediately the confidential guardians of the rights and liberties of the people. With these advantages, it can hardly be supposed that the adverse party would have an equal chance for a favorable issue.

But the legislative party would not only be able to plead their cause most successfully with the people. They would probably be constituted themselves the judges. The same influence which had gained them an election into the legislature, would gain them a seat in the convention. If this should not be the case with all, it would probably be the case with many, and pretty certainly with those leading characters, on whom every thing depends in such bodies. The convention in short would be composed chiefly of men, who had been, who actually were, or who expected to be, members of the department whose conduct was arraigned. They would consequently be parties to the very question to be decided by them.

It might however sometimes happen, that appeals would be made under circumstances less adverse to the executive and judiciary departments. The usurpations of the legislature might be so flagrant and so sudden, as to admit of no specious colouring. A strong party among themselves might take side with the other branches. The executive power might be in the hands of a peculiar favorite of the people. In such a posture of things, the public decision might be less swayed by prepossessions in favor of the legislative party. But still it could never be expected to turn on the true merits of the question. It would inevitably be connected with the spirit of pre-existing parties, or of parties springing out of the question itself. It would be connected with persons of distinguished character and extensive influence in the community. It would be pronounced by the very men who had been agents in, or opponents of the measures, to which the decision would relate. The *passions* therefore not *the reason,* of the public, would sit in judgment. But it is the reason of the public alone that ought to controul and regulate the government. The passions ought to be controuled and regulated by the government.

We found in the last paper that mere declarations in the written constitution, are not sufficient to restrain the several departments within their legal limits. It appears in this, that occasional appeals to the people would be neither a proper nor an effectual provision, for that purpose. How far the provisions of a different nature contained in the plan above quoted, might be adequate, I do not examine. Some of them are unquestionably founded on sound political principles, and all of them are framed with singular ingenuity and precision.

PUBLIUS.

Federalist 50

To the People of the State of New York.
It may be contended perhaps, that instead of *occasional* appeals to the people, which are liable to the objections urged against them, *periodical* appeals are the proper and adequate means *of preventing and correcting infractions of the Constitution.*

It will be attended to, that in the examination of these expedients, I confine myself to their aptitude for *enforcing* the Constitution by keeping the several departments of power within their due bounds, without particularly considering them, as provisions for *altering* the Constitution itself. In the first view, appeals to the people at fixed periods, appear to be nearly as ineligible, as appeals on particular occasions as they emerge. If the periods be separated by short intervals, the measures to be reviewed and rectified, will have been of recent date, and will be connected with all the circumstances which tend to viciate and pervert the result of occasional revisions. If the periods be distant from each other, the same remark will be applicable to all recent measures, and in proportion as the remoteness of the others may favor a dispassionate review of them, this advantage is inseparable from inconveniencies which seem to counterbalance it. In the first place, a distant prospect of public censure would be a very feeble restraint on power from those excesses, to which it might be urged by the force of present motives. Is it to be imagined, that a legislative assembly, consisting of a hundred or two hundred members, eagerly bent on some favorite object, and breaking through the restraints of the Constitution in pursuit of it, would be arrested in their career, by considerations drawn from a censorial revision of their conduct at the future distance of ten, fifteen or twenty years? In the next place, the abuses would often have compleated their mischievous effects, before the remedial provision would be applied. And in the last place, where this might not be the case, they would be of long standing, would have taken deep root, and would not easily be extirpated.

The scheme of revising the Constitution in order to correct recent breaches of it, as well as for other purposes, has been actually tried in one of the States. One of the objects of the council of censors, which met in Pennsylvania, in 1783 and 1784, was, as we have seen,[1] to enquire "whether the Constitution had been violated, and whether the legislative and executive departments had encroached on each other." This important and novel experiment in politics, merits in several points of view, very particular attention. In some of them it may perhaps, as a single experiment, made under circumstances somewhat peculiar, be thought to be not absolutely conclusive. But as applied to the case under consideration, it involves some facts which I venture to remark, as a compleat and satisfactory illustration of the reasoning which I have employed.

First. It appears from the names of the gentlemen, who composed the council, that some at least of its most active and leading members, had also been active and leading characters in the parties which pre-existed in the State.

Secondly. It appears that the same active and leading members of

---

[1] See Essay 48.

the council, had been active and influential members of the legislative and executive branches, within the period to be reviewed; and even patrons or opponents of the very measures to be thus brought to the test of the Constitution. Two of the members had been Vice-Presidents of the State, and several others, members of the executive council, within the seven preceding years. One of them had been Speaker, and a number of others distinguished members of the legislative assembly, within the same period.

Thirdly. Every page of their proceedings witnesses the effect of all these circumstances on the temper of their deliberations. Throughout the continuance of the council, it was split into two fixed and violent parties. The fact is acknowledged and lamented by themselves. Had this not been the case, the face of their proceedings exhibit a proof equally satisfactory. In all questions, however unimportant in themselves, or unconnected with each other, the same names, stand invariably contrasted on the opposite columns. Every unbiassed observer, may infer without danger of mistake, and at the same time, without meaning to reflect on either party, or any individuals of either party, that unfortunately *passion,* not *reason,* must have presided over their decisions. When men exercise their reason coolly and freely, on a variety of distinct questions, they inevitably fall into different opinions, on some of them. When they are governed by a common passion, their opinions if they are so to be called, will be the same.

Fourthly. It is at least problematical, whether the decisions of this body, do not, in several instances, misconstrue the limits prescribed for the legislative and executive departments, instead of reducing and limiting them within their constitutional places.

Fifthly. I have never understood that the decisions of the council on constitutional questions, whether rightly or erroneously formed, have had any effect in varying the practice founded on legislative constructions. It even appears, if I mistake not, that in one instance, the contemporary Legislature denied the constructions of the council, and actually prevailed in the contest.

This censorial body therefore, proves at the same time, by its researches, the existence of the disease; and by its example, the inefficacy of the remedy.

This conclusion cannot be invalidated by alledging that the State in which the experiment was made, was at that crisis, and had been for a long time before, violently heated and distracted by the rage of party. Is it to be presumed, that at any future septennial epoch, the same State will be free from parties? Is it to be presumed that any other

State, at the same or any other given period, will be exempt from them? Such an event ought to be neither presumed nor desired; because an extinction of parties necessarily implies either a universal alarm for the public safety, or an absolute extinction of liberty.

Were the precaution taken of excluding from the assemblies elected by the people to revise the preceding administration of the government, all persons who should have been concerned in the government within the given period, the difficulties would not be obviated. The important task would probably devolve on men, who with inferior capacities, would in other respects, be little better qualified. Although they might not have been personally concerned in the administration, and therefore not immediately agents in the measures to be examined; they would probably have been involved in the parties connected with these measures, and have been elected under their auspices.

PUBLIUS.

[MADISON]

Federalist 51

*The Same Subject Continued with the Same View and Concluded,
February 6, 1788*

Modern commentators generally regard Federalist 51 *as second in importance only to* Federalist 10. *Madison begins by observing that the only effective way to maintain the desired separation of powers must be found in the design of the institutions themselves and in their "mutual relations." The argument that unfolds rests upon the famous assertion that "Ambition must be made to counteract ambition. The interest of the man must be connected with the constitutional rights of the place." Madison thus concedes that officeholders will have ambitions that are not entirely healthy in themselves, but which may somehow be yoked to the public service if they support the just powers of the particular office each occupies. This raises an interesting question: Should one have a consistent and disinterested philosophy about the proper powers of each department that would exist independently of the office one held, or does Madison's argument expect that one's philosophy is simply a function of the position one occupies?*

A different question arises when Madison turns to the specific institutional solution the Constitution proposes to the problem of preserving the separation of powers in a republican regime where "the legislative authority, necessarily, predominates." In the course of refuting the Anti-Federalist obsession with the Senate, Madison uses this essay to justify the "qualified connection" between the "weaker department" of the executive and "the weaker branch of the stronger department." This can only mean the Senate, which shares the appointment and treaty powers with the president. But why would Madison call the Senate the "weaker branch" of Congress, when it exercises additional powers that its coordinate institution, the House of Representatives, lacks, and when its members, with their six-year terms, would be more insulated from the ordinary pressures of politics? Simply by posing the question in this way, Madison indicated that he regarded the capacity to claim to speak for the people at large as the decisive factor of republican politics.

To the People of the State of New York.

To what expedient then shall we finally resort for maintaining in practice the necessary partition of power among the several departments, as laid down in the constitution? The only answer that can be given is, that as all the exterior provisions are found to be inadequate, the defect must be supplied, by so contriving the interior structure of the government, as that its several constituent parts may, by their mutual relations, be the means of keeping each other in their proper places. Without presuming to undertake a full developement of this important idea, I will hazard a few general observations, which may perhaps place it in a clearer light, and enable us to form a more correct judgment of the principles and structure of the government planned by the convention.

In order to lay a due foundation for that separate and distinct exercise of the different powers of government, which to a certain extent, is admitted on all hands to be essential to the preservation of liberty, it is evident that each department should have a will of its own; and consequently should be so constituted, that the members of each should have as little agency as possible in the appointment of the members of the others. Were this principle rigorously adhered to, it would require that all the appointments for the supreme executive, legislative, and judiciary magistracies, should be drawn from the same fountain of authority, the people, through channels, having no communication whatever with one another. Perhaps such a plan of constructing the several departments would be less difficult in practice than it may in contemplation appear. Some difficulties however, and some additional expence, would attend the execution of it. Some deviations therefore from the principle must be admitted. In the constitution of the judiciary department in particular, it might be inexpedient to insist rigorously on the principle; first, because peculiar qualifications being essential in the members, the primary consideration ought to be to select that mode of choice, which best secures these qualifications; secondly, because the permanent tenure by which the appointments are held in that department, must soon destroy all sense of dependence on the authority conferring them.

It is equally evident that the members of each department should be as little dependent as possible on those of the others, for the emoluments annexed to their offices. Were the executive magistrate, or the judges, not independent of the legislature in this particular, their independence in every other would be merely nominal.

But the great security against a gradual concentration of the several powers in the same department, consists in giving to those who administer each department, the necessary constitutional means, and personal motives; to resist encroachments of the others. The provision for defence must in this, as in all other cases, be made commensurate to the danger of attack. Ambition must be made to counteract ambition. The interest of the man must be connected with the constitutional rights of the place. It may be a reflection on human nature, that such devices should be necessary to controul the abuses of government. But what is government itself but the greatest of all reflections on human nature? If men were angels, no government would be necessary. If angels were to govern men, neither external nor internal controuls on government would be necessary. In framing a government which is to be administered by men over men, the great difficulty lies in this: You must first enable the government to controul the governed; and in the next place, oblige it to controul itself. A dependence on the people is no doubt the primary controul on the government; but experience has taught mankind the necessity of auxiliary precautions.

This policy of supplying by opposite and rival interests, the defect of better motives, might be traced through the whole system of human affairs, private as well as public. We see it particularly displayed in all the subordinate distributions of power; where the constant aim is to divide and arrange the several offices in such a manner as that each may be a check on the other; that the private interest of every individual, may be a centinel over the public rights. These inventions of prudence cannot be less requisite in the distribution of the supreme powers of the state.

But it is not possible to give to each department an equal power of self defence. In republican government the legislative authority, necessarily, predominates. The remedy for this inconveniency is, to divide the legislature into different branches; and to render them by different modes of election, and different principles of action, as little connected with each other, as the nature of their common functions, and their common dependence on the society, will admit. It may even be necessary to guard against dangerous encroachments by still further precautions. As the weight of the legislative authority requires that it should be thus divided, the weakness of the executive may require, on the other hand, that it should be fortified. An absolute negative, on the legislature, appears at first view to be the natural defence with which the executive magistrate should be armed. But perhaps it would be neither altogether safe, nor alone sufficient. On ordinary occasions, it might not be exerted with the requisite firmness; and on extraordinary occasions, it might be perfidiously abused. May not this defect of an absolute negative be supplied, by some qualified connection between this weaker department, and the weaker branch of the stronger department, by which the latter may be led to support the constitutional rights of the former, without being too much detached from the rights of its own department?

If the principles on which these observations are founded be just, as I persuade myself they are, and they be applied as a criterion, to the several state constitutions, and to the federal constitution, it will be found, that if the latter does not perfectly correspond with them, the former are infinitely less able to bear such a test.

There are moreover two considerations particularly applicable to the federal system of America, which place that system in a very interesting point of view.

First. In a single republic, all the power surrendered by the people, is submitted to the administration of a single government; and usurpations are guarded against by a division of the government into distinct and separate departments. In the compound republic of America, the power surrendered by the people, is first divided between two distinct governments, and then the portion allotted to each, subdivided among distinct and separate departments. Hence a double security arises to the rights of the people. The different governments will controul each other; at the same time that each will be controuled by itself.

Second. It is of great importance in a republic, not only to guard the society against the oppression of its rulers; but to guard one part of the society against the injustice of the other part. Different interests necessarily exist in different classes of citizens. If a majority be united by a common interest, the rights of the minority will be insecure. There are but two methods of providing against this evil: The one by creating a will in the community independent of the majority, that is, of the society itself, the other by comprehending in the society so many separate descriptions of citizens, as will render an unjust combination of a majority of the whole, very improbable, if not impracticable. The first method prevails in all governments possessing an hereditary or self appointed authority. This at best is but a precarious security; because a power independent of the society may as well espouse the unjust views of the major, as the rightful interests, of the minor party, and may possibly be turned against both parties. The second method will be exemplified in the federal republic of the United States. Whilst all authority in it will be derived from and dependent on the society, the society itself will be broken into so many parts, interests and classes of citizens, that the rights of individuals or of the minority, will be in little danger from interested combinations of the majority. In a free government, the security for civil rights must be the same as for religious rights. It consists in the one case in the multiplicity of interests, and in the other, in the multiplicity of sects. The degree of security in both cases will depend on the number of interests and sects; and this may be presumed to depend on the extent of country and number of people comprehended under the same government. This view of the subject must particularly recommend a proper federal system to all the sincere and considerate friends of republican government: Since it shews that in exact proportion as the territory of the union may be formed into more circumscribed confederacies or states, oppressive combinations of a majority will be facilitated, the best security under the republican form, for the rights of every class of citizens, will be diminished; and consequently, the stability and independence of some member of the government, the only other security, must be proportionally increased. Justice is the end of government. It is the end of civil society. It ever has been, and ever will be pursued, until it be obtained, or until liberty be lost in the pursuit. In a society under the forms of which the stronger faction can readily unite and oppress the weaker, anarchy may as truly be said to reign, as in a state of nature where the weaker individual is not secured against the violence of the stronger: And as in the latter state even the stronger individuals are prompted by the uncertainty of their condition, to submit to a government which may protect the weak as well as themselves: So in the former state, will the more powerful factions or parties be gradually induced by a like motive, to wish for a government which will protect all parties, the weaker as well as the more powerful. It can be little doubted, that if the state of Rhode Island was separated from the confederacy, and left to itself, the insecurity of rights under the popular form of government within such narrow limits, would be displayed by such reiterated oppressions of factious majorities, that some power altogether independent of the people would soon be called for by the voice of the very factions whose misrule had proved the necessity of it. In the extended republic of the United States, and among the great variety of interests, parties and sects which it embraces, a coalition of a majority of the whole society could seldom take place on any other principles than those of justice and the general good; and there being thus less danger to a minor from the will of the major party, there must be less pretext also, to provide for the security of the former, by introducing into the government a will not dependent on the latter; or in other words, a will independent of the society itself. It is no less certain than it is important, notwithstanding the contrary opinions which have been entertained, that the larger the society, provided it lie within a practicable sphere, the more duly capable it will be of self government. And happily for the *republican cause,* the practicable sphere may be carried to a very great extent, by a judicious modification and mixture of the *federal principle.*

PUBLIUS.

[MADISON]

Federalist 53

The Same Subject Continued (Concerning the House of Representatives) with a View of the Term of the Service of the Members, February 9, 1788

After completing the discussion of separated powers, Publius turned next to Congress, beginning with the House of Representatives, the only institution of the new government to be elected directly by the people. Although Anti-Federalists professed to worry more about the Senate, they were also troubled by the character of the lower house, which did not conform to popular norms of representation. Many Americans believed their elected representatives should regularly return to the body of the people, to live under the same laws they had enacted, and to ensure this would happen, they supported the principle of the annual election of legislators. This practice would keep representatives closely accountable to their constituents, reminding lawmakers that they had not been elevated to a privileged estate. Anti-Federalists were quick to try the Constitution by these principles. Members of the House would serve two-year terms, be elected either in large districts or statewide, and conduct their business in a distant national capital. Together these conditions would insulate them from the voters, stripping them of the "sympathy" they should feel for ordinary people.

In this essay, Madison rebuts these criticisms, in part by noting the real security afforded by requiring elections at regular intervals, but also by explaining why the nature of the business the national government will conduct requires giving representatives adequate time to master issues more novel and complicated than the petty matters that ordinarily preoccupied state lawmakers.

To the People of the State of New York.

I shall here perhaps be reminded of a current observation, "that where annual elections end, tyranny begins." If it be true as has often been remarked, that sayings which become proverbial, are generally founded in reason, it is not less true that when once established, they are often applied to cases to which the reason of them does not extend. I need not look for a proof beyond the case before us. What is the reason on which this proverbial observation is founded? No man will subject himself to the ridicule of pretending that any natural connection subsists between the sun or the seasons, and the period within which human virtue can bear the temptations of power. Happily for mankind, liberty is not in this respect confined to any single point of time; but lies within extremes, which afford sufficient latitude for all the variations which may be required by the various situations and circumstances of civil society. The election of magistrates might be, if it were found expedient, as in some instances it actually has been, daily, weekly, or monthly, as well as annual; and if circumstances may require a deviation from the rule on one side, why not also on the other side? Turning our attention to the periods established among ourselves, for the election of the most numerous branches of the state legislatures, we find them by no means coinciding any more in this instance, than in the elections of other civil magistrates. In Connecticut and Rhode-Island, the periods are half-yearly. In the other states, South-Carolina excepted, they are annual. In South-Carolina, they are biennial; as is proposed in the federal government. Here is a difference, as four to one, between the longest and shortest periods; and yet it would be not easy to shew that Connecticut or Rhode-Island is better governed, or enjoys a greater share of rational liberty than South-Carolina; or that either the one or the other of these states are distinguished in these respects, and by these causes, from the states whose elections are different from both.

In searching for the grounds of this doctrine, I can discover but one, and that is wholly inapplicable to our case. The important distinction so well understood in America between a constitution established by the people, and unalterable by the government; and a law established by the government, and alterable by the government, seems to have been little understood and less observed in any other country. Wherever the supreme power of legislation has resided, has been supposed to reside also, a full power to change the form of the government. Even in Great-Britain, where the principles of political and civil liberty have been most discussed; and where we hear most of the rights of the constitution, it is maintained that the authority of the parliament is transcendent and uncontroulable, as well with regard to the constitution, as the ordinary objects of legislative provision. They have accordingly, in several instances, actually changed, by legislative acts, some of the most fundamental articles of the government. They have in particular, on several occasions, changed the periods of election; and on the last occasion, not only introduced septennial, in place of triennial, elections; but by the same act continued themselves in place four years beyond the term for which they were elected by the people. An attention to these dangerous practices has produced a very natural alarm in the votaries of free government, of which frequency of elections is the corner stone; and has led them to seek for some security to liberty against the danger to which it is exposed. Where no constitution paramount to the government, either existed or could be obtained, no constitutional security similar to that established in the United States, was to be attempted. Some other security therefore was to be sought for; and what better security would the case admit, than that of selecting and appealing to some simple and familiar portion of time, as a standard for measuring the danger of innovations, for fixing the national sentiment, and for uniting the patriotic exertions. The most simple and familiar portion of time, applicable to the subject, was that of a year; and hence the doctrine has been inculcated by a laudable zeal to erect some barrier against the gradual innovations of an unlimited government, that the advance towards tyranny was to be calculated by the distance of departure from the fixed point of annual elections. But what necessity can there be of applying this expedient to a government, limited as the federal government will be, by the authority of a paramount constitution? Or who will pretend that the liberties of the people of America will not be more secure under biennial elections, unalterably fixed by such a constitution, than those of any other nation would be, where elections were annual or even more frequent, but subject to alterations by the ordinary power of the government?

The second question stated is, whether biennial elections be necessary or useful? The propriety of answering this question in the affirmative will appear from several very obvious considerations.

No man can be a competent legislator who does not add to an upright intention and a sound judgment, a certain degree of knowledge of the subjects on which he is to legislate. A part of this knowledge may be acquired by means of information which lie within the compass of men in private as well as public stations. Another part can only be attained, or at least thoroughly attained, by actual experience in the station which requires the use of it. The period of service ought therefore in all such cases to bear some proportion to the extent of practical knowledge, requisite to the due performance of the service. The period of legislative service established in most of the states for the more numerous branch is, as we have seen, one year. The question then may be put into this simple form; does the period of two years bear no greater proportion to the knowledge requisite for federal legislation, than one year does to the knowledge requisite for state legislation? The very statement of the question in this form, suggests the answer that ought to be given to it.

In a single state the requisite knowledge, relates to the existing laws which are uniform throughout the state, and with which all the citizens are more or less conversant; and to the general affairs of the state, which lie within a small compass, are not very diversified, and occupy much of the attention and conversation of every class of people. The great theatre of the United States presents a very different scene. The laws are so far from being uniform, that they vary in every state; whilst the public affairs of the union are spread throughout a very extensive region, and are extremely diversified by the local affairs connected with them, and can with difficulty be correctly learnt in any other place, than in the central councils, to which a knowledge of them will be brought by the representatives of every part of the empire. Yet some knowledge of the affairs, and even of the laws of all the states, ought to be possessed by the members from each of the states. How can foreign trade be properly regulated by uniform laws, without some acquaintance with the commerce, the ports, the usages, and the regulations, of the different states? How can the trade between the different states be duly regulated without some knowledge of their relative situations in these and other points? How can taxes be judiciously imposed, and effectually collected, if they be not accommodated to the different laws and local circumstances relating to these objects in the different states? How can uniform regulations for the militia be duly provided without a similar knowledge of many internal circumstances by which the states are distinguished from each other? These are the principal objects of federal legislation, and suggest most forceably, the extensive information which the representatives ought to acquire. The other inferior objects will require a proportional degree of information with regard to them.

It is true that all these difficulties will by degrees be very much diminished. The most laborious task will be the proper inauguration of the government, and the primeval formation of a federal code. Improvements on the first draught will every year become both easier and fewer. Past transactions of the government will be a ready and accurate source of information to new members. The affairs of the union will become more and more objects of curiosity and conversation among the citizens at large. And the increased intercourse among those of different states will contribute not a little to diffuse a mutual knowledge of their affairs, as this again will contribute to a general assimilation of their manners and laws. But with all these abatements the business of federal legislation must continue so far to exceed both in novelty and difficulty, the legislative business of a single state as to justify the longer period of service assigned to those who are to transact it.

A branch of knowledge which belongs to the acquirements of a federal representative, and which has not been mentioned, is that of foreign affairs. In regulating our own commerce he ought to be not only acquainted with the treaties between the United States and other nations, but also with the commercial policy and laws of other nations. He ought not to be altogether ignorant of the law of nations, for that as far as it is a proper object of municipal legislation is submitted to the federal government. And although the house of representatives is not immediately to participate in foreign negotiations and arrangements, yet from the necessary connection between the several branches of public affairs, those particular branches will frequently deserve attention in the ordinary course of legislation, and will sometimes demand particular legislative sanction and cooperation. Some portion of this knowledge may no doubt be acquired in a man's closet; but some of it also can only be derived from the public sources of information; and all of it will be acquired to best effect by a practical attention to the subject during the period of actual service in the legislature.

There are other considerations of less importance perhaps, but which are not unworthy of notice. The distance which many of the representatives will be obliged to travel, and the arrangements rendered necessary by that circumstance, might be much more serious objections with fit men to this service if limited to a single year than if extended to two years. No argument can be drawn on this subject from the case of the delegates to the existing Congress. They are elected annually it is true; but their re-election is considered by the legislative assemblies almost as a matter of course. The election of the representatives by the people would not be governed by the same principle.

A few of the members, as happens in all such assemblies, will possess superior talents, will by frequent re-elections, become members of long standing; will be thoroughly masters of the public business, and perhaps not unwilling to avail themselves of those advantages. The greater the proportion of new members, and the less the information of the bulk of the members, the more apt will they be to fall into the snares that may be laid for them. This remark is no less applicable to the relation which will subsist between the house of representatives and the senate.

It is an inconveniency mingled with the advantages of our frequent elections, even in single states where they are large and hold but one legislative session in the year, that spurious elections cannot be investigated and annulled in time for the decision to have its due effect. If a return can be obtained, no matter by what unlawful means, the irregular member, who takes his seat of course, is sure of holding it a sufficient time, to answer his purposes. Hence a very pernicious encouragement is given to the use of unlawful means for obtaining irregular returns. Were elections for the federal legislature to be annual, this practice might become a very serious abuse, particularly in the more distant states. Each house is, as it necessarily must be, the judge of the elections, qualifications and returns of its members, and whatever improvements may be suggested by experience for simplifying and accelerating the process in disputed cases. So great a portion of a year would unavoidably elapse, before an illegitimate member could be dispossessed of his seat, that the prospect of such an event, would be little check to unfair and illicit means of obtaining a seat. All these considerations taken together warrant us in affirming that biennial elections will be as useful to the affairs of the public, as we have seen that they will be safe to the liberties of the people.

PUBLIUS.

[MADISON]

Federalist 54

The Same Subject Continued with a View to the Ratio of Representation,
February 12, 1788

At the Federal Convention, there had been two great struggles over representation. One involved the equal representation of states in the Senate; the other was whether to count slaves in the apportionment of seats in the House of Representatives. Many northern delegates found this idea both morally reprehensible and politically illogical. Unlike women, children, or propertyless men, who were also disenfranchised, slaves could not be regarded as citizens in any sense of the term; they had no rights at all. But southern delegates responded that slaves contributed significantly to the national economy; that it was legitimate to factor both population and wealth into the allocation of representation; and that the South, as a minority region fearful of northern domination, required the additional representation it would gain if slaves were counted. Northern delegates acceded to this claim as an expedient compromise. The result was the formula apportioning both representation in the House and direct taxation among the states according to the three-fifths rule: that is, a slave would count as three-fifths of a free person. That ratio was first used in 1783, when Congress sought to amend the Confederation to apportion the expenses of the Union on the basis of population. The congressional delegate who originally proposed this arbitrary number was none other than Madison.

In this essay, Madison uses a unique device, found nowhere else in The Federalist, to defend the Convention's decision. Rather than present the argument as the opinion of Publius, he assigns the task to someone else — the invented voice of "one of our southern brethren" — and closes the case for the clause by observing that "although [the reasoning] may appear to be a little strained in some points, yet . . . it fully reconciles me" to the compromise proposed. Reconciliation is not the same as conviction; it implies acceptance rather than persuasion.

But however "strained" the argument may appear, it reflects an important facet of the law of slavery: the inherent tension in treating people as property. Although the law treated slaves primarily as property, it also had to reckon with the fact that slaves were people, capable of committing and undertaking acts for which they or their masters might be held accountable in ways that property could not.

To the People of the State of New York.

The next view which I shall take of the House of Representatives, relates to the apportionment of its members to the several States, which is to be determined by the same rule with that of direct taxes.

It is not contended that the number of people in each State ought not to be the standard for regulating the proportion of those who are to represent the people of each State. The establishment of the same rule for the apportionment of taxes, will probably be as little contested; though the rule itself in this case, is by no means founded on the same principle. In the former case, the rule is understood to refer to the personal rights of the people, with which it has a natural and universal connection. In the latter, it has reference to the proportion of wealth, of which it is in no case a precise measure, and in ordinary cases a very unfit one. But notwithstanding the imperfection of the rule as applied to the relative wealth and contributions of the States, it is evidently the least exceptionable among the practicable rules; and had too recently obtained the general sanction of America, not to have found a ready preference with the Convention.

All this is admitted, it will perhaps be said: But does it follow from an admission of numbers for the measure of representation, or of slaves combined with free citizens, as a ratio of taxation, that slaves ought to be included in the numerical rule of representation? Slaves are considered as property, not as persons. They ought therefore to be comprehended in estimates of taxation which are founded on property, and to be excluded from representation which is regulated by a census of persons. This is the objection, as I understand it, stated in its full force. I shall be equally candid in stating the reasoning which may be offered on the opposite side.

We subscribe to the doctrine, might one of our southern brethren observe, that representation relates more immediately to persons, and taxation more immediately to property, and we join in the application of this distinction to the case of our slaves. But we must deny the fact that slaves are considered merely as property, and in no respect whatever as persons. The true state of the case is, that they partake of both these qualities; being considered by our laws, in some respects, as persons, and in other respects, as property. In being compelled to labor not for himself, but for a master; in being vendible by one master to another master; and in being subject at all times to be restrained in his liberty, and chastised in his body, by the capricious will of another, the slave may appear to be degraded from the human rank, and classed with those irrational animals, which fall under the legal denomination of property. In being protected on the other hand in his life & in his limbs, against the violence of all others, even the master of his labor and his liberty; and in being punishable himself for all violence committed against others; the slave is no less evidently regarded by the law as a member of the society; not as a part of the irrational creation; as a moral person, not as a mere article of property. The Foederal Constitution therefore, decides with great propriety on the case of our slaves, when it views them in the mixt character of persons and of property. This is in fact their true character. It is the character bestowed on them by the laws under which they live; and it will not be denied that these are the proper criterion; because it is only under the pretext that the laws have transformed the negroes into subjects of property, that a place is disputed them in the computation of numbers; and it is admitted that if the laws were to restore the rights which have been taken away, the negroes could no longer be refused an equal share of representation with the other inhabitants.

This question may be placed in another light. It is agreed on all sides, that numbers are the best scale of wealth and taxation, as they are the only proper scale of representation. Would the Convention have been impartial or consistent, if they had rejected the slaves from the list of inhabitants when the shares of representation were to be calculated; and inserted them on the lists when the tariff of contributions was to be adjusted? Could it be reasonably expected that the southern States would concur in a system which considered their slaves in some degree as men, when burdens were to be imposed, but refused to consider them in the same light when advantages were to be conferred? Might not some surprize also be expressed that those who reproach the southern States with the barbarous policy of considering as property a part of their human brethren, should themselves contend that the government to which all the States are to be parties, ought to consider this unfortunate race more compleatly in the unnatural light of property, than the very laws of which they complain!

It may be replied perhaps that slaves are not included in the estimate of representatives in any of the States possessing them. They neither vote themselves, nor increase the votes of their masters. Upon what principle then ought they to be taken into the foederal estimate of representation? In rejecting them altogether, the Constitution would in this respect have followed the very laws which have been appealed to, as the proper guide.

This objection is repelled by a single observation. It is a fundamental principle of the proposed Constitution, that as the aggregate number of representatives allotted to the several States, is to be determined by a foederal rule founded on the aggregate number of inhabitants, so the right of choosing this allotted number in each State is to be exercised by such part of the inhabitants, as the State itself may designate. The qualifications on which the right of suffrage depend, are not perhaps the same in any two States. In some of the States the difference is very material. In every State, a certain proportion of inhabitants are deprived of this right by the Constitution of the State, who will be included in the census by which the Foederal Constitution apportions the representatives. In this point of view, the southern States might retort the complaint, by insisting, that the principle laid down by the Convention required that no regard should be had to the policy of particular States towards their own inhabitants; and consequently, that the slaves as inhabitants should have been admitted into the census according to their full number, in like manner with other inhabitants, who by the policy of other States, are not admitted to all the rights of citizens. A rigorous adherence however to this principle is wa[i]ved by those who would be gainers by it. All that they ask is, that equal moderation be shewn on the other side. Let the case of the slaves be considered as it is in truth a peculiar one. Let the compromising expedient of the Constitution be mutually adopted, which regards them as inhabitants, but as debased by servitude below the equal level of free inhabitants, which regards the *slave* as divested of two fifth of the *man*.

After all may not another ground be taken on which this article of the Constitution, will admit of a still more ready defence? We have hitherto proceeded on the idea that representation related to persons only, and not at all to property. But is it a just idea? Government is instituted no less for protection of the property, than of the persons of individuals. The one as well as the other, therefore may be considered as represented by those who are charged with the government. Upon this principle it is, that in several of the States, and particularly in the

State of New-York, one branch of the government is intended more especially to be the guardian of property, and is accordingly elected by that part of the society which is most interested in this object of government. In the Foederal Constitution, this policy does not prevail. The rights of property are committed into the same hands with the personal rights. Some attention ought therefore to be paid to property in the choice of those hands.[1]

For another reason the votes allowed in the Foederal Legislature to the people of each State, ought to bear some proportion to the comparative wealth of the States. States have not like individuals, an influence over each other arising from superior advantages of fortune. If the law allows an opulent citizen but a single vote in the choice of his representative, the respect and consequence which he derives from his fortunate situation, very frequently guide the votes of others to the objects of his choice; and through this imperceptible channel the rights of property are conveyed into the public representation. A State possesses no such influence over other States. It is not probable that the richest State in the confederacy will ever influence the choice of a single representative in any other State. Nor will the representatives of the larger and richer States possess any other advantage in the Foederal Legislature over the representatives of other States, than what may result from their superior number alone; as far therefore as their superior wealth and weight may justly entitle them to any advantage, it ought to be secured to them by a superior share of representation. The new Constitution is in this respect materially different from the existing confederation as well as from that of the United Netherlands, and other similar confederacies. In each of the latter the efficacy of the foederal resolutions depends on the subsequent and voluntary resolutions of the States composing the Union. Hence the States, though possessing an equal vote in the public councils, have an unequal influence, corresponding with the unequal importance of these subsequent and voluntary resolutions. Under the proposed Constitution, the foederal acts will take effect without the necessary intervention of the individual States. They will depend merely on the majority of votes in the Foederal Legislature, and consequently each vote whether proceeding from a larger or a smaller State, or a State

---

[1]Madison here addresses a concern that particularly troubled him during this period: the relation between the protection of the civil rights that all free persons enjoy, on the one hand, and the special importance of protecting the rights of property, which may be unevenly distributed throughout society, on the other. One method of protection for the latter might be to give the upper house of a legislature a special obligation to represent property, for example, by restricting the suffrage for its members to citizens possessing more wealth than would be required to vote for representatives in the lower house.

more or less wealthy or powerful, will have an equal weight and efficacy; in the same manner as the votes individually given in a State Legislature, by the representatives of unequal counties or other districts, have each a precise equality of value and effect; or if there be any difference in the case, it proceeds from the difference in the personal character of the individual representative, rather than from any regard to the extent of the district from which he comes.

Such is the reasoning which an advocate for the southern interests might employ on this subject: And although it may appear to be a little strained in some points, yet on the whole, I must confess, that it fully reconciles me to the scale of representation, which the Convention have established.

In one respect the establishment of a common measure for representation and taxation will have a very salutary effect. As the accuracy of the census to be obtained by the Congress, will necessarily depend in a considerable degree on the disposition, if not the cooperation of the States, it is of great importance that the States should feel as little bias as possible to swell or to reduce the amount of their numbers. Were their share of representation alone to be governed by this rule they would have an interest in exaggerating their inhabitants. Were the rule to decide their share of taxation alone, a contrary temptation would prevail. By extending the rule to both objects, the States will have opposite interests, which will controul and ballance each other; and produce the requisite impartiality.

PUBLIUS.

[MADISON]

Federalist 62

Concerning the Constitution of the Senate with Regard to the
Qualifications of the Members, the Manner of Appointing Them, the Equality
of Representation, the Number of the Senators and the Duration of Their
Appointments, February 27, 1788

After devoting ten essays (52–61) to the House of Representatives, Publius next turned his attention to the Senate, the one institution about which Anti-Federalists harbored their gravest suspicions. Madison had long believed that a well-designed upper house had a critical role to play in providing the "wisdom and steadiness" that he found so absent from American legislation. But privately he, too, retained doubts about the *new Senate the Constitution would create. He had been one of a handful of delegates to oppose the Convention's early decision to allow the state legislatures to elect senators, because he understood that the idea that each legislature was equal in authority to other legislatures could be translated into a claim for the political equality of the states they governed. Madison had also bitterly opposed the "compromise" giving each state two senators. Given the importance that both decisions played in the politics of the Convention, it is striking to see how little attention Madison pays to them here. With those provisions dispatched, however, he warms to his subject as he describes the beneficial effect that the Senate will have on national lawmaking. Here Madison's reservations about the key political decisions the Convention had taken in forming the Senate give way to his hopes that it will emerge as the one institution best prepared to endow the national government with stability.*

To the People of the State of New York.

Having examined the constitution of the house of representatives, and answered such of the objections against it as seemed to merit notice, I enter next on the examination of the senate. The heads into which this member of the government may be considered, are I. the qualifications of senators. II. the appointment of them by the state legislatures. III. the equality of representation in the senate. IV. the number of senators, and the term for which they are to be elected. V. the powers vested in the senate.

I. The qualifications proposed for senators, as distinguished from those of representatives, consist in a more advanced age, and a longer period of citizenship. A senator must be thirty years of age at least; as a representative, must be twenty-five. And the former must have been a citizen nine years; as seven years are required for the latter. The propriety of these distinctions is explained by the nature of the senatorial trust; which requiring greater extent of information and stability of character, requires at the same time that the senator should have reached a period of life most likely to supply these advantages; and which participating immediately in transactions with foreign nations, ought to be exercised by none who are not thoroughly weaned from the prepossessions and habits incident to foreign birth and education. The term of nine years appears to be a prudent mediocrity between a total exclusion of adopted citizens, whose merit and talents may claim a share in the public confidence; and an indiscriminate and hasty admission of them, which might create a channel for foreign influence on the national councils.

II. It is equally unnecessary to dilate on the appointment of senators by the state legislatures. Among the various modes which might have been devised for constituting this branch of the government, that which has been proposed by the convention is probably the most congenial with the public opinion. It is recommended by the double advantage of favouring a select appointment, and of giving to the state governments such an agency in the formation of the federal government, as must secure the authority of the former; and may form a convenient link between the two systems.

III. The equality of representation in the senate is another point, which, being evidently the result of compromise between the opposite pretensions of the large and the small states, does not call for much discussion. If indeed it be right that among a people thoroughly incorporated into one nation, every district ought to have a *proportional* share in the government; and that among independent and sovereign states bound together by a simple league, the parties however unequal in size, ought to have an *equal* share in the common councils, it does not appear to be without some reason, that in a compound republic partaking both of the national and federal character, the government ought to be founded on a mixture of the principles of proportional and equal representation. But it is superfluous to try by the standards of theory, a part of the constitution which is allowed on all hands to be the result not of theory, but "of a spirit of amity, and that mutual deference and concession which the peculiarity of our political situation rendered indispensable."[1] A common government with powers equal to its objects, is called for by the voice, and still more loudly by the political situation of America. A government founded on principles more consonant to the wishes of the larger states, is not likely to be obtained from the smaller states. The only option then for the former lies between the proposed government and a government still more objectionable. Under this alternative the advice of prudence must be, to embrace the lesser evil; and instead of indulging a fruitless anticipation of the possible mischiefs which may ensue, to contemplate rather the advantageous consequences which may qualify the sacrifice.

In this spirit it may be remarked, that the equal vote allowed to each state, is at once a constitutional recognition of the portion of sov-

---

[1] *"of a spirit of amity . . .":* Madison quotes from the covering letter of September 17, 1787, signed by George Washington, that accompanied the submission of the proposed Constitution from the Federal Convention to the Continental Congress.

ereignty remaining in the individual states, and an instrument for preserving that residuary sovereignty. So far the equality ought to be no
less acceptable to the large than to the small states; since they are not
less solicitous to guard by every possible expedient against an
improper consolidation of the states into one simple republic.

Another advantage accruing from this ingredient in the constitution
of the senate, is the additional impediment it must prove against
improper acts of legislation. No law or resolution can now be passed
without the concurrence first of a majority of the people, and then of a
majority of the states. It must be acknowledged that this complicated
check on legislation may in some instances be injurious as well as beneficial; and that the peculiar defence which it involves in favour of the
smaller states would be more rational, if any interests common to
them, and distinct from those of the other states, would otherwise be
exposed to peculiar danger. But as the larger states will always be able
by their power over the supplies to defeat unreasonable exertions of
this prerogative of the lesser states; and as the facility and excess of
law-making seem to be the diseases to which our governments are
most liable, it is not impossible that this part of the constitution may be
more convenient in practice than it appears to many in contemplation.

IV. The number of senators and the duration of their appointment
come next to be considered. In order to form an accurate judgment on
both these points, it will be proper to enquire into the purposes which
are to be answered by a senate; and in order to ascertain these it will
be necessary to review the inconveniencies which a republic must suffer from the want of such an institution.

First. It is a misfortune incident to republican government, though
in a less degree than to other governments, that those who administer
it, may forget their obligations to their constituents, and prove unfaith-
ful to their important trust. In this point of view, a senate, as a second
branch of the legislative assembly, distinct from, and dividing the
power with, a first, must be in all cases a salutary check on the government. It doubles the security to the people, by requiring the concurrence of two distinct bodies in schemes of usurpation or perfidy,
where the ambition or corruption of one, would otherwise be sufficient. This is a precaution founded on such clear principles, and now
so well understood in the United States, that it would be more than
superfluous to enlarge on it. I will barely remark that as the improbability of sinister combinations will be in proportion to the dissimilarity
in the genius of the two bodies; it must be politic to distinguish them
from each other by every circumstance which will consist with a due

harmony in all proper measures, and with the genuine principles of republican government.

Secondly. The necessity of a senate is not less indicated by the propensity of all single and numerous assemblies, to yield to the impulse of sudden and violent passions, and to be seduced by factious leaders, into intemperate and pernicious resolutions. Examples on this subject might be cited without number; and from proceedings within the United States, as well as from the history of other nations. But a position that will not be contradicted need not be proved. All that need be remarked is that a body which is to correct this infirmity ought itself be free from it, and consequently ought to be less numerous. It ought moreover to possess great firmness, and consequently ought to hold its authority by a tenure of considerable duration.

Thirdly. Another defect to be supplied by a senate lies in a want of due acquaintance with the objects and principles of legislation. It is not possible that an assembly of men called for the most part from pursuits of a private nature, continued in appointment for a short time, and led by no permanent motive to devote the intervals of public occupation to a study of the laws, the affairs and the comprehensive interests of their country, should, if left wholly to themselves, escape a variety of important errors in the exercise of their legislative trust. It may be affirmed, on the best grounds, that no small share of the present embarrassments of America is to be charged on the blunders of our governments; and that these have proceeded from the heads rather than the hearts of most of the authors of them. What indeed are all the repealing, explaining and amending laws, which fill and disgrace our voluminous codes, but so many monuments of deficient wisdom; so many impeachments exhibited by each succeeding, against each preceding session; so many admonitions to the people of the value of those aids which may be expected from a well constituted senate?

A good government implies two things; first, fidelity to the object of government, which is the happiness of the people; secondly, a knowledge of the means by which that object can be best attained. Some governments are deficient in both these qualities: Most governments are deficient in the first. I scruple not to assert that in the American governments, too little attention has been paid to the last. The federal constitution avoids this error; and what merits particular notice, it provides for the last in a mode which increases the security for the first.

Fourthly. The mutability in the public councils, arising from a rapid succession of new members, however qualified they may be, points out in the strongest manner, the necessity of some stable institution in the government. Every new election in the states, is found to change one half of the representatives. From this change of men must proceed a change of opinions; and from a change of opinions, a change of measures. But a continual change even of good measures is inconsistent with every rule of prudence, and every prospect of success. The remark is verified in private life, and becomes more just as well as more important, in national transactions.

To trace the mischievous effects of a mutable government would fill a volume. I will hint a few only, each of which will be perceived to be a source of innumerable others.

In the first place it forfeits the respect and confidence of other nations, and all the advantages connected with national character. An individual who is observed to be inconstant to his plans, or perhaps to carry on his affairs without any plan at all, is marked at once by all prudent people as a speedy victim to his own unsteadiness and folly. His more friendly neighbours may pity him; but all will decline to connect their fortunes with his; and not a few will seize the opportunity of making their fortunes out of his. One nation is to another what one individual is to another; with this melancholy distinction perhaps, that the former with fewer of the benevolent emotions than the latter, are under fewer restraints also from taking undue advantage of the indiscretions of each other. Every nation consequently whose affairs betray a want of wisdom and stability, may calculate on every loss which can be sustained from the more systematic policy of its wiser neighbours. But the best instruction on this subject is unhappily conveyed to America by the example of her own situation. She finds that she is held in no respect by her friends; that she is the derision of her enemies; and that she is a prey to every nation which has an interest in speculating on her fluctuating councils and embarrassed affairs.

The internal effects of a mutable policy are still more calamitous. It poisons the blessings of liberty itself. It will be of little avail to the people that the laws are made by men of their own choice, if the laws be so voluminous that they cannot be read, or so incoherent that they cannot be understood; if they be repealed or revised before they are promulged, or undergo such incessant changes that no man who knows what the law is to-day can guess what it will be to-morrow. Law is defined to be a rule of action; but how can that be a rule, which is little known and less fixed?

Another effect of public instability is the unreasonable advantage it gives to the sagacious, the enterprising and the moneyed few, over the industrious and uninformed mass of the people. Every new regulation concerning commerce or revenue, or in any manner affecting the value of the different species of property, presents a new harvest to those who watch the change, and can trace its consequences; a harvest reared not by themselves but by the toils and cares of the great body of their fellow citizens. This is a state of things in which it may be said with some truth that laws are made for the *few* not for the *many*.

In another point of view great injury results from an unstable government. The want of confidence in the public councils damps every useful undertaking; the success and profit of which may depend on a continuance of existing arrangements. What prudent merchant will hazard his fortunes in any new branch of commerce, when he knows not but that his plans may be rendered unlawful before they can be executed? What farmer or manufacturer will lay himself out for the encouragement given to any particular cultivation or establishment, when he can have no assurance that his preparatory labors and advances will not render him a victim to an inconstant government? In a word no great improvement or laudable enterprise, can go forward, which requires the auspices of a steady system of national policy.

But the most deplorable effect of all is that diminution of attachment and reverence which steals into the hearts of the people, towards a political system which betrays so many marks of infirmity, and disappoints so many of their flattering hopes. No government any more than an individual will long be respected, without being truly respectable, nor be truly respectable without possessing a certain portion of order and stability.

PUBLIUS.

[MADISON]

Federalist 63

A Further View of the Constitution of the Senate in Regard to the Duration of Appointment of Its Members, March 1, 1788

In his last essay as Publius, Madison concludes his defense of the contributions the Senate will make to instilling stability, wisdom, and "a due sense of national character" in the federal government. But the essay is revealing for another reason. Madison was enough of a republican in principle to believe that government must always be held accountable to the will of the people. But he also doubted the capacity of the people to reach informed judgments about complicated issues, and he feared their capacity to act impulsively and impetuously. A well-constructed Senate, insulated from these impulses, was the institutional solution that would enable the government to remain responsible to the people's true interests without becoming too responsive to their immediate passions. Madison thus closes his contributions to The Federalist *with a candid statement of his own deepest concerns about the character of republican politics. He repeats the distinction between a republic and a democracy drawn in earlier essays, and uses the final paragraph to remind readers that even should the Senate aspire to become the independent aristocracy that Anti-Federalists repeatedly denounced, the House of Representatives, with the dominant voice of the people on its side, would be able to preserve the Constitution.*

To the People of the State of New York.

A fifth desideratum illustrating the utility of a Senate, is the want of a due sense of national character. Without a select and stable member of the government, the esteem of foreign powers will not only be forfeited by an unenlightened and variable policy, proceeding from the causes already mentioned; but the national councils will not possess that sensibility to the opinion of the world, which is perhaps not less necessary in order to merit, than it is to obtain, its respect and confidence.

An attention to the judgment of other nations is important to every government for two reasons: The one is, that independently of the merits of any particular plan or measure, it is desireable on various accounts, that it should appear to other nations as the offspring of a wise and honorable policy: The second is that in doubtful cases, particularly where the national councils may be warped by some strong passion, or momentary interest, the presumed or known opinion of the impartial world, may be the best guide that can be followed. What has not America lost by her want of character with foreign nations? And how many errors and follies would she not have avoided, if the justice and propriety of her measures had in every instance been previously tried by the light in which they would probably appear to the unbiassed part of mankind?

Yet however requisite a sense of national character may be, it is evident that it can never be sufficiently possessed by a numerous and changeable body. It can only be found in a number so small, that a sensible degree of the praise and blame of public measures may be the portion of each individual; or in an assembly so durably invested with public trust, that the pride and consequence of its members may be sensibly incorporated with the reputation and prosperity of the community. The half-yearly representatives of Rhode-Island, would probably have been little affected in their deliberations on the iniquitous measures of that state, by arguments drawn from the light in which such measures would be viewed by foreign nations, or even by the sister states; whilst it can scarcely be doubted, that if the concurrence of a select and stable body had been necessary, a regard to national character alone, would have prevented the calamities under which that misguided people is now labouring.

I add as a *sixth* defect, the want in some important cases of a due responsibility in the government to the people, arising from that frequency of elections, which in other cases produces this responsibility. This remark will perhaps appear not only new but paradoxical. It must nevertheless be acknowledged, when explained, to be as undeniable as it is important.

Responsibility in order to be reasonable must be limited to objects within the power of the responsible party; and in order to be effectual, must relate to operations of that power, of which a ready and proper judgment can be formed by the constituents. The objects of government may be divided into two general classes; the one depending on measures which have singly an immediate and sensible operation; the other depending on a succession of well chosen and well connected measures, which have a gradual and perhaps unobserved operation. The importance of the latter description to the collective and permanent welfare of every country needs no explanation. And yet it is evident, that an assembly elected for so short a term as to be unable to provide more than one or two links in a chain of measures, on which the general welfare may essentially depend, ought not to be answerable for the final result, any more than a steward or tenant, engaged for one year, could be justly made to answer for places or improvements, which could not be accomplished in less than half a dozen years. Nor is it possible for the people to estimate the *share* of influence which their annual assemblies may respectively have on events resulting from the mixed transactions of several years. It is sufficiently difficult at any rate to preserve a personal responsibility in the members of a *numerous* body, for such acts of the body as have an immediate, detached and palpable operation on its constituents.

The proper remedy for this defect must be an additional body in the legislative department, which, having sufficient permanency to provide for such objects as require a continued attention, and a train of measures, may be justly and effectually answerable for the attainment of those objects.

Thus far I have considered the circumstances which point out the necessity of a well constructed senate, only as they relate to the representatives of the people. To a people as little blinded by prejudice, or corrupted by flattery, as those whom I address, I shall not scruple to add, that such an institution may be sometimes necessary, as a defence to the people against their own temporary errors and delusions. As the cool and deliberate sense of the community ought in all governments, and actually will in all free governments ultimately prevail over the views of its rulers; so there are particular moments in public affairs, when the people stimulated by some irregular passion, or some illicit advantage, or misled by the artful misrepresentations of interested men, may call for measures which they themselves will afterwards be the most ready to lament and condemn. In these critical moments, how salutary will be the interference of some temperate and respectable body of citizens, in order to check the misguided career, and to suspend the blow meditated by the people against themselves, until reason, justice and truth, can regain their authority over the public mind? What bitter anguish would not the people of Athens have often escaped, if their government had contained so provident a safeguard against the tyranny of their own passions? Popular liberty might then have escaped the indelible reproach of decreeing to the same citizens, the hemlock on one day, and statues on the next.[1]

It may be suggested that a people spread over an extensive region, cannot like the crouded inhabitants of a small district, be subject to the infection of violent passions; or to the danger of combining in the pursuit of unjust measures. I am far from denying that this is a distinction of peculiar importance. I have on the contrary endeavoured in a former paper, to shew that it is one of the principal recommendations of a confederated republic. At the same time this advantage ought not to be considered as superseding the use of auxiliary precautions. It may even be remarked that the same extended situation which will exempt the people of America from some of the dangers incident to lesser republics, will expose them to the inconveniency of remaining for a longer time, under the influence of those misrepresentations

---

[1] *the hemlock on one day, and statues on the next:* In a democracy ruled by a fickle people, a leader might be one day condemned to death, and the next day have a monument erected in his honor.

which the combined industry of interested men may succeed in distributing among them.

It adds no small weight to all these considerations, to recollect, that history informs us of no long lived republic which had not a senate. Sparta, Rome and Carthage are in fact the only states to whom that character can be applied. In each of the two first there was a senate for life. The constitution of the senate in the last, is less known. Circumstantial evidence makes it probable that it was not different in this particular from the two others. It is at least certain that it had some quality or other which rendered it an anchor against popular fluctuations; and that a smaller council drawn out of the senate was appointed not only for life; but filled up vacancies itself. These examples, though as unfit for the imitation, as they are repugnant to the genius of America, are notwithstanding, when compared with the fugitive and turbulent existence of other antient republics, very instructive proofs of the necessity of some institution that will blend stability with liberty. I am not unaware of the circumstances which distinguish the American from other popular governments, as well antient as modern; and which render extreme circumspection necessary in reasoning from the one case to the other. But after allowing due weight to this consideration, it may still be maintained that there are many points of similitude which render these examples not unworthy of our attention. Many of the defects as we have seen, which can only be supplied by a senatorial institution, are common to a numerous assembly frequently elected by the people, and to the people themselves. There are others peculiar to the former, which require the controul of such an institution. The people can never wilfully betray their own interests: But they may possibly be betrayed by the representatives of the people; and the danger will be evidently greater where the whole legislative trust is lodged in the hands of one body of men, than where the concurrence of separate and dissimilar bodies is required in every public act.

The difference most relied on between the American and other republics, consists in the principle of representation, which is the pivot on which the former move, and which is supposed to have been unknown to the latter, or at least to the antient part of them. The use which has been made of this difference, in reasonings contained in former papers, will have shewn that I am disposed neither to deny its existence nor to under value its importance. I feel the less restraint therefore in observing that the position concerning the ignorance of the antient government on the subject of representation is by no means precisely true in the latitude commonly given to it. Without entering into a disquisition which here would be misplaced, I will refer to a few known facts in support of what I advance.

In the most pure democracies of Greece, many of the executive functions were performed not by the people themselves, but by officers elected by the people, and *representing* the people in their *executive* capacity.

Prior to the reform of Solon, Athens was governed by nine Archons, annually *elected by the people at large.* The degree of power delegated to them seems to be left in great obscurity. Subsequent to that period, we find an assembly first of four and afterwards of six hundred members, annually *elected by the people;* and *partially* representing them in their *legislative* capacity; since they were not only associated with the people in the function of making laws; but had the exclusive right of originating legislative propositions to the people. The senate of Carthage also, whatever might be its power or the duration of its appointment, appears to have been *elective* by the suffrages of the people. Similar instances might be traced in most if not all the popular governments of antiquity.

Lastly in Sparta, we meet with the Ephori, and in Rome with the Tribunes; two bodies, small indeed in number, but annually *elected by the whole body of the people,* and considered as the *representatives* of the people, almost in their *plenipotentiary* capacity. The Cosmi of Crete were also annually *elected by the people;* and have been considered by some authors as an institution analogous to those of Sparta and Rome; with this difference only that in the election of that representative body, the right of suffrage was communicated to a part only of the people.

From these facts, to which many others might be added, it is clear that the principle of representation was neither unknown to the antients, nor wholly overlooked in their political constitutions. The true distinction between these and the American Governments lies *in the total exclusion of the people in their collective capacity* from any share in the *latter,* and not in the *total exclusion of representatives of the people,* from the administration of the *former.* The distinction however thus qualified must be admitted to leave a most advantageous superiority in favor of the United States. But to ensure to this advantage its full effect, we must be careful not to separate it from the other advantage, of an extensive territory. For it cannot be believed that any form of representative government, could have succeeded within the narrow limits occupied by the democracies of Greece.

In answer to all these arguments, suggested by reason, illustrated by examples, and enforced by our own experience, the jealous adversary of the constitution will probably content himself with repeating, that a senate appointed not immediately by the people, and for the term of six years, must gradually acquire a dangerous preeminence in the government, and finally transform it into a tyrannical aristocracy.

To this general answer the general reply ought to be sufficient; that liberty may be endangered by the abuses of liberty, as well as by the abuses of power; that there are numerous instances of the former as well as of the latter; and that the former rather than the latter is apparently most to be apprehended by the United States. But a more particular reply may be given.

Before such a revolution can be effected, the senate, it is to be observed, must in the first place corrupt itself; must next corrupt the state legislatures, must then corrupt the house of representatives, and must finally corrupt the people at large. It is evident that the senate must be first corrupted, before it can attempt an establishment of tyranny. Without corrupting the state legislatures, it cannot prosecute the attempt, because the periodical change of members would otherwise regenerate the whole body. Without exerting the means of corruption with equal success on the house of representatives, the opposition of that co-equal branch of the government would inevitably defeat the attempt; and without corrupting the people themselves, a succession of new representatives would speedily restore all things to their pristine order. Is there any man who can seriously persuade himself, that the proposed senate can, by any possible means within the compass of human address, arrive at the object of a lawless ambition, through all these obstructions?

If reason condemns the suspicion, the same sentence is pronounced by experience. The constitution of Maryland furnishes the most apposite example. The senate of that state is elected, as the federal senate will be, indirectly by the people; and for a term less by one year only, than the federal senate. It is distinguished also by the remarkable prerogative of filling up its own vacancies within the term of its appointment: and at the same time, is not under the controul of any such rotation, as is provided for the federal senate. There are some other lesser distinctions, which would expose the former to colorable objections that do not lie against the latter. If the federal senate therefore really contained the danger which has been so loudly proclaimed, some symptoms at least of a like danger ought by this time to have been betrayed by the senate of Maryland; but no such symptoms have appeared. On the contrary the jealousies at first entertained by men of the same description with those who view with terror the correspondent part of the federal constitution, have been gradually extinguished by the progress of the experiment; and the Maryland constitution is daily deriving from the salutary operations of this part of it, a reputation in which it will probably not be rivalled by that of any state in the union.

But if any thing could silence the jealousies on this subject, it ought to be the British example. The senate there, instead of being elected for a term of six years, and of being unconfined to particular families or fortunes, is an hereditary assembly of opulent nobles. The house of representatives, instead of being elected for two years and by the whole body of the people, is elected for seven years; and in very great proportion, by a very small proportion of the people. Here unquestionably ought to be seen in full display, the aristocratic usurpations and tyranny, which are at some future period to be exemplified in the United States. Unfortunately however for the antifederal argument the British history informs us, that this hereditary assembly has not even been able to defend itself against the continual encroachments of the house of representatives; and that it no sooner lost the support of the monarch, than it was actually crushed by the weight of the popular branch.[2]

As far as antiquity can instruct us on this subject, its examples support the reasoning which we have employed. In Sparta the Ephori, the annual representatives of the people, were found an overmatch for the senate for life, continually gained on its authority, and finally drew all power into their own hands. The tribunes of Rome, who were the representatives of the people, prevailed, it is well known, in almost every contest with the senate for life, and in the end gained the most complete triumph over it. This fact is the more remarkable, as unanimity was required in every act of the tribunes, even after their number was augmented to ten. It proves the irresistable force possessed by that branch of a free government, which has the people on its side. To these examples might be added that of Carthage, whose senate, according to the testimony of Polybius, instead of drawing all power into its vortex, had at the commencement of the second punic war, lost almost the whole of its original portion.

Besides the conclusive evidence resulting from this assemblage of facts, that the federal senate will never be able to transform itself, by

[2]Madison here seems to allude both to the ongoing shift of power within Parliament to the House of Commons, and to the period of the Commonwealth (1649–60) when the Puritan revolutionaries who controlled the House of Commons actually abolished the House of Lords.

gradual usurpations, into an independent and aristocratic body; we are warranted in believing that if such a revolution should ever happen from causes which the foresight of man cannot guard against, the house of representatives with the people on their side will at all times be able to bring back the constitution to its primitive form and principles. Against the force of the immediate representatives of the people, nothing will be able to maintain even the constitutional authority of the senate, but such a display of enlightened policy, and attachment to the public good, as will divide with that branch of the legislature, the affections and support of the entire body of the people themselves.

PUBLIUS.

[JAY]

Federalist 64

A Further View of the Constitution of the Senate in Regard to the Power of Making Treaties, March 5, 1788

After writing four of the first five essays, illness prevented John Jay from contributing to the series. Federalist 64, his last essay, was his only substantive commentary on the Constitution, but it addresses a key provision that Jay, as secretary for foreign affairs, was well qualified to discuss. The clause of the Constitution authorizing the president to make treaties "by and with the Advice and Consent of the Senate" was controversial for several reasons. First, it supported the image of the Senate as the dominant and most dangerous branch of government. Second, the inclusion of treaties under the supremacy clause would enable the Senate and president to make agreements with foreign nations that would bind the nation and its citizens, even though the people's directly elected representative had no role in treaty formation. Third was the fear that even with the two-thirds majority required to approve a treaty, particular regions might find their essential interests sacrificed to the demands of diplomacy. This fear was especially strong in the South, where Jay's willingness during the Spanish negotiations of 1786 to yield American navigation rights on the Mississippi still rankled.

Jay uses this essay to offer measured responses to all these concerns. He takes particular care to explain the advantages of including the president in the treaty-making process, and the importance of recognizing that treaties deserve, indeed require, to be regarded as legally binding in every sense of the term.

To the People of the State of New York.

It is a just and not a new observation, that enemies to particular persons and opponents to particular measures, seldom confine their censures to such things only in either, as are worthy of blame. Unless on this principle it is difficult to explain the motives of their conduct, who condemn the proposed constitution in the aggregate, and treat with severity some of the most unexceptionable articles in it.

The 2d. section gives power to the president *"by and with the advice and consent of the senate to make treaties* PROVIDED TWO THIRDS OF THE SENATORS PRESENT CONCUR."

The power of making treaties is an important one, especially as it relates to war, peace and commerce; and it should not be delegated but in such a mode, and with such precautions, as will afford the highest security, that it will be exercised by men the best qualified for the purpose, and in the manner most conducive to the public good. The convention appears to have been attentive to both these points—they have directed the president to be chosen by select bodies of electors to be deputed by the people for that express purpose; and they have committed the appointment of senators to the state legislatures. This mode has in such cases, vastly the advantage of elections by the people in their collective capacity, where the activity of party zeal taking advantage of the supineness, the ignorance, and the hopes and fears of the unwary and interested, often places men in office by the votes of a small proportion of the electors.

As the select assemblies for choosing the president, as well as the state legislatures who appoint the senators will in general be composed of the most enlightened and respectable citizens, there is reason to presume that their attention and their votes will be directed to those men only who have become the most distinguished by their abilities and virtue, and in whom the people perceive just grounds for confidence. The constitution manifests very particular attention to this object. By excluding men under thirty five from the first office, and those under thirty from the second, it confines the electors to men of whom the people have had time to form a judgment, and with respect to whom they will not be liable to be deceived by those brilliant appearances of genius and patriotism, which like transient meteors sometimes mislead as well as dazzle. If the observation be well founded, that wise kings will always be served by able ministers, it is fair to argue that as an assembly of select electors possess in a greater degree than kings, the means of extensive and accurate information relative to men and characters, so will their appointments bear at least equal marks of discretion and discernment. The inference which naturally results from these considerations is this, that the president and senators so chosen will always be of the number of those who best understand our national interests, whether considered in relation to the several states or to foreign nations, who are best able to promote those interests, and whose reputation for integrity inspires and merits confidence. With such men the power of making treaties may be safely lodged.

Although the absolute necessity of system in the conduct of any business, is universally known and acknowledged, yet the high importance of it in national affairs has not yet become sufficiently impressed on the public mind. They who wish to commit the power under consideration to a popular assembly, composed of members constantly coming and going in quick succession, seem not to recollect that such a body must necessarily be inadequate to the attainment of those great objects, which require to be steadily contemplated in all their relations and circumstances, and which can only be approached and achieved by measures, which not only talents, but also exact information and often much time are necessary to concert and to execute. It was wise therefore in the convention to provide not only that the power of making treaties should be committed to able and honest men, but also that they should continue in place a sufficient time to become perfectly acquainted with our national concerns, and to form and introduce a system for the management of them. The duration prescribed is such as will give them an opportunity of greatly extending their political informations and of rendering their accumulating experience more and more beneficial to their country. Nor has the convention discovered less prudence in providing for the frequent elections of senators in such a way, as to obviate the inconvenience of periodically transferring those great affairs entirely to new men, for by leaving a considerable residue of the old ones in place, uniformity and order, as well as a constant succession of official information, will be preserved.

There are few who will not admit that the affairs of trade and navigation should be regulated by a system cautiously formed and steadily pursued; and that both our treaties and our laws should correspond with, and be made to promote it. It is of much consequence that this correspondence and conformity be carefully maintained, and they who assent to the truth of this position, will see and confess that it is well provided for by making the concurrence of the senate necessary both to treaties and to laws.

It seldom happens in the negociation of treaties of whatever nature, but that perfect *secrecy* and immediate *dispatch* are sometimes requisite. There are cases where the most useful intelligence may be obtained, if the persons possessing it can be relieved from apprehensions of discovery. Those apprehensions will operate on those persons whether they are actuated by mercenary or friendly motives, and there doubtless are many of both descriptions, who would rely on the secrecy of the president, but who would not confide in that of the senate, and still less in that of a large popular assembly. The convention have done well therefore in so disposing of the power of making treaties, that although the president must in forming them act by the advice and consent of the senate, yet he will be able to manage the business of intelligence in such manner as prudence may suggest.

They who have turned their attention to the affairs of men, must have perceived that there are tides in them. Tides, very irregular in their duration, strength and direction, and seldom found to run twice exactly in the same manner or measure. To discern and to profit by these tides in national affairs, is the business of those who preside over them; and they who have had much experience on this head inform us, that there frequently are occasions when days, nay even when hours are precious. The loss of a battle, the death of a Prince, the removal of a minister, or other circumstances intervening to change the present posture and aspect of affairs, may turn the most favorable tide into a course opposite to our wishes. As in the field, so in the cabinet, there are moments to be seized as they pass, and they who preside in either, should be left in capacity to improve them. So often and so essentially have we heretofore suffered from the want of secrecy and dispatch, that the Constitution would have been inexcusably defective if no attention had been paid to those objects. Those matters which in negociations usually require the most secrecy and the most dispatch, are those preparatory and auxiliary measures which are no otherwise important in a national view, than as they tend to facilitate the attainment of the objects of the negociation. For these the president will find no difficulty to provide, and should any circumstance occur which requires the advice and consent of the senate, he may at any time convene them. Thus we see that the constitution provides that our negociations for treaties shall have every advantage which can be derived from talents, information, integrity, and deliberate investigations on the one hand, and from secrecy and dispatch on the other.

But to this plan as to most others that have ever appeared, objections are contrived and urged.

Some are displeased with it, not on account of any errors or defects in it, but because as the treaties when made are to have the force of laws, they should be made only by men invested with legislative authority. These gentlemen seem not to consider that the judgments of our courts, and the commissions constitutionally given by our governor, are as valid and as binding on all persons whom they concern, as the laws passed by our legislature are. All constitutional acts of power, whether in the executive or in the judicial departments, have as much legal validity and obligation as if they proceeded from the Legislature, and therefore whatever name be given to the power of making treaties, or however obligatory they may be when made, certain it is that the people may with much propriety commit the power to a distinct body from the legislature, the executive or judicial. It surely does not follow that because they have given the power of making laws to the Legislature, that therefore they should likewise give them power to do every other act of sovereignty by which the citizens are to be bound and affected.

Others, though content that treaties should be made in the mode proposed, are averse to their being the *supreme* laws of the land. They insist and profess to believe, that treaties, like acts of assembly, should be repealable at pleasure. This idea seems to be new and peculiar to this country, but new errors as well as new truths often appear. These gentlemen would do well to reflect that a treaty is only another name for a bargain; and that it would be impossible to find a nation who would make any bargain with us, which should be binding on them *absolutely,* but on us only so long and so far as we may think proper to be bound by it. They who make laws may without doubt amend or repeal them, and it will not be disputed that they who make treaties may alter or cancel them; but still let us not forget that treaties are made not by only one of the contracting parties, but by both, and consequently that as the consent of both was essential to their formation at first, so must it ever afterwards be to alter or cancel them. The proposed Constitution therefore has not in the least extended the obligation of treaties. They are just as binding, and just as far beyond the lawful reach of legislative acts now, as they will be at any future period, or under any form of government.

However useful jealousy may be in republics, yet when, like Bile in the natural, it abounds too much in the body politic; the eyes of both become very liable to be deceived by the delusive appearances which that malady casts on surrounding objects. From this cause probably proceed the fears and apprehensions of some, that the President and Senate may make treaties without an equal eye to the interests of all the States. Others suspect that the two-thirds will oppress the remaining third, and ask whether those gentlemen are made sufficiently responsible for their conduct—whether if they act corruptly they can be punished; and if they make disadvantageous treaties, how are we to get rid of those treaties?

As all the States are equally represented in the senate, and by men the most able and the most willing to promote the interests of their constituents, they will all have an equal degree of influence in that body, especially while they continue to be careful in appointing proper persons, and to insist on their punctual attendance. In proportion as the United States assume a national form, and a national character, so will the good of the whole be more and more an object of attention; and the government must be a weak one indeed, if it should forget that the good of the whole can only be promoted by advancing the good of each of the parts or members which compose the whole. It will not be in the power of the president and senate to make any treaties, by which they and their families and estates will not be equally bound and affected with the rest of the community; and having no private interest distinct from that of the nation, they will be under no temptations to neglect the latter.

As to corruption, the case is not supposable, he must either have been very unfortunate in his intercourse with the world, or possess a heart very susceptible of such impressions, who can think it probable that the president and two-thirds of the senate will ever be capable of such unworthy conduct. The idea is too gross and too invidious to be entertained. But in such a case, if it should ever happen, the treaty so obtained from us would, like all other fraudulent contracts, be null and void by the laws of nations.

With respect to their responsibility, it is difficult to conceive how it could be encreased. Every consideration that can influence the human mind, such as honor, oaths, reputation, conscience, the love of country, and family affections and attachments, afford security for their fidelity. In short, as the constitution has taken the utmost care that they shall be men of talents and integrity, we have reason to be persuaded that the treaties they make will be as advantageous as all circumstances considered could be made; and so far as the fear of punishment and disgrace can operate, that motive to good behaviour is amply afforded by the article on the subject of impeachments.

PUBLIUS.

[HAMILTON]

Federalist 70

The Same View Continued (Concerning the Constitution of the President) in Relation to the Unity of the Executive, with an Examination of the Project of an Executive Council, March 15, 1788

After opening the discussion of the executive department in Federalist 67, Hamilton devoted the next two essays to the electoral college and to a comparison of the presidency with the crown of Britain and the governorship of New York. But it was only with this essay that he began to speak frankly and robustly about the positive advantages that an "energetic" executive could lend to republican government. His mission was to combat the common view that a vigorous executive, which smacked of monarchy, was incompatible with the basic principles of republicanism. Most of the state constitutions, with the notable exceptions of those of New York and Massachusetts, had left the executive politically dependent on the legislature and often yoked governors to act in conjunction with executive councils. The Constitution gave the president potential political independence, through the system of presidential electors, and while it contemplated the establishment of subordinate departments, the first sentence of Article II clearly stated that the executive power would reside in a single individual. To many Anti-Federalists, that augured a dangerous reversion to monarchical principles.

To counter that argument, Hamilton launches a strong defense of the advantages of a unitary executive — the president — arguing that a plural executive will serve only to mask the responsibility for decisions and therefore make it more difficult for the people to know whom to hold accountable. Moreover, a plural executive is potentially a divided executive, and that would introduce dissent and confusion into the office where they are least needed.

To the People of the State of New York.
There is an idea, which is not without its advocates, that a vigorous executive is inconsistent with the genius of republican government.

The enlightened well wishers to this species of government must at least hope that the supposition is destitute of foundation; since they can never admit its truth, without at the same time admitting the condemnation of their own principles. Energy in the executive is a leading character in the definition of good government. It is essential to the protection of the community against foreign attacks: It is not less essential to the steady administration of the laws, to the protection of property against those irregular and high handed combinations, which sometimes interrupt the ordinary course of justice, to the security of liberty against the enterprises and assaults of ambition, of faction and of anarchy. Every man the least conversant in Roman story knows how often that republic was obliged to take refuge in the absolute power of a single man, under the formidable title of dictator, as well against the intrigues of ambitious individuals, who aspired to the tyranny, and the seditions of whole classes of the community, whose conduct threatened the existence of all government, as against the invasions of external enemies, who menaced the conquest and destruction of Rome.

There can be no need however to multiply arguments or examples on this head. A feeble executive implies a feeble execution of the government. A feeble execution is but another phrase for a bad execution: And a government ill executed, whatever it may be in theory, must be in practice a bad government.

Taking it for granted, therefore, that all men of sense will agree in the necessity of an energetic executive; it will only remain to inquire, what are the ingredients which constitute this energy—how far can they be combined with those other ingredients which constitute safety in the republican sense? And how far does this combination characterise the plan, which has been reported by the convention?

The ingredients, which constitute energy in the executive, are first unity, secondly duration, thirdly an adequate provision for its support, fourthly competent powers.

The circumstances which constitute safety in the republican sense are, Ist. a due dependence on the people, secondly a due responsibility.

Those politicians and statesmen, who have been the most celebrated for the soundness of their principles, and for the justness of their views, have declared in favor of a single executive and a numerous legislature. They have with great propriety considered energy as the most necessary qualification of the former, and have regarded this as most applicable to power in a single hand; while they have with equal propriety considered the latter as best adapted to deliberation and wisdom, and best calculated to conciliate the confidence of the people and to secure their privileges and interests.

That unity is conducive to energy will not be disputed. Decision, activity, secrecy, and dispatch will generally characterise the proceedings of one man, in a much more eminent degree, than the proceedings of any greater number; and in proportion as the number is increased, these qualities will be diminished.

This unity may be destroyed in two ways; either by vesting the power in two or more magistrates of equal dignity and authority; or by vesting it ostensibly in one man, subject in whole or in part to the controul and co-operation of others, in the capacity of counsellors to him. Of the first the two consuls of Rome may serve as an example; of the last we shall find examples in the constitutions of several of the states. New-York and New-Jersey, if I recollect right, are the only states, which have entrusted the executive authority wholly to single men.* Both these methods of destroying the unity of the executive have their partisans; but the votaries of an executive council are the most numerous. They are both liable, if not to equal, to similar objections; and may in most lights be examined in conjunction.

The experience of other nations will afford little instruction on this head. As far however as it teaches any thing, it teaches us not to be inamoured of plurality in the executive. We have seen that the Achæans on an experiment of two Prætors, were induced to abolish one. The Roman history records many instances of mischiefs to the republic from the dissentions between the consuls, and between the military tribunes, who were at times substituted to the consuls. But it gives us no specimens of any peculiar advantages derived to the state, from the circumstance of the plurality of those magistrates. That the dissentions between them were not more frequent, or more fatal, is matter of astonishment; until we advert to the singular position in which the republic was almost continually placed and to the prudent policy pointed out by the circumstances of the state, and pursued by the consuls, of making a division of the government between them. The Patricians engaged in a perpetual struggle with the Plebians for the preservation of their antient authorities and dignities; the consuls, who were generally chosen out of the former body, were commonly united by the personal interest they had in the defence of the privileges of their order. In addition to this motive of union, after the arms of the republic had considerably expanded the bounds of its empire, it

---

*New-York has no council except for the single purpose of appointing to offices; New-Jersey has a council, whom the governor may consult. But I think from the terms of the constitution their resolutions do not bind him.

became an established custom with the consuls to divide the administration between themselves by lot; one of them remaining at Rome to govern the city and its environs; the other taking the command in the more distant provinces. This expedient must no doubt have had great influence in preventing those collisions and rivalships, which might otherwise have embroiled the peace of the republic.

But quitting the dim light of historical research, and attaching ourselves purely to the dictates of reason and good sense, we shall discover much greater cause to reject than to approve the idea of plurality in the executive, under any modification whatever.

Wherever two or more persons are engaged in any common enterprize or pursuit, there is always danger of difference of opinion. If it be a public trust or office in which they are cloathed with equal dignity and authority, there is peculiar danger of personal emulation and even animosity. From either and especially from all these causes, the most bitter dissentions are apt to spring. Whenever these happen, they lessen the respectability, weaken the authority, and distract the plans and operations of those whom they divide. If they should unfortunately assail the supreme executive magistracy of a country, consisting of a plurality of persons, they might impede or frustrate the most important measures of the government, in the most critical emergencies of the state. And what is still worse, they might split the community into the most violent and irreconcilable factions, adhering differently to the different individuals who composed the magistracy.

Men often oppose a thing merely because they have had no agency in planning it, or because it may have been planned by those whom they dislike. But if they have been consulted and have happened to disapprove, opposition then becomes in their estimation an indispensable duty of self love. They seem to think themselves bound in honor, and by all the motives of personal infallibility to defeat the success of what has been resolved upon, contrary to their sentiments. Men of upright, benevolent tempers have too many opportunities of remarking with horror, to what desperate lengths this disposition is sometimes carried, and how often the great interests of society are sacrificed to the vanity, to the conceit and to the obstinacy of individuals, who have credit enough to make their passions and their caprices interesting to mankind. Perhaps the question now before the public may in its consequences afford melancholy proofs of the effects of this despicable frailty, or rather detestable vice in the human character.

Upon the principles of a free government, inconveniencies from the source just mentioned must necessarily be submitted to in the formation of the legislature; but it is unnecessary and therefore unwise to introduce them into the constitution of the executive. It is here too that they may be most pernicious. In the legislature, promptitude of decision is oftener an evil than a benefit. The differences of opinion, and the jarrings of parties in that department of the government, though they may sometimes obstruct salutary plans, yet often promote deliberation and circumspection; and serve to check excesses in the majority. When a resolution too is once taken, the opposition must be at an end. That resolution is a law, and resistance to it punishable. But no favourable circumstances palliate or atone for the disadvantages of dissention in the executive department. Here they are pure and unmixed. There is no point at which they cease to operate. They serve to embarrass and weaken the execution of the plan or measure, to which they relate, from the first step to the final conclusion of it. They constantly counteract those qualities in the executive, which are the most necessary ingredients in its composition, vigour and expedition, and this without any counterballancing good. In the conduct of war, in which the energy of the executive is the bulwark of the national security, every thing would be to be apprehended from its plurality.

It must be confessed that these observations apply with principal weight to the first case supposed, that is to a plurality of magistrates of equal dignity and authority; a scheme the advocates for which are not likely to form a numerous sect: But they apply, though not with equal, yet with considerable weight, to the project of a council, whose concurrence is made constitutionally necessary to the operations of the ostensible executive. An artful cabal[1] in that council would be able to distract and to enervate the whole system of administration. If no such cabal should exist, the mere diversity of views and opinions would alone be sufficient to tincture the exercise of the executive authority with a spirit of habitual feebleness and dilatoriness.

But one of the weightiest objections to a plurality in the executive, and which lies as much against the last as the first plan, is that it tends to conceal faults, and destroy responsibility. Responsibility is of two kinds, to censure and to punishment. The first is the most important of the two; especially in an elective office. Man, in public trust, will much oftener act in such a manner as to render him unworthy of being any longer trusted, than in such a manner as to make him obnoxious to legal punishment. But the multiplication of the executive

---

[1]*cabal:* a conspiracy, or a knot of conspirators.

adds to the difficulty of detection in either case. It often becomes impossible, amidst mutual accusations, to determine on whom the blame or the punishment of a pernicious measure, or series of pernicious measures ought really to fall. It is shifted from one to another with so much dexterity, and under such plausible appearances, that the public opinion is left in suspense about the real author. The circumstances which may have led to any national miscarriage or misfortune are sometimes so complicated, that where there are a number of actors who may have had different degrees and kinds of agency, though we may clearly see upon the whole that there has been mismanagement, yet it may be impracticable to pronounce to whose account the evil which may have been incurred is truly chargeable.

"I was overruled by my council. The council were so divided in their opinions, that it was impossible to obtain any better resolution on the point." These and similar pretexts are constantly at hand, whether true or false. And who is there that will either take the trouble or incur the odium of a strict scrutiny into the secret springs of the transaction? Should there be found a citizen zealous enough to undertake the unpromising task, if there happen to be a collusion between the parties concerned, how easy is it to cloath the circumstances with so much ambiguity, as to render it uncertain what was the precise conduct of any of those parties?

In the single instance in which the governor of this state is coupled with a council, that is in the appointment to offices, we have seen the mischiefs of it in the view now under consideration. Scandalous appointments to important offices have been made. Some cases indeed have been so flagrant, that ALL PARTIES have agreed in the impropriety of the thing. When enquiry has been made, the blame has been laid by the governor on the members of the council; who on their part have charged it upon his nomination: While the people remain altogether at a loss to determine by whose influence their interests have been committed to hands so unqualified, and so manifestly improper. In tenderness to individuals, I forbear to descend to particulars.

It is evident from these considerations, that the plurality of the executive tends to deprive the people of the two greatest securities they can have for the faithful exercise of any delegated power; first, the restraints of public opinion, which lose their efficacy as well on account of the division of the censure attendant on bad measures among a number, as on account of the uncertainty on whom it ought to fall; and secondly, the opportunity of discovering with facility and clearness the misconduct of the persons they trust, in order either to their removal from office, or to their actual punishment, in cases which admit of it.

In England the king is a perpetual magistrate; and it is a maxim, which has obtained for the sake of the public peace, that he is unaccountable for his administration, and his person sacred. Nothing therefore can be wiser in that kingdom than to annex to the king a constitutional council, who may be responsible to the nation for the advice they give. Without this there would be no responsibility whatever in the executive department; an idea inadmissible in a free government. But even there the king is not bound by the resolutions of his council, though they are answerable for the advice they give. He is the absolute master of his own conduct, in the exercise of his office; and may observe or disregard the council given to him at his sole discretion.

But in a republic, where every magistrate ought to be personally responsible for his behaviour in office, the reason which in the British constitution dictates the propriety of a council not only ceases to apply, but turns against the institution. In the monarchy of Great-Britain, it furnishes a substitute for the prohibited responsibility of the chief magistrate; which serves in some degree as a hostage to the national justice for his good behaviour. In the American republic it would serve to destroy, or would greatly diminish the intended and necessary responsibility of the chief magistrate himself.

The idea of a council to the executive, which has so generally obtained in the state constitutions, has been derived from that maxim of republican jealousy, which considers power as safer in the hands of a number of men than of a single man. If the maxim should be admitted to be applicable to the case, I should contend that the advantage on that side would not counterballance the numerous disadvantages on the opposite side. But I do not think the rule at all applicable to the executive power. I clearly concur in opinion in this particular with a writer whom the celebrated Junius pronounces to be "deep, solid and ingenious," that, "the executive power is more easily confined when it is one": That it is far more safe there should be a single object for the jealousy and watchfulness of the people; and in a word that all multiplication of the executive is rather dangerous than friendly to liberty.

A little consideration will satisfy us, that the species of security sought for in the multiplication of the executive is unattainable. Numbers must be so great as to render combination difficult; or they are rather a source of danger than of security. The united credit and influence of several individuals must be more formidable to liberty than the credit and influence of either of them separately. When power therefore is placed in the hands of so small a number of men, as to admit of their interests and views being easily combined in a common enterprise, by an artful leader, it becomes more liable to abuse and more dangerous when abused, than if it be lodged in the hands of one man; who from the very circumstance of his being alone will be more narrowly watched and more readily suspected, and who cannot unite so great a mass of influence as when he is associated with others. The Decemvirs of Rome, whose name denotes their number,* were more to be dreaded in their usurpation than any ONE of them would have been. No person would think of proposing an executive much more numerous than that body, from six to a dozen have been suggested for the number of the council. The extreme of these numbers is not too great for an easy combination; and from such a combination America would have more to fear, than from the ambition of any single individual. A council to a magistrate, who is himself responsible for what he does, are generally nothing better than a clog upon his good intentions; are often the instruments and accomplices of his bad, and are almost always a cloak to his faults.

I forbear to dwell upon the subject of expence; though it be evident that if the council should be numerous enough to answer the principal end, aimed at by the institution, the salaries of the members, who must be drawn from their homes to reside at the seat of government, would form an item in the catalogue of public expenditures, too serious to be incurred for an object of equivocal utility.

I will only add, that prior to the appearance of the constitution, I rarely met with an intelligent man from any of the states, who did not admit as the result of experience, that the UNITY of the Executive of this state was one of the best of the distinguishing features of our constitution.

PUBLIUS.

* Ten.

Federalist 71

The Same View Continued in Regard to the Duration of the Office,
March 18, 1788

During the debates at the Federal Convention, two questions about the executive had repeatedly vexed the delegates: the method of election, and the tenure the president should enjoy once elected. The shorter the term to be served, the more dependent on Congress the president might become; the longer the term, the more the president might start to develop monarchical cravings and ambitions. And as with the other political departments, supporters of the Constitution had to explain why the principle of annual elections should not apply to the executive. That principle rested on the healthy suspicion that holders of high office would naturally seek to exploit their positions for selfish ends. But those who recognized, with Hamilton, that some of the ends of government require prolonged planning and oversight were now inclined to perceive the advantages of giving the president a significant and fixed term in office. Hamilton defends this position in terms similar to Madison's defense of the Senate. Even in republican governments, there are institutions that need to be insulated from the passing fancies and passions of the people, if the more durable interests of the polity are to be preserved and advanced.

To the People of the State of New York.
Duration in office has been mentioned as the second requisite to the energy of the executive authority. This has relation to two objects: To the personal firmness of the Executive Magistrate in the employment of his constitutional powers; and to the stability of the system of administration which may have been adopted under his auspices. With regard to the first, it must be evident, that the longer the duration in office, the greater will be the probability of obtaining so important an advantage. It is a general principle of human nature, that a man will be interested in whatever he possesses, in proportion to the firmness or precariousness of the tenure, by which he holds it; will be less attached to what he holds by a momentary or uncertain title, than to what he enjoys by a durable or certain title; and of course will be willing to risk more for the sake of the one, than for the sake of the other.

This remark is not less applicable to a political privilege, or honor, or trust, than to any article of ordinary property. The inference from it is, that a man acting in the capacity of Chief Magistrate, under a consciousness, that in a very short time he *must* lay down his office, will be apt to feel himself too little interested in it, to hazard any material censure or perplexity, from the independent exertion of his powers, or from encountering the ill-humors, however transient, which may happen to prevail either in a considerable part of the society itself, or even in a predominant faction in the legislative body. If the case should only be, that he *might* lay it down, unless continued by a new choice; and if he should be desirous of being continued, his wishes conspiring with his fears would tend still more powerfully to corrupt his integrity, or debase his fortitude. In either case feebleness and irresolution must be the characteristics of the station.

There are some, who would be inclined to regard the servile pliancy of the executive to a prevailing current, either in the community, or in the Legislature, as its best recommendation. But such men entertain very crude notions, as well of the purposes for which government was instituted, as of the true means by which the public happiness may be promoted. The republican principle demands, that the deliberate sense of the community should govern the conduct of those to whom they entrust the management of their affairs; but it does not require an unqualified complaisance to every sudden breese of passion, or to every transient impulse which the people may receive from the arts of men, who flatter their prejudices to betray their interests. It is a just observation, that the people commonly *intend* the PUBLIC GOOD. This often applies to their very errors. But their good sense would despise the adulator, who should pretend that they always *reason right* about the *means* of promoting it. They know from experience, that they sometimes err; and the wonder is, that they so seldom err as they do; beset as they continually are by the wiles of parasites and sycophants, by the snares of the ambitious, the avaricious, the desperate; by the artifices of men, who possess their confidence more than they deserve it, and of those who seek to possess, rather than to deserve it. When occasions present themselves in which the interests of the people are at variance with their inclinations, it is the duty of the persons whom they have appointed to be the guardians of those interests, to withstand the temporary delusion, in order to give them time and opportunity for more cool and sedate reflection. Instances might be cited, in which a conduct of this kind has saved the people from very fatal consequences of their own mistakes, and has procured lasting monuments of their gratitude to the men, who had courage and magnanimity enough to serve them at the peril of their displeasure.

But however inclined we might be to insist upon an unbounded complaisance in the executive to the inclinations of the people, we can with no propriety contend for a like complaisance to the humors of the Legislature. The latter may sometimes stand in opposition to the former; and at other times the people may be entirely neutral. In either supposition, it is certainly desirable that the executive should be in a situation to dare to act his own opinion with vigor and decision.

The same rule, which teaches the propriety of a partition between the various branches of power, teaches us likewise that this partition ought to be so contrived as to render the one independent of the other. To what purpose separate the executive, or the judiciary, from the legislative, if both the executive and the judiciary are so constituted as to be at the absolute devotion of the legislative? Such a separation must be merely nominal and incapable of producing the ends for which it was established. It is one thing to be subordinate to the laws, and another to be dependent on the legislative body. The first comports with, the last violates, the fundamental principles of good government; and whatever may be the forms of the Constitution, unites all power in the same hands. The tendency of the legislative authority to absorb every other, has been fully displayed and illustrated by examples, in some preceding numbers.[1] In governments purely republican, this tendency is almost irresistable. The representatives of the people, in a popular assembly, seem sometimes to fancy that they are the people themselves; and betray strong symptoms of impatience and disgust at the least sign of opposition from any other quarter; as if the exercise of its rights by either the executive or judiciary, were a breach of their privilege and an outrage to their dignity. They often appear disposed to exert an imperious controul over the other departments; and as they commonly have the people on their side, they always act with such momentum as to make it very difficult for the other members of the government to maintain the balance of the Constitution.

It may perhaps be asked how the shortness of the duration in office can affect the independence of the executive on the legislature, unless the one were possessed of the power of appointing or displacing the other? One answer to this enquiry may be drawn from the principle already remarked, that is from the slender interest a man is apt to take

[1] See Essays 48 and 49.

in a short lived advantage, and the little inducement it affords him to expose himself on account of it to any considerable inconvenience or hazard. Another answer, perhaps more obvious, though not more conclusive, will result from the consideration of the influence of the legislative body over the people, which might be employed to prevent the re-election of a man, who by an upright resistance to any sinister project of that body, should have made himself obnoxious to its resentment.

It may be asked also whether a duration of four years would answer the end proposed, and if it would not, whether a less period which would at least be recommended by greater security against ambitious designs, would not for that reason be preferable to a longer period, which was at the same time too short for the purpose of inspiring the desired firmness and independence of the magistrate?

It cannot be affirmed, that a duration of four years or any other limited duration would completely answer the end proposed; but it would contribute towards it in a degree which would have a material influence upon the spirit and character of the government. Between the commencement and termination of such a period there would always be a considerable interval, in which the prospect of annihilation would be sufficiently remote not to have an improper effect upon the conduct of a man endued with a tolerable portion of fortitude; and in which he might reasonably promise himself, that there would be time enough, before it arrived, to make the community sensible of the propriety of the measures he might incline to pursue. Though it be probable, that as he approached the moment when the public were by a new election to signify their sense of his conduct, his confidence and with it, his firmness would decline; yet both the one and the other would derive support from the opportunities, which his previous continuance in the station had afforded him of establishing himself in the esteem and good will of his constituents. He might then hazard with safety, in proportion to the proofs he had given of his wisdom and integrity, and to the title he had acquired to the respect and attachment of his fellow citizens. As on the one hand, a duration of four years will contribute to the firmness of the executive in a sufficient degree to render it a very valuable ingredient in the composition; so on the other, it is not long enough to justify any alarm for the public liberty. If a British House of Commons, from the most feeble beginnings, *from the mere power of assenting or disagreeing to the imposition of a new tax,* have by rapid strides, reduced the prerogatives of the crown and the privileges of the nobility within the limits they conceived to be compatible with the principles of a free government;

while they raised themselves to the rank and consequence of a coequal branch of the Legislature; if they have been able in one instance to abolish both the royalty and the aristocracy, and to overturn all the ancient establishments as well in the church as State; if they have been able on a recent occasion to make the monarch tremble at the prospect of an innovation* attempted by them; what would be to be feared from an elective magistrate of four years duration, with the confined authorities of a President of the United States? What but that he might be unequal to the task which the Constitution assigns him? I shall only add that if his duration be such as to leave a doubt of his firmness, that doubt is inconsistent with a jealousy of his encroachments.

PUBLIUS.

*This was the case with respect to Mr. Fox's India bill which was carried in the House of Commons, and rejected in the House of Lords, to the entire satisfaction, as it is said, of the people.

[HAMILTON]

Federalist 72

The Same View Continued in Regard to the Re-eligibility of the President,
March 19, 1788

Closely related to the length of the term the president would serve was the question of eligibility for reelection. The Convention initially favored a single term of seven years, but the eventual decision for a four-year term was accompanied by a removal of the restriction on additional terms. Some delegates worried that this decision would encourage presidents to grasp for power, but the decisive view, which Hamilton clearly shares, was that the promise of reelection would inspire the right kind of ambitions in incumbents. As Hamilton observes in this essay, "the love of fame," which was "the ruling passion of the noblest minds," might inspire presidents to "undertake extensive and arduous enterprises for the public benefit." But would a president do so if an arbitrary restriction prevented him from seeing the measure through or enjoying the acclaim to come from success? From this query, Hamilton proceeds to identify the "ill effects" that a flat prohibition against reelection would produce.

These observations, like others in Hamilton's essays on the presidency, illustrate the traits that distinguished this gifted public servant from most of *his contemporaries. Hamilton appreciated the possibilities of executive leadership in ways that remained alien to most American republicans. Madison wanted to improve the quality of legislative deliberation while protecting the executive from legislative manipulation, but he did not expect that the president would play a decisive role in framing the public agenda. By contrast, Hamilton understood that vigorous leadership from the executive would often carry Congress along in its wake. As secretary of the treasury under President George Washington after 1789, he set out to demonstrate just what that possibility could mean in practice, in the process driving Madison, his ally and coauthor in 1787–88, into opposition.*

To the People of the State of New York.

The administration of government, in its largest sense, comprehends all the operations of the body politic, whether legislative, executive or judiciary, but in its most usual and perhaps in its most precise signification, it is limited to executive details, and falls peculiarly within the province of the executive department. The actual conduct of foreign negotiations, the preparatory plans of finance, the application and disbursement of the public monies, in conformity to the general appropriations of the legislature, the arrangement of the army and navy, the direction of the operations of war; these and other matters of a like nature constitute what seems to be most properly understood by the administration of government. The persons therefore, to whose immediate management these different matters are committed, ought to be considered as the assistants or deputies of the chief magistrate; and, on this account, they ought to derive their offices from his appointment, at least from his nomination, and ought to be subject to his superintendence. This view of the subject will at once suggest to us the intimate connection between the duration of the executive magistrate in office, and the stability of the system of administration. To reverse and undo what has been done by a predecessor is very often considered by a successor, as the best proof he can give of his own capacity and desert; and, in addition to this propensity, where the alteration has been the result of public choice, the person substituted is warranted in supposing, that the dismission of his predecessor has proceeded from a dislike to his measures, and that the less he resembles him the more he will recommend himself to the favor of his constituents. These considerations, and the influence of personal confidences and attachments, would be likely to induce every new president to promote a change of men to fill the subordinate stations; and these causes together could not fail to occasion a disgraceful and ruinous mutability in the administration of the government.

With a positive duration of considerable extent, I connect the circumstance of re-eligibility. The first is necessary to give to the officer himself the inclination and the resolution to act his part well, and to the community time and leisure to observe the tendency of his measures, and thence to form an experimental estimate of their merits. The last is necessary to enable the people, when they see reason to approve of his conduct, to continue him in the station, in order to prolong the utility of his talents and virtues, and to secure to the government, the advantage of permanency in a wise system of administration.

Nothing appears more plausible at first sight, nor more ill founded upon close inspection, than a scheme, which in relation to the present point has had some respectable advocates—I mean that of continuing the chief magistrate in office for a certain time, and then excluding him from it, either for a limited period, or for ever after. This exclusion whether temporary or perpetual would have nearly the same effects; and these effects would be for the most part rather pernicious than salutary.

One ill effect of the exclusion would be a diminution of the inducements to good behaviour. There are few men who would not feel much less zeal in the discharge of a duty, when they were conscious that the advantages of the station, with which it was connected, must be relinquished at a determinate period, then when they were permitted to entertain a hope of *obtaining* by *meriting* a continuance of them. This position will not be disputed, so long as it is admitted that the desire of reward is one of the strongest incentives of human conduct, or that the best security for the fidelity of mankind is to make their interest coincide with their duty. Even the love of fame, the ruling passion of the noblest minds, which would prompt a man to plan and undertake extensive and arduous enterprises for the public benefit, requiring considerable time to mature and perfect them, if he could flatter himself with the prospect of being allowed to finish what he had begun, would on the contrary deter him from the undertaking, when he foresaw that he must quit the scene, before he could accomplish the work, and must commit that, together with his own reputation, to hands which might be unequal or unfriendly to the task. The most to be expected from the generality of men, in such a situation, is the negative merit of not doing harm instead of the positive merit of doing good.

Another ill effect of the exclusion would be the temptation to sordid views, to peculation,[1] and in some instances, to usurpation. An avaricious man, who might happen to fill the offices, looking forward to a time when he must at all events yield up the emoluments he enjoyed, would feel a propensity, not easy to be resisted by such a man, to make the best use of the opportunity he enjoyed, while it lasted; and might not scruple to have recourse to the most corrupt expedients to make the harvest as abundant as it was transitory; though the same man probably, with a different prospect before him, might content himself with the regular perquisites of his station, and might even be unwilling to risk the consequences of an abuse of his opportunities. His avarice might be a guard upon his avarice. Add to this, that the same man might be vain or ambitious as well as avaricious. And if he could expect to prolong his honors, by his good conduct, he might hesitate to sacrifice his appetite for them to his appetite for gain. But with the prospect before him of approaching and inevitable annihilation, his avarice would be likely to get the victory over his caution, his vanity or his ambition.

An ambitious man too, when he found himself seated on the summit of his country's honors, when he looked forward to the time at which he must descend from the exalted eminence forever; and reflected that no exertion of merit on his part could save him from the unwelcome reverse: Such a man, in such a situation, would be much more violently tempted to embrace a favorable conjuncture for attempting the prolongation of his power, at every personal hazard, than if he had the probability of answering the same end by doing his duty.

Would it promote the peace of the community, or the stability of the government, to have half a dozen men who had had credit enough to be raised to the seat of the supreme magistracy, wandering among the people like discontented ghosts, and sighing for a place which they were destined never more to possess?

A third ill effect of the exclusion would be the depriving the community of the advantage of the experience gained by the chief magistrate in the exercise of his office. That experience is the parent of wisdom is an adage, the truth of which is recognized by the wisest as well as the simplest of mankind. What more desirable or more essential than this quality in the governors of nations? Where more desirable or more essential than in the first magistrate of a nation? Can it

[1] *peculation:* embezzlement.

be wise to put this desirable and essential quality under the ban of the constitution; and to declare that the moment it is acquired, its possessor shall be compelled to abandon the station in which it was acquired, and to which it is adapted? This nevertheless is the precise import of all those regulations, which exclude men from serving their country, by the choice of their fellow citizens, after they have, by a course of service fitted themselves for doing it with a greater degree of utility.

A fourth ill effect of the exclusion would be the banishing men from stations, in which in certain emergencies of the state their presence might be of the greatest moment to the public interest or safety. There is no nation which has not at one period or another experienced an absolute necessity of the services of particular men, in particular situations, perhaps it would not be too strong to say, to the preservation of its political existence. How unwise therefore must be every such self-denying ordinance, as serves to prohibit a nation from making use of its own citizens, in the manner best suited to its exigences and circumstances! Without supposing the personal essentiality of the man, it is evident that a change of the chief magistrate, at the breaking out of a war, or at any similar crisis, for another even of equal merit, would at all times be detrimental to the community; inasmuch as it would substitute inexperience to experience and would tend to unhinge and set afloat the already settled train of the administration.

A fifth ill effect of the exclusion would be, that it would operate as a constitutional interdiction of stability in the administration. By *necessitating* a change of men, in the first office in the nation, it would necessitate a mutability of measures. It is not generally to be expected, that men will vary; and measures remain uniform. The contrary is the usual course of things. And we need not be apprehensive there will be too much stability, while there is even the option of changing; nor need we desire to prohibit the people from continuing their confidence, where they think it may be safely placed, and where by constancy on their part they may obviate the fatal inconveniences of fluctuating councils and a variable policy.

These are some of the disadvantages, which would flow from the principle of exclusion. They apply most forcibly to the scheme of a perpetual exclusion; but when we consider that even a partial exclusion would always render the re-admission of the person a remote and precarious object, the observations which have been made will apply nearly as fully to one case as to the other.

What are the advantages promised to counterballance these disadvantages? They are represented to be Ist. Greater independence in the magistrate: 2dly. Greater security to the people. Unless the exclusion be perpetual there will be no pretence to infer the first advantage. But even in that case, may he have no object beyond his present station to which he may sacrifice his independence? May he have no connections, no friends, for whom he may sacrifice it? May he not be less willing, by a firm conduct, to make personal enemies, when he acts under the impression, that a time is fast approaching, on the arrival of which he not only MAY, but MUST be exposed to their resentments, upon an equal, perhaps upon an inferior footing? It is not an easy point to determine whether his independence would be most promoted or impaired by such an arrangement.

As to the second supposed advantage, there is still greater reason to entertain doubts concerning it. If the exclusion were to be perpetual, a man of irregular ambition, of whom alone there could be reason in any case to entertain apprehensions, would with infinite reluctance yield to the necessity of taking his leave forever of a post, in which his passion for power and pre-eminence had acquired the force of habit. And if he had been fortunate or adroit enough to conciliate the good will of people he might induce them to consider as a very odious and unjustifiable restraint upon themselves, a provision which was calculated to debar them of the right of giving a fresh proof of their attachment to a favorite. There may be conceived circumstances, in which this disgust of the people, seconding the thwarted ambition of such a favourite, might occasion greater danger to liberty, than could ever reasonably be dreaded from the possibility of a perpetuation in office, by the voluntary suffrages of the community, exercising a constitutional privilege.

There is an excess of refinement in the idea of disabling the people to continue in office men, who had entitled themselves, in their opinion, to approbation and confidence; the advantages of which are at best speculative and equivocal; and are overbalanced by disadvantages far more certain and decisive.

PUBLIUS.

Federalist 75

The Same View Continued in Relation to the Power of Making Treaties, March 26, 1788

John Jay had already discussed the treaty power in Federalist *64, but in this essay Hamilton doubles back to pursue two questions Jay had neglected. One concerned the likelihood that the power would be abused by a small faction. Here Hamilton had in mind the recurring Anti-Federalist charge that because as few as two-thirds of a quorum (half the membership plus one) of the Senate could make a treaty, fewer than ten treacherous senators could theoretically conclude a treaty sacrificing the national interest. Hamilton uses the closing paragraph of this essay to identify drawbacks in requiring treaties to be confirmed by two-thirds of the whole membership of the Senate, rather than two-thirds of a quorum.*

The other question involved determining where to locate a treaty power shared by president and Senate in the overall scheme of the constitutional separation of powers. Here Hamilton follows a passage in John Locke's Second Treatise of Government *(1689), where Locke described "the federative power"—the power to deal with foreign nations—as a distinct function that could not be lumped under the conventional heading of executive or legislative power. By combining the Senate and president in the making of a treaty, the Constitution seemingly joined the two branches in the executive function of determining how treaties were to be negotiated (through the "advice" of the Senate, which could be given beforehand) and the legislative function of making treaties "the supreme law of the land" (through the "consent" of the Senate). Hamilton's careful effort to delineate the respective role of the two institutions anticipates the repeated jockeying between the president and Congress that would take place over ensuing decades—and centuries. Within a few years, Hamilton helped to sharpen the debate when, as the author of the letters of "Pacificus" (1793), he argued that the conduct of foreign relations and the negotiation of treaties were essentially the prerogatives of the president.*

To the People of the State of New York.
The president is to have power "by and with the advice and consent of the senate, to make treaties, provided two-thirds of the senators present concur." Though this provision has been assailed on different

grounds, with no small degree of vehemence, I scruple not to declare my firm persuasion, that it is one of the best digested and most unexceptionable parts of the plan. One ground of objection is, the trite topic of the intermixture of powers; some contending that the president ought alone to possess the power of making treaties; and others, that it ought to have been exclusively deposited in the senate. Another source of objection is derived from the small number of persons by whom a treaty may be made: Of those who espouse this objection, a part are of opinion that the house of representatives ought to have been associated in the business, while another part seem to think that nothing more was necessary than to have substituted two-thirds of all the members of the senate to two-thirds of the members *present*. As I flatter myself the observations made in a preceding number, upon this part of the plan, must have sufficed to place it to a discerning eye in a very favourable light,[1] I shall here content myself with offering only some supplementary remarks, principally with a view to the objections which have been just stated.

With regard to the intermixture of powers, I shall rely upon the explanations already given, in other places of the true sense of the rule,[2] upon which that objection is founded; and shall take it for granted, as an inference from them, that the union of the executive with the senate, in the article of treaties, is no infringement of that rule. I venture to add that the particular nature of the power of making treaties indicates a peculiar propriety in that union. Though several writers on the subject of government place that power in the class of executive authorities, yet this is evidently an arbitrary disposition: For if we attend carefully to its operation, it will be found to partake more of the legislative than of the executive character, though it does not seem strictly to fall within the definition of either of them. The essence of the legislative authority is to enact laws, or in other words to prescribe rules for the regulation of the society. While the execution of the laws and the employment of the common strength, either for this purpose or for the common defence, seem to comprise all the functions of the executive magistrate. The power of making treaties is plainly neither the one nor the other. It relates neither to the execution of the subsisting laws, nor to the enaction of new ones, and still less to an exertion of the common strength. Its objects are CONTRACTS with foreign nations, which have the force of law, but derive it from

[1]See Essay 64.
[2]See Essays 47 and 48.

the obligations of good faith. They are not rules prescribed by the sovereign to the subject, but agreements between sovereign and sovereign. The power in question seems therefore to form a distinct department, and to belong properly neither to the legislative nor to the executive. The qualities elsewhere detailed, as indispensable in the management of foreign negotiations,[3] point out the executive as the most fit agent in those transactions; while the vast importance of the trust, and the operation of treaties as laws, plead strongly for the participation of the whole or a part of the legislative body in the office of making them.

However proper or safe it may be in governments where the executive magistrate is an hereditary monarch, to commit to him the entire power of making treaties, it would be utterly unsafe and improper to entrust that power to an elective magistrate of four years duration. It has been remarked upon another occasion, and the remark is unquestionably just, that an hereditary monarch, though often the oppressor of his people, has personally too much at stake in the government to be in any material danger of being corrupted by foreign powers. But a man raised from the station of a private citizen to the rank of chief magistrate, possessed of but a moderate or slender fortune, and looking forward to a period not very remote, when he may probably be obliged to return to the station from which he was taken, might sometimes be under temptations to sacrifice his duty to his interest, which it would require superlative virtue to withstand. An avaricious man might be tempted to betray the interests of the state to the acquisition of wealth. An ambitious man might make his own aggrandizement, by the aid of a foreign power, the price of his treachery to his constituents. The history of human conduct does not warrant that exalted opinion of human virtue which would make it wise in a nation to commit interests of so delicate and momentous a kind as those which concern its intercourse with the rest of the world to the sole disposal of a magistrate, created and circumstanced, as would be a president of the United States.

To have entrusted the power of making treaties to the senate alone, would have been to relinquish the benefits of the constitutional agency of the president, in the conduct of foreign negotiations. It is true, that the senate would in that case have the option of employing him in this capacity; but they would also have the option of letting it alone; and pique or cabal might induce the latter rather than the for-

[3]See Essay 64.

mer. Besides this, the ministerial servant of the senate could not be expected to enjoy the confidence and respect of foreign powers in the same degree with the constitutional representative of the nation; and of course would not be able to act with an equal degree of weight or efficacy. While the union would from this cause lose a considerable advantage in the management of its external concerns, the people would lose the additional security, which would result from the co-operation of the executive. Though it would be imprudent to confide in him solely so important a trust; yet it cannot be doubted, that his participation in it would materially add to the safety of the society. It must indeed be clear to a demonstration, that the joint possession of the power in question by the president and senate would afford a greater prospect of security, than the separate possession of it by either of them. And whoever has maturely weighed the circumstances, which must concur in the appointment of a president will be satisfied, that the office will always bid fair to be filled by men of such characters as to render their concurrence in the formation of treaties peculiarly desirable, as well on the score of wisdom as on that of integrity.

The remarks made in a former number, which has been alluded to in an other part of this paper, will apply with conclusive force against the admission of the house of representatives to a share in the formation of treaties.[4] The fluctuating, and taking its future increase into the account, the multitudinous composition of that body, forbid us to expect in it those qualities which are essential to the proper execution of such a trust. Accurate and comprehensive knowledge of foreign politics; a steady and systematic adherence to the same views; a nice and uniform sensibility to national character, decision, *secrecy* and dispatch; are incompatible with the genius of a body so variable and so numerous. The very complication of the business by introducing a necessity of the concurrence of so many different bodies, would of itself afford a solid objection. The greater frequency of the calls upon the house of representatives, and the greater length of time which it would often be necessary to keep them together when convened, to obtain their sanction in the progressive stages of a treaty, would be source of so great inconvenience and expence, as alone ought to condemn the project.

The only objection which remains to be canvassed is that which would substitute the proportion of two thirds of all the members

[4]See Essay 64.

composing the senatorial body to that of two thirds of the members *present*. It has been shewn under the second head of our inquiries that all provisions which require more than the majority of any body to its resolutions have a direct tendency to embarrass the operations of the government and an indirect one to subject the sense of the majority to that of the minority. This consideration seems sufficient to determine our opinion, that the convention have gone as far in the endeavour to secure the advantage of numbers in the formation of treaties as could have been reconciled either with the activity of the public councils or with a reasonable regard to the major sense of the community. If two thirds of the whole number of members had been required, it would in many cases from the non attendance of a part amount in practice to a necessity of unanimity. And the history of every political establishment in which this principle has prevailed is a history of impotence, perplexity and disorder. Proofs of this position might be adduced from the examples of the Roman tribuneship, the Polish diet and the states general of the Netherlands; did not an example at home render foreign precedents unnecessary.[5]

To require a fixed proportion of the whole body would not in all probability contribute to the advantages of a numerous agency, better than merely to require a proportion of the attending members. The former by making a determinate number at all times requisite to a resolution diminishes the motives to punctual attendance. The latter by making the capacity of the body to depend on a *proportion* which may be varied by the absence or presence of a single member, has the contrary effect. And as, by promoting punctuality, it tends to keep the body complete, there is great likelihood that its resolutions would generally be dictated by as great a number in this case as in the other; while there would be much fewer occasions of delay. It ought not to be forgotten that under the existing confederation two members *may* and usually *do* represent a state; whence it happens that Congress, who now are solely invested with *all the powers* of the union, rarely consists of a greater number of persons than would compose the intended senate. If we add to this, that as the members vote by states, and that where there is only a single member present from a state, his vote is lost, it will justify a supposition that the active voices in the senate, where the members are to vote individually, would rarely fall short in

---

[5] Hamilton alludes to the rule requiring amendments to the Articles of Confederation to receive the unanimous approval of all thirteen states. He may also be alluding to the repeated problems that the Continental Congress had encountered in maintaining a quorum after 1783.

number of the active voices in the existing Congress. When in addition to these considerations we take into view the cooperation of the president, we shall not hesitate to infer that the people of America would have greater security against an improper use of the power of making treaties, under the new constitution, than they now enjoy under the confederation. And when we proceed still one step further, and look forward to the probable augmentation of the senate, by the erection of new states, we shall not only perceive ample ground of confidence in the sufficiency of the numbers, to whose agency that power will be entrusted; but we shall probably be led to conclude that a body more numerous than the senate would be likely to become, would be very little fit for the proper discharge of the trust.

PUBLIUS.

[HAMILTON]

Federalist 78

A View of the Constitution of the Judicial Department in Relation to the Tenure of Good Behavior, May 28, 1788

The Federal Convention devoted far less attention to the judiciary than it paid to the other two departments of government. But the records of debate clearly indicate that the framers expected the judiciary to play a leading role in policing the boundaries between national and state governments. They considered, and rejected, the idea that Congress should exercise a veto over state laws, or that the national government should be empowered to use armed force against delinquent states. Instead, they assumed that federal judges would resolve disputes where national and state jurisdictions seemed to overlap, in the process clarifying which powers were properly exercised by which level of government. The supremacy clause explicitly bound state judges to enforce the Constitution and national laws and treaties against the rival authority of state constitutions and statutes; and it followed, implicitly but necessarily, that federal judges would exercise a similar authority. State judges had to be bound because their loyalty was more problematic; federal judges would exercise this power as a matter of course.

One leading Anti-Federalist, writing as Brutus, offered a particularly incisive critique of the potential misuse of judicial power. Brutus may well have been Robert Yates, one of the two New York delegates who had left the Convention for good in early July. In several of his essays, Brutus suggested that the federal judiciary would act as anything but the neutral, impartial umpire that Federalists imagined. Would not federal judges have a strong incentive, he wondered, to favor interpretations of the Constitution that would increase the scope of national power, the better to enhance their own authority?

Hamilton's Federalist 78 can be read, in part, as an answer to Brutus, but to modern commentators, it also ranks with Federalist 10 and 51 as the third in a trinity of major statements expressing the underlying theory of the Constitution. It has that status because Hamilton's defense of the concept of judicial review in this essay heralds the doctrine that would soon be articulated by the Supreme Court, especially during the three and a half decades when John Marshall, a Hamilton ally, served as the nation's third chief justice (1801–35). The doctrine of judicial review holds that courts have the authority and duty to measure ordinary acts of government—statutes or executive actions—against the standard of the Constitution, and to prevent their enforcement or administration when that standard is transgressed. That function has been especially important in the realm of federalism, where federal courts frequently review and overturn the legislative acts of the states. But it also applies within the realm of national government itself, where Congress and the executive also become the objects of judicial review.

So great is the authority that the Supreme Court enjoys that Hamilton's description of the judiciary as "the least dangerous" branch of government now seems almost ironic. But this essay, along with Chief Justice Marshall's opinion in Marbury v. Madison (1803), are essential starting points for any inquiry into the origins of judicial review. Hamilton grounds his analysis on two major points. The first evokes the theory of popular sovereignty. When judges overturn laws, Hamilton argues, they are not truly defying the popular majorities for whom legislatures are presumed to speak but rather enforcing the more authoritative majority whose voice informs the Constitution itself.

The second major argument rests on Hamilton's defense of an independent judiciary—a point we take so for granted that its importance is easily missed. The legal and political tradition of eighteenth-century America did not place great confidence in the idea of judges as determinants of law; juries were often regarded as the true decision makers, while judges were treated more as presiding officers. But Hamilton and other Federalists were now prepared to argue the merits of an independent and professional judiciary as a superior source of legal authority, especially in the difficult area of enforcing a written constitution.

We proceed now to an examination of the judiciary department of the proposed government.

In unfolding the defects of the existing confederation, the utility and necessity of a federal judicature have been clearly pointed out. It is the less necessary to recapitulate the considerations there urged; as the propriety of the institution in the abstract is not disputed: The only questions which have been raised being relative to the manner of constituting it, and to its extent. To these points therefore our observations shall be confined.

The manner of constituting it seems to embrace these several objects—1st. The mode of appointing the judges. 2d. The tenure by which they are to hold their places. 3d. The partition of the judiciary authority between different courts, and their relations to each other.

First. As to the mode of appointing the judges: This is the same with that of appointing the officers of the union in general, and has been so fully discussed in the two last numbers, that nothing can be said here which would not be useless repetition.[1]

Second. As to the tenure by which the judges are to hold their places: This chiefly concerns their duration in office; the provisions for their support; and the precautions for their responsibility.

According to the plan of the convention, all the judges who may be appointed by the United States are to hold their offices *during good behaviour,* which is conformable to the most approved of the state constitutions; and among the rest, to that of this state. Its propriety having been drawn into question by the adversaries of that plan, is no light symptom of the rage for objection which disorders their imaginations and judgments. The standard of good behaviour for the continuance in office of the judicial magistracy is certainly one of the most valuable of the modern improvements in the practice of government. In a monarchy it is an excellent barrier to the despotism of the prince: In a republic it is a no less excellent barrier to the encroachments and oppressions of the representative body. And it is the best expedient which can be devised in any government, to secure a steady, upright and impartial administration of the laws.

Whoever attentively considers the different departments of power must perceive, that in a government in which they are separated from each other, the judiciary, from the nature of its functions, will always

---

[1] Hamilton had devoted the previous two essays to justifying the provision of the Constitution empowering the president to "nominate, and, by and with the advice and consent of the Senate, . . . appoint ambassadors, other public ministers and consuls, judges of the Supreme Court. . . ."

be the least dangerous to the political rights of the constitution; because it will be least in a capacity to annoy or injure them. The executive not only dispenses the honors, but holds the sword of the community. The legislature not only commands the purse, but prescribes the rules by which the duties and rights of every citizen are to be regulated. The judiciary on the contrary has no influence over either the sword or the purse, no direction either of the strength or of the wealth of the society, and can take no active resolution whatever. It may truly be said to have neither Force nor Will, but merely judgment; and must ultimately depend upon the aid of the executive arm even for the efficacy of its judgments.

This simple view of the matter suggests several important consequences. It proves incontestibly that the judiciary is beyond comparison the weakest of the three departments of power;* that it can never attack with success either of the other two; and that all possible care is requisite to enable it to defend itself against their attacks. It equally proves, that though individual oppression may now and then proceed from the courts of justice, the general liberty of the people can never be endangered from that quarter: I mean, so long as the judiciary remains truly distinct from both the legislative and executive. For I agree that "there is no liberty, if the power of judging be not separated from the legislative and executive powers."† And it proves, in the last place, that as liberty can have nothing to fear from the judiciary alone, but would have every thing to fear from its union with either of the other departments; that as all the effects of such an union must ensue from a dependence of the former on the latter, notwithstanding a nominal and apparent separation; that as from the natural feebleness of the judiciary, it is in continual jeopardy of being overpowered, awed or influenced by its co-ordinate branches; and that as nothing can contribute so much to its firmness and independence, as permanency in office, this quality may therefore be justly regarded as an indispensable ingredient in its constitution; and in a great measure as the citadel of the public justice and the public security.

The complete independence of the courts of justice is peculiarly essential in a limited constitution. By a limited constitution I understand one which contains certain specified exceptions to the legislative authority; such for instance as that it shall pass no bills of attainder, no *ex post facto* laws, and the like. Limitations of this kind can be pre-

---

*The celebrated Montesquieu speaking of them says, "of the three powers above mentioned, the JUDICIARY is next to nothing." Spirit of Laws, vol. 1, page 186.
†Idem. page 181.

served in practice no other way than through the medium of the courts of justice; whose duty it must be to declare all acts contrary to the manifest tenor of the constitution void. Without this, all the reservations of particular rights or privileges would amount to nothing.

Some perplexity respecting the right of the courts to pronounce legislative acts void, because contrary to the constitution, has arisen from an imagination that the doctrine would imply a superiority of the judiciary to the legislative power. It is urged that the authority which can declare the acts of another void, must necessarily be superior to the one whose acts may be declared void. As this doctrine is of great importance in all the American constitutions, a brief discussion of the grounds on which it rests cannot be unacceptable.

There is no position which depends on clearer principles, than that every act of a delegated authority, contrary to the tenor of the commission under which it is exercised, is void. No legislative act therefore contrary to the constitution can be valid. To deny this would be to affirm that the deputy is greater than his principal; that the servant is above his master; that the representatives of the people are superior to the people themselves; that men acting by virtue of powers may do not only what their powers do not authorise, but what they forbid.

If it be said that the legislative body are themselves the constitutional judges of their own powers, and that the construction they put upon them is conclusive upon the other departments, it may be answered, that this cannot be the natural presumption, where it is not to be collected from any particular provisions in the constitution. It is not otherwise to be supposed that the constitution could intend to enable the representatives of the people to substitute their *will* to that of their constituents. It is far more rational to suppose that the courts were designed to be an intermediate body between the people and the legislature, in order, among other things, to keep the latter within the limits assigned to their authority. The interpretation of the laws is the proper and peculiar province of the courts. A constitution is in fact, and must be, regarded by the judges as a fundamental law. It therefore belongs to them to ascertain its meaning as well as the meaning of any particular act proceeding from the legislative body. If there should happen to be an irreconcileable variance between the two, that which has the superior obligation and validity ought of course to be preferred; or in other words, the constitution ought to be preferred to the statute, the intention of the people to the intention of their agents.

Nor does this conclusion by any means suppose a superiority of the judicial to the legislative power. It only supposes that the power of the people is superior to both; and that where the will of the legislature declared in its statutes, stands in opposition to that of the people declared in the constitution, the judges ought to be governed by the latter, rather than the former. They ought to regulate their decisions by the fundamental laws, rather than by those which are not fundamental.

This exercise of judicial discretion in determining between two contradictory laws, is exemplified in a familiar instance. It not uncommonly happens, that there are two statutes existing at one time, clashing in whole or in part with each other, and neither of them containing any repealing clause or expression. In such a case, it is the province of the courts to liquidate and fix their meaning and operation: So far as they can by any fair construction be reconciled to each other; reason and law conspire to dictate that this should be done. Where this is impracticable, it becomes a matter of necessity to give effect to one, in exclusion of the other. The rule which has obtained in the courts for determining their relative validity is that the last in order of time shall be preferred to the first. But this is mere rule of construction, not derived from any positive law, but from the nature and reason of the thing. It is a rule not enjoined upon the courts by legislative provision, but adopted by themselves, as consonant to truth and propriety, for the direction of their conduct as interpreters of the law. They thought it reasonable, that between the interfering acts of an *equal* authority, that which was the last indication of its will, should have the preference.

But in regard to the interfering acts of a superior and subordinate authority, of an original and derivative power, the nature and reason of the thing indicate the converse of that rule as proper to be followed. They teach us that the prior act of a superior ought to be preferred to the subsequent act of an inferior and subordinate authority; and that, accordingly, whenever a particular statute contravenes the constitution, it will be the duty of the judicial tribunals to adhere to the latter, and disregard the former.

It can be of no weight to say, that the courts on the pretence of a repugnancy, may substitute their own pleasure to the constitutional intentions of the legislature. This might as well happen in the case of two contradictory statutes; or it might as well happen in every adjudication upon any single statute. The courts must declare the sense of the law; and if they should be disposed to exercise WILL instead of JUDGMENT, the consequence would equally be the substitution of their pleasure to that of the legislative body. The observation, if it proved any thing, would prove that there ought to be no judges distinct from that body.

If then the courts of justice are to be considered as the bulwarks of a limited constitution against legislative encroachments, this consideration will afford a strong argument for the permanent tenure of judicial offices, since nothing will contribute so much as this to that independent spirit in the judges, which must be essential to the faithful performance of so arduous a duty.

This independence of the judges is equally requisite to guard the constitution and the rights of individuals from the effects of those ill humours which the arts of designing men, or the influence of particular conjunctures, sometimes disseminate among the people themselves, and which, though they speedily give place to better information and more deliberate reflection, have a tendency in the mean time to occasion dangerous innovations in the government, and serious oppressions of the minor party in the community. Though I trust the friends of the proposed constitution will never concur with its enemies* in questioning that fundamental principle of republican government, which admits the right of the people to alter or abolish the established constitution whenever they find it inconsistent with their happiness; yet it is not to be inferred from this principle, that the representatives of the people, whenever a momentary inclination happens to lay hold of a majority of their constituents incompatible with the provisions in the existing constitution, would on that account be justifiable in a violation of those provisions; or that the courts would be under a greater obligation to connive at infractions in this shape, than when they had proceeded wholly from the cabals of the representative body. Until the people have by some solemn and authoritative act annulled or changed the established form, it is binding upon themselves collectively, as well as individually; and no presumption, or even knowledge of their sentiments, can warrant their representatives in a departure from it, prior to such an act. But it is easy to see that it would require an uncommon portion of fortitude in the judges to do their duty as faithful guardians of the constitution, where legislative invasions of it had been instigated by the major voice of the community.

But it is not with a view to infractions of the constitution only that the independence of the judges may be an essential safeguard against the effects of occasional ill humours in the society. These sometimes extend no farther than to the injury of the private rights of particular classes of citizens, by unjust and partial laws. Here also the firmness of the judicial magistracy is of vast importance in mitigating the severity,

---

*Vide Protest of the minority of the convention of Pennsylvania, Martin's speech, &c.

and confining the operation of such laws. It not only serves to moderate the immediate mischiefs of those which may have been passed, but it operates as a check upon the legislative body in passing them; who, perceiving that obstacles to the success of an iniquitous intention are to be expected from the scruples of the courts, are in a manner compelled by the very motives of the injustice they meditate, to qualify their attempts. This is a circumstance calculated to have more influence upon the character of our governments, than but few may be aware of. The benefits of the integrity and moderation of the judiciary have already been felt in more states than one; and though they may have displeased those whose sinister expectations they may have disappointed, they must have commanded the esteem and applause of all the virtuous and disinterested. Considerate men of every description ought to prize whatever will tend to beget or fortify that temper in the courts; as no man can be sure that he may not be to-morrow the victim of a spirit of injustice, by which he may be a gainer to-day. And every man must now feel that the inevitable tendency of such a spirit is to sap the foundations of public and private confidence, and to introduce in its stead, universal distrust and distress.

That inflexible and uniform adherence to the rights of the constitution and of individuals, which we perceive to be indispensable in the courts of justice, can certainly not be expected from judges who hold their offices by a temporary commission. Periodical appointments, however regulated, or by whomsoever made, would in some way or other be fatal to their necessary independence. If the power of making them was committed either to the executive or legislature, there would be danger of an improper complaisance to the branch which possessed it; if to both, there would be an unwillingness to hazard the displeasure of either; if to the people, or to persons chosen by them for the special purpose, there would be too great a disposition to consult popularity, to justify a reliance that nothing would be consulted but the constitution and the laws.

There is yet a further and a weighty reason for the permanency of the judicial offices; which is deducible from the nature of the qualifications they require. It has been frequently remarked with great propriety, that a voluminous code of laws is one of the inconveniences necessarily connected with the advantages of a free government. To avoid an arbitrary discretion in the courts, it is indispensable that they should be bound down by strict rules and precedents, which serve to define and point out their duty in every particular case that comes before them; and it will readily be conceived from the variety of controversies which grow out of the folly and wickedness of mankind, that the records of those precedents must unavoidably swell to a very considerable bulk, and must demand long and laborious study to acquire a competent knowledge of them. Hence it is that there can be but few men in the society, who will have sufficient skill in the laws to qualify them for the stations of judges. And making the proper deductions for the ordinary depravity of human nature, the number must be still smaller of those who unite the requisite integrity with the requisite knowledge. These considerations apprise us, that the government can have no great option between fit characters; and that a temporary duration in office, which would naturally discourage such characters from quitting a lucrative line of practice to accept a seat on the bench, would have a tendency to throw the administration of justice into hands less able, and less well qualified to conduct it with utility and dignity. In the present circumstances of this country, and in those in which it is likely to be for a long time to come, the disadvantages on this score would be greater than they may at first sight appear; but it must be confessed that they are far inferior to those which present themselves under the other aspects of the subject.

Upon the whole there can be no room to doubt that the convention acted wisely in copying from the models of those constitutions which have established *good behaviour* as the tenure of their judicial offices in point of duration; and that so far from being blameable on this account, their plan would have been inexcuseably defective if it had wanted this important feature of good government. The experience of Great Britain affords an illustrious comment on the excellence of the institution.

PUBLIUS.

[HAMILTON]

Federalist 81

A Further View of the Judicial Department in Relation to the Distribution of Its Authority, May 28, 1788

Federalist 81 returns to examine the proper place of courts within the constitutional system. Hamilton again rebuts the claim that an unelected judiciary will emerge as the dominant institution of government. In Britain, the House of Lords acted as the highest court of appeal, and Parliament could always use its ordinary legislative power to revise an objectionable rule of legal interpretation. With the power of judicial review, however, the Supreme Court's authority to evaluate legislation on constitutional grounds implied that its decisions might indeed be final and superior—unless corrected through the difficult and unwieldy process of constitutional amendment. In defending judicial resolution of constitutional questions, Hamilton relies in part on the advantages that judges with life tenure will enjoy over elected officials in reaching the correct decision, but also on the supposition that judges will be unlikely to abuse this power.

Hamilton then proceeds to discuss a number of other objections to the broader construction of a federal judiciary. One set of these objections held that Article III of the Constitution would gravely weaken the authority of juries. Although the Constitution required jury trials in criminal matters, it did not do so in civil suits involving, for example, disputes over property, and this led some Anti-Federalists to allege that the right to jury trial in civil matters had been effectively abolished. Moreover, the provision extending the appellate jurisdiction of the Supreme Court to questions of law and fact alike could be interpreted to imply that the traditional fact-finding power of juries—the power to ascertain what had really happened—was also being undermined. This danger seemed all the more alarming because many eighteenth-century Americans believed that juries were generally competent to decide matters of law and fact, and that all forms of legal jurisdiction not permitting jury deliberation posed a grave threat to the rights and liberties of the citizen. In the concluding section of this essay, Hamilton, a skillful attorney himself, sets out to answer these concerns in a lawyerly way, in large part by noting that the new Congress would retain authority to lay down additional rules for the role of juries and appellate courts.

Let us now return to the partition of the judiciary authority between different courts, and their relations to each other.

"The judicial power of the United States is (by the plan of the convention) to be vested in one supreme court, and in such inferior courts as the congress may from time to time ordain and establish."*

That there ought to be one court of supreme and final jurisdiction is a proposition which has not been, and is not likely to be contested. The reasons for it have been assigned in another place,[1] and are too obvious to need repetition. The only question that seems to have been raised concerning it, is whether it ought to be a distinct body, or a

---

*Article 3. Sec. 1.
[1] *in another place: Federalist 22*, not included in this text.

branch of the legislature. The same contradiction is observable in regard to this matter, which has been remarked in several other cases. The very men who object to the senate as a court of impeachments, on the ground of an improper intermixture of powers, advocate, by implication at least, the propriety of vesting the ultimate decision of all causes in the whole, or in a part of the legislative body.

The arguments or rather suggestions, upon which this charge is founded, are to this effect: "The authority of the proposed supreme court of the United States, which is to be a separate and independent body, will be superior to that of the legislature. The power of construing the laws, according to the *spirit* of the constitution, will enable that court to mould them into whatever shape it may think proper; especially as its decisions will not be in any manner subject to the revision or correction of the legislative body. This is as unprecedented as it is dangerous. In Britain, the judicial power in the last resort, resides in the house of lords, which is a branch of the legislature; and this part of the British government has been imitated in the state constitutions in general. The parliament of Great-Britain, and the legislatures of the several states, can at any time rectify by law, the exceptionable decisions of their respective courts. But the errors and usurpations of the supreme court of the United States will be uncontrolable and remediless." This, upon examination, will be found to be altogether made up of false reasoning upon misconceived fact.

In the first place, there is not a syllable in the plan under consideration, which *directly* empowers the national courts to construe the laws according to the spirit of the constitution, or which gives them any greater latitude in this respect, than may be claimed by the courts of every state. I admit however, that the constitution ought to be the standard of construction for the laws, and that wherever there is an evident opposition, the laws ought to give place to the constitution. But this doctrine is not deducible from any circumstance peculiar to the plan of the convention; but from the general theory of a limited constitution; and as far as it is true, is equally applicable to most, if not to all the state governments. There can be no objection therefore, on this account, to the federal judicature, which will not lie against the local judicatures in general, and which will not serve to condemn every constitution that attempts to set bounds to the legislative discretion.

But perhaps the force of the objection may be thought to consist in the particular organization of the proposed supreme court; in its being composed of a distinct body of magistrates, instead of being one of the branches of the legislature, as in the government of Great-Britain and in that of this state. To insist upon this point, the authors of the objection must renounce the meaning they have laboured to annex to the celebrated maxim requiring a separation of the departments of power. It shall nevertheless be conceded to them, agreeably to the interpretation given to that maxim in the course of these papers, that it is not violated by vesting the ultimate power of judging in a *part* of the legislative body. But though this be not an absolute violation of that excellent rule; yet it verges so nearly upon it, as on this account alone to be less eligible than the mode preferred by the convention. From a body which had had even a partial agency in passing bad laws, we could rarely expect a disposition to temper and moderate them in the application. The same spirit, which had operated in making them, would be too apt to operate in interpreting them: Still less could it be expected, that men who had infringed the constitution, in the character of legislators, would be disposed to repair the breach, in the character of judges. Nor is this all: Every reason, which recommends the tenure of good behaviour for judicial offices, militates against placing the judiciary power in the last resort in a body composed of men chosen for a limited period. There is an absurdity in referring the determination of causes in the first instance to judges of permanent standing, and in the last to those of a temporary and mutable constitution. And there is a still greater absurdity in subjecting the decisions of men selected for their knowledge of the laws, acquired by long and laborious study, to the revision and control of men, who for want of the same advantage cannot but be deficient in that knowledge. The members of the legislature will rarely be chosen with a view to those qualifications which fit men for the stations of judges; and as on this account there will be great reason to apprehend all the ill consequences of defective information; so on account of the natural propensity of such bodies to party divisions, there will be no less reason to fear, that the pestilential breath of faction may poison the fountains of justice. The habit of being continually marshalled on opposite sides, will be too apt to stifle the voice both of law and of equity.

These considerations teach us to applaud the wisdom of those states, who have committed the judicial power in the last resort, not to a part of the legislature, but to distinct and independent bodies of men. Contrary to the supposition of those, who have represented the plan of the convention in this respect as novel and unprecedented, it is but a copy of the constitutions of New-Hampshire, Massachusetts, Pennsylvania, Delaware, Maryland, Virginia, North-Carolina, South-

Carolina and Georgia; and the preference which has been given to these models is highly to be commended.

It is not true, in the second place, that the parliament of Great Britain, or the legislatures of the particular states, can rectify the exceptionable decisions of their respective courts, in any other sense than might be done by a future legislature of the United States. The theory neither of the British, nor the state constitutions, authorises the revisal of a judicial sentence, by a legislative act. Nor is there any thing in the proposed constitution more than in either of them, by which it is forbidden. In the former as well as in the latter, the impropriety of the thing, on the general principles of law and reason, is the sole obstacle. A legislature without exceeding its province cannot reverse a determination once made, in a particular case; though it may prescribe a new rule for future cases. This is the principle, and it applies in all its consequences, exactly in the same manner and extent, to the state governments, as to the national government, now under consideration. Not the least difference can be pointed out in any view of the subject.

It may in the last place be observed that the supposed danger of judiciary encroachments on the legislative authority, which has been upon many occasions reiterated, is in reality a phantom. Particular misconstructions and contraventions of the will of the legislature may now and then happen; but they can never be so extensive as to amount to an inconvenience, or in any sensible degree to affect the order of the political system. This may be inferred with certainty from the general nature of the judicial power; from the objects to which it relates; from the manner in which it is exercised; from its comparative weakness, and from its total incapacity to support its usurpations by force. And the inference is greatly fortified by the consideration of the important constitutional check, which the power of instituting impeachments, in one part of the legislative body, and of determining upon them in the other, would give to that body upon the members of the judicial department. This is alone a complete security. There never can be danger that the judges, by a series of deliberate usurpations on the authority of the legislature, would hazard the united resentment of the body entrusted with it, while this body was possessed of the means of punishing their presumption by degrading them from their stations. While this ought to remove all apprehensions on the subject, it affords at the same time a cogent argument for constituting the senate a court for the trial of impeachments.

Having now examined, and I trust removed the objections to the distinct and independent organization of the supreme court, I proceed to consider the propriety of the power of constituting inferior courts,* and the relations which will subsist between these and the former.

The power of constituting inferior courts is evidently calculated to obviate the necessity of having recourse to the supreme court, in every case of federal cognizance. It is intended to enable the national government to institute or *authorise* in each state or district of the United States, a tribunal competent to the determination of matters of national jurisdiction within its limits.

But why, it is asked, might not the same purpose have been accomplished by the instrumentality of the state courts? This admits of different answers. Though the fitness and competency of those courts should be allowed in the utmost latitude; yet the substance of the power in question, may still be regarded as a necessary part of the plan, if it were only to empower the national legislature to commit to them the cognizance of causes arising out of the national constitution. To confer the power of determining such causes upon the existing courts of the several states, would perhaps be as much "to constitute tribunals," as to create new courts with the like power. But ought not a more direct and explicit provision to have been made in favour of the state courts? There are, in my opinion, substantial reasons against such a provision: The most discerning cannot foresee how far the prevalency of a local spirit may be found to disqualify the local tribunals for the jurisdiction of national causes; whilst every man may discover that courts constituted like those of some of the states, would be improper channels of the judicial authority of the union. State judges, holding their offices during pleasure, or from year to year, will be too little independent to be relied upon for an inflexible execution of the national laws. And if there was a necessity for confiding the original cognizance of causes arising under those laws to them, there would be a correspondent necessity for leaving the door of appeal as wide as possible. In proportion to the grounds of confidence in, or diffidence of the subordinate tribunals, ought to be the facility or difficulty of appeals. And well satisfied as I am of the propriety of the

---

*This power has been absurdly represented as intended to abolish all the county courts in the several states, which are commonly called inferior courts. But the expressions of the constitution are to constitute "tribunals INFERIOR TO THE SUPREME COURT," and the evident design of the provision is to enable the institution of local courts subordinate to the supreme, either in states or larger districts. It is ridiculous to imagine that county courts were in contemplation.

appellate jurisdiction in the several classes of causes to which it is extended by the plan of the convention, I should consider every thing calculated to give in practice, an *unrestrained course* to appeals as a source of public and private inconvenience.

I am not sure but that it will be found highly expedient and useful to divide the United States into four or five, or half a dozen districts; and to institute a federal court in each district, in lieu of one in every state. The judges of these courts, with the aid of the state judges, may hold circuits for the trial of causes in the several parts of the respective districts. Justice through them may be administered with ease and dispatch; and appeals may be safely circumscribed within a very narrow compass. This plan appears to me at present the most eligible of any that could be adopted, and in order to it, it is necessary that the power of constituting inferior courts should exist in the full extent in which it is to be found in the proposed constitution.

These reasons seem sufficient to satisfy a candid mind, that the want of such a power would have been a great defect in the plan. Let us now examine in what manner the judicial authority is to be distributed between the supreme and the inferior courts of the union.

The supreme court is to be invested with original jurisdiction, only "in cases affecting ambassadors, other public ministers and consuls, and those in which a STATE shall be a party." Public ministers of every class, are the immediate representatives of their sovereigns. All questions in which they are concerned, are so directly connected with the public peace, that as well for the preservation of this, as out of respect to the sovereignties they represent, it is both expedient and proper, that such questions should be submitted in the first instance to the highest judicatory of the nation. Though consuls have not in strictness a diplomatic character, yet as they are the public agents of the nations to which they belong, the same observation is in a great measure applicable to them. In cases in which a state might happen to be a party, it would ill suit its dignity to be turned over to an inferior tribunal.

Though it may rather be a digression from the immediate subject of this paper, I shall take occasion to mention here, a supposition which has excited some alarm upon very mistaken grounds: It has been suggested that an assignment of the public securities of one state to the citizens of another, would enable them to prosecute that state in the federal courts for the amount of those securities. A suggestion which the following considerations prove to be without foundation.

It is inherent in the nature of sovereignty, not to be amenable to the suit of an individual *without its consent.* This is the general sense and the general practice of mankind; and the exemption, as one of the attributes of sovereignty, is now enjoyed by the government of every state in the union. Unless therefore, there is a surrender of this immunity in the plan of the convention, it will remain with the states, and the danger intimated must be merely ideal. The circumstances which are necessary to produce an alienation of state sovereignty, were discussed in considering the article of taxation, and need not be repeated here.[2] A recurrence to the principles there established will satisfy us, that there is no colour to pretend that the state governments, would by the adoption of that plan, be divested of the privilege of paying their own debts in their own way, free from every constraint but that which flows from the obligations of good faith. The contracts between a nation and individuals are only binding on the conscience of the sovereign, and have no pretensions to a compulsive force. They confer no right of action independent of the sovereign will. To what purpose would it be to authorise suits against states, for the debts they owe? How could recoveries be enforced? It is evident that it could not be done without waging war against the contracting state; and to ascribe to the federal courts, by mere implication, and in destruction of a pre-existing right of the state governments, a power which would involve such a consequence, would be altogether forced and unwarrantable.

Let us resume the train of our observations; we have seen that the original jurisdiction of the supreme court would be confined to two classes of causes, and those of a nature rarely to occur. In all other causes of federal cognizance, the original jurisdiction would appertain to the inferior tribunals, and the supreme court would have nothing more than an appellate jurisdiction, "with such *exceptions,* and under such *regulations* as the congress shall make."

The propriety of this appellate jurisdiction has been scarcely called in question in regard to matters of law; but the clamours have been loud against it as applied to matters of fact. Some well intentioned men in this state, deriving their notions from the language and forms which obtain in our courts, have been induced to consider it as an implied supersedure of the trial by jury, in favour of the civil law mode of trial, which prevails in our courts of admiralty, probates and chancery. A technical sense has been affixed to the term "appellate," which in our law parlance is commonly used in reference to appeals in the course of the civil law. But if I am not misinformed, the same meaning would not be given to it in any part of New-England. There an appeal from

[2] See Essay 32.

one jury to another is familiar both in language and practice, and is even a matter of course, until there have been two verdicts on one side. The word "appellate" therefore will not be understood in the same sense in New-England as in New-York, which shews the impropriety of a technical interpretation derived from the jurisprudence of any particular state. The expression taken in the abstract, denotes nothing more than the power of one tribunal to review the proceedings of another, either as to the law or fact, or both. The mode of doing it may depend on ancient custom or legislative provision, (in a new government it must depend on the latter) and may be with or without the aid of a jury, as may be judged adviseable. If therefore the re-examination of a fact, once determined by a jury, should in any case be admitted under the proposed constitution, it may be so regulated as to be done by a second jury, either by remanding the cause to the court below for a second trial of the fact, or by directing an issue immediately out of the supreme court.

But it does not follow that the re-examination of a fact once ascertained by a jury, will be permitted in the supreme court. Why may it not be said, with the strictest propriety, when a writ of error is brought from an inferior to a superior court of law in this state, that the latter has jurisdiction of the fact, as well as the law? It is true it cannot institute a new enquiry concerning the fact, but it takes cognizance of it as it appears upon the record, and pronounces the law arising upon it.* This is jurisdiction of both fact and law, nor is it even possible to separate them. Though the common law courts of this state ascertain disputed facts by a jury, yet they unquestionably have jurisdiction of both fact and law; and accordingly, when the former is agreed in the pleadings, they have no recourse to a jury, but proceed at once to judgment. I contend therefore on this ground, that the expressions, "appellate jurisdiction, both as to law and fact," do not necessarily imply a re-examination in the supreme court of facts decided by juries in the inferior courts.

The following train of ideas may well be imagined to have influenced the convention in relation to this particular provision. The appellate jurisdiction of the supreme court (may it have been argued) will extend to causes determinable in different modes, some in the course of the COMMON LAW, and others in the course of the CIVIL LAW. In the former, the revision of the law only, will be, generally speaking, the

---

*This word is a compound of JUS and DICTIO, juris, dictio, or a speaking or pronouncing of the law.

proper province of the supreme court; in the latter, the re-examination of the fact is agreeable to usage, and in some cases, of which prize causes are an example, might be essential to the preservation of the public peace. It is therefore necessary, that the appellate jurisdiction should, in certain cases, extend in the broadest sense to matters of fact. It will not answer to make an express exception of cases, which shall have been originally tried by a jury, because in the courts of some of the states, *all causes* are tried in this mode;* and such an exception would preclude the revision of matters of fact, as well where it might be proper, as where it might be improper. To avoid all inconveniencies, it will be safest to declare generally, that the supreme court shall possess appellate jurisdiction, both as to law and *fact,* and that this jurisdiction shall be subject to such *exceptions* and regulations as the national legislature may prescribe. This will enable the government to modify it in such a manner as will best answer the ends of public justice and security.

This view of the matter, at any rate puts it out of all doubt that the supposed *abolition* of the trial by jury, by the operation of this provision, is fallacious and untrue. The legislature of the United States would certainly have full power to provide that in appeals to the supreme court there should be no re-examination of facts where they had been tried in the original causes by juries. This would certainly be an authorised exception; but if for the reason already intimated it should be thought too extensive, it might be qualified with a limitation to such causes only as are determinable at common law in that mode of trial.

The amount of the observations hitherto made on the authority of the judicial department is this—that it has been carefully restricted to those causes which are manifestly proper for the cognizance of the national judicature, that in the partition of this authority a very small portion of original jurisdiction has been reserved to the supreme court, and the rest consigned to the subordinate tribunals—that the supreme court will possess an appellate jurisdiction both as to law and fact in all the cases referred to them, but subject to any *exceptions* and *regulations* which may be thought adviseable; that this appellate jurisdiction does in no case *abolish* the trial by jury, and that an ordinary degree of prudence and integrity in the national councils will insure us solid advantages from the establishment of the proposed judiciary, without exposing us to any of the inconveniencies which have been predicted from that source.

PUBLIUS.

---

*I hold that the states will have concurrent jurisdiction with the subordinate federal judicatories, in many cases of federal cognizance, as will be explained in my next paper.

Federalist 84

Concerning Several Miscellaneous Objections, May 28, 1788

Because The Federalist *was a defense of the Constitution as it was written, there was no obvious reason to discuss its principal omission: the lack of a declaration or bill of rights, enumerating essential liberties of the citizen. Anti-Federalists began criticizing this oversight as soon as the Constitution was published. That objection gathered new force in the early months of 1788, when the Massachusetts convention became the first to urge the speedy adoption of amendments after the Constitution was ratified. Federalists balked at considering the structural amendments that their opponents desired most, but the idea of accepting additional articles affirming rights offered a basis for conciliating Anti-Federalists without altering the essential features of the Constitution. In several of the later ratification conventions — including Virginia and New York — Federalists had to agree to recommend amendments to the first Congress under the Constitution in order to secure ratification.*

Yet beyond the politics of proposing amendments, a deeper debate about the meaning of bills of rights was unfolding. James Wilson, a prominent framer and Federalist from Pennsylvania, launched this discussion in a widely reported public address delivered at the statehouse where the Constitution was drafted. To add a bill of rights to a government of limited delegated powers might be a mistake, Wilson warned, because it could be read to imply that the government possessed other, unenumerated powers that it had not in fact been granted. That statement quickly became a lightning rod for criticism. After all, Anti-Federalists quickly replied, the Constitution contained a provision prohibiting the suspension of habeas corpus, *even though it nowhere suggested that the national government might otherwise have authority to revoke this famous writ against unlawful detention.*

Hamilton was entering this debate at a late point, but he nonetheless affirmed Wilson's position while adding a new riposte of his own. The Constitution was its own bill of rights, Hamilton asserted, not through the enumeration of fundamental liberties, but because its formula for balanced popular government would provide the essential security that a mere statement of rights could not.

In the course of the foregoing review of the constitution I have taken notice of, and endeavoured to answer, most of the objections which have appeared against it. There however remain a few which either did not fall naturally under any particular head, or were forgotten in their proper places. These shall now be discussed; but as the subject has been drawn into great length, I shall so far consult brevity as to comprise all my observations on these miscellaneous points in a single paper.

The most considerable of these remaining objections is, that the plan of the convention contains no bill of rights. Among other answers given to this, it has been upon different occasions remarked, that the constitutions of several of the states are in a similar predicament. I add, that New-York is of this number. And yet the opposers of the new system in this state, who profess an unlimited admiration for its constitution, are among the most intemperate partizans of a bill of rights. To justify their zeal in this matter, they alledge two things; one is, that though the constitution of New-York has no bill of rights prefixed to it, yet it contains in the body of it various provisions in favour of particular privileges and rights, which in substance amount to the same thing; the other is, that the constitution adopts in their full extent the common and statute law of Great-Britain, by which many other rights not expressed in it are equally secured.

To the first I answer, that the constitution proposed by the convention contains, as well as the constitution of this state, a number of such provisions.

Independent of those, which relate to the structure of the government, we find the following: Article I. section 3. clause 7. "Judgment in cases of impeachment shall not extend further than to removal from office, and disqualification to hold and enjoy any office of honour, trust or profit under the United States; but the party convicted shall nevertheless be liable and subject to indictment, trial, judgment and punishment, according to law." Section 9. of the same article, clause 2. "The privilege of the writ of *habeas corpus* shall not be suspended, unless when in cases of rebellion or invasion the public safety may require it." Clause 3. "No bill of attainder or *ex post facto* law shall be passed." Clause 7. "No title of nobility shall be granted by the United States: And no person holding any office of profit or trust under them, shall, without the consent of the congress, accept of any present, emolument, office or title, of any kind whatever, from any king, prince or foreign state." Article III. section 2. clause 3. "The trial of all crimes, except in cases of impeachment, shall be by jury; and such trial shall be held in the state where the said crimes shall have been committed; but when not committed within any state, the trial shall be

at such place or places as the congress may by law have directed."
Section 3, of the same article, "Treason against the United States shall
consist only in levying war against them, or in adhering to their enemies, giving them aid and comfort. No person shall be convicted of
treason unless on the testimony of two witnesses to the same overt
act, or on confession in open court." And clause 3, of the same section.
"The congress shall have power to declare the punishment of treason,
but no attainder of treason shall work corruption of blood, or forfei-
ture, except during the life of the person attainted."

It may well be a question whether these are not upon the whole, of
equal importance with any which are to be found in the constitution of
this state. The establishment of the writ of *habeas corpus,* the prohibition of *ex post facto* laws, and of TITLES OF NOBILITY, *to which we have
no corresponding provisions in our constitution,* are perhaps greater
securities to liberty and republicanism than any it contains. The creation of crimes after the commission of the fact, or in other words, the
subjecting of men to punishment for things which, when they were
done, were breaches of no law, and the practice of arbitrary imprison-
ments have been in all ages the favourite and most formidable instruments of tyranny. The observations of the judicious Blackstone*,[1] in
reference to the latter, are well worthy of recital. "To bereave a man of
life (says he) or by violence to confiscate his estate, without accusation or trial, would be so gross and notorious an act of despotism, as
must at once convey the alarm of tyranny throughout the whole
nation; but confinement of the person by secretly hurrying him to
goal, where his sufferings are unknown or forgotten, is a less public, a
less striking, and therefore *a more dangerous engine* of arbitrary government." And as a remedy for this fatal evil, he is every where peculiarly emphatical in his encomiums on the *habeas corpus* act, which in
one place he calls "the BULWARK of the British constitution."†

Nothing need be said to illustrate the importance of the prohibition
of titles of nobility. This may truly be denominated the corner stone of
republican government; for so long as they are excluded, there can
never be serious danger that the government will be any other than
that of the people.

To the second, that is, to the pretended establishment of the common
and statute law by the constitution, I answer, that they are expressly

---

*Vide Blackstone's Commentaries, vol. 1, page 136.
[1]Sir William Blackstone's *Commentaries on the Laws of England* were the most
authoritative summary of the subject available, and possibly more widely read in America than in Britain.
†Idem, vol. 4, page 438.

made subject "to such alterations and provisions as the legislature shall from time to time make concerning the same." They are therefore at any moment liable to repeal by the ordinary legislative power, and of course have no constitutional sanction. The only use of the declaration was to recognize the ancient law, and to remove doubts which might have been occasioned by the revolution. This consequently can be considered as no part of a declaration of rights, which under our constitutions must be intended as limitations of the power of the government itself.

It has been several times truly remarked, that bills of rights are in their origin, stipulations between kings and their subjects, abridgments of prerogative in favor of privilege, reservations of rights not surrendered to the prince. Such was MAGNA CHARTA, obtained by the Barons, sword in hand, from king John. Such were the subsequent confirmations of that charter by subsequent princes. Such was the *petition of right* assented to by Charles the First, in the beginning of his reign. Such also was the declaration of right presented by the lords and commons to the prince of Orange in 1688, and afterwards thrown into the form of an act of parliament, called the bill of rights. It is evident, therefore, that according to their primitive signification, they have no application to constitutions professedly founded upon the power of the people, and executed by their immediate representatives and servants. Here, in strictness, the people surrender nothing, and as they retain every thing, they have no need of particular reservations. "WE THE PEOPLE of the United States, to secure the blessings of liberty to ourselves and our posterity, do *ordain* and *establish* this constitution for the United States of America." Here is a better recognition of popular rights than volumes of those aphorisms which make the principal figure in several of our state bills of rights, and which would sound much better in a treatise of ethics than in a constitution of government.

But a minute detail of particular rights is certainly far less applicable to a constitution like that under consideration, which is merely intended to regulate the general political interests of the nation, than to a constitution which has the regulation of every species of personal and private concerns. If therefore the loud clamours against the plan of the convention on this score, are well founded, no epithets of reprobation will be too strong for the constitution of this state. But the truth is, that both of them contain all, which in relation to their objects, is reasonably to be desired.

I go further, and affirm that bills of rights, in the sense and in the extent in which they are contended for, are not only unnecessary in the proposed constitution, but would even be dangerous. They would contain various exceptions to powers which are not granted; and on this very account, would afford a colourable pretext to claim more than were granted. For why declare that things shall not be done which there is no power to do? Why for instance, should it be said, that the liberty of the press shall not be restrained, when no power is given by which restrictions may be imposed? I will not contend that such a provision would confer a regulating power; but it is evident that it would furnish, to men disposed to usurp, a plausible pretence for claiming that power. They might urge with a semblance of reason, that the constitution ought not to be charged with the absurdity of providing against the abuse of an authority, which was not given, and that the provision against restraining the liberty of the press afforded a clear implication, that a power to prescribe proper regulations concerning it, was intended to be vested in the national government. This may serve as a specimen of the numerous handles which would be given to the doctrine of constructive powers, by the indulgence of an injudicious zeal for bills of rights.

On the subject of the liberty of the press, as much has been said, I cannot forbear adding a remark or two: In the first place, I observe that there is not a syllable concerning it in the constitution of this state, and in the next, I contend that whatever has been said about it in that of any other state, amounts to nothing. What signifies a declaration that "the liberty of the press shall be inviolably preserved?" What is the liberty of the press? Who can give it any definition which would not leave the utmost latitude for evasion? I hold it to be impracticable; and from this, I infer, that its security, whatever fine declarations may be inserted in any constitution respecting it, must altogether depend on public opinion, and on the general spirit of the people and of the government.* And here, after all, as intimated upon another occasion, must we seek for the only solid basis of all our rights.

*To show that there is a power in the constitution by which the liberty of the press may be affected, recourse has been had to the power of taxation. It is said that duties may be laid upon publications so high as to amount to a prohibition. I know not by what logic it could be maintained that the declarations in the state constitutions, in favour of the freedom of the press, would be a constitutional impediment to the imposition of duties upon publications by the state legislatures. It cannot certainly be pretended that any degree of duties, however low, would be an abridgement of the liberty of the press. We know that newspapers are taxed in Great-Britain, and yet it is notorious that the press no where enjoys greater liberty than in that country. And if duties of any kind may be laid without a violation of that liberty, it is evident that the extent must depend on legislative discretion, regulated by public opinion; so that after all, general declarations respecting the liberty of the press will give it no greater security than it will have without them. The same invasions of it may be effected under the state constitutions which contain those declarations through the means of taxation, as under the proposed constitution which has nothing of the kind. It would be quite as significant to declare that government ought to be free, that taxes ought not to be excessive, &c., as that the liberty of the press ought not to be restrained.

There remains but one other view of this matter to conclude the point. The truth is, after all the declamation we have heard, that the constitution is itself in every rational sense, and to every useful purpose, A BILL OF RIGHTS. The several bills of rights, in Great-Britain, form its constitution, and conversely the constitution of each state is its bill of rights. And the proposed constitution, if adopted, will be the bill of rights of the union. Is it one object of a bill of rights to declare and specify the political privileges of the citizens in the structure and administration of the government? This is done in the most ample and precise manner in the plan of the convention, comprehending various precautions for the public security, which are not to be found in any of the state constitutions. Is another object of a bill of rights to define certain immunities and modes of proceeding, which are relative to personal and private concerns? This we have seen has also been attended to, in a variety of cases, in the same plan. Adverting therefore to the substantial meaning of a bill of rights, it is absurd to allege that it is not to be found in the work of the convention. It may be said that it does not go far enough, though it will not be easy to make this appear; but it can with no propriety be contended that there is no such thing. It certainly must be immaterial what mode is observed as to the order of declaring the rights of the citizens, if they are to be found in any part of the instrument which establishes the government. And hence it must be apparent that much of what has been said on this subject rests merely on verbal and nominal distinctions, which are entirely foreign from the substance of the thing.

Another objection, which has been made, and which from the frequency of its repetition it is to be presumed is relied on, is of this nature:—It is improper (say the objectors) to confer such large powers, as are proposed, upon the national government; because the seat of that government must of necessity be too remote from many of the states to admit of a proper knowledge on the part of the constituent, of the conduct of the representative body. This argument, if it proves any thing, proves that there ought to be no general government whatever. For the powers which it seems to be agreed on all hands, ought to be vested in the union, cannot be safely intrusted to a body which is not under every requisite controul. But there are satisfactory reasons to shew that the objection is in reality not well founded. There is in most of the arguments which relate to distance a palpable illusion of the imagination. What are the sources of information by which the people in Montgomery county[2] must regulate their judgment of the conduct

---

[2] A county in northern New York, far distant from the capital in New York City.

of their representatives in the state legislature? Of personal observation they can have no benefit. This is confined to the citizens on the spot. They must therefore depend on the information of intelligent men, in whom they confide—and how must these men obtain their information? Evidently from the complection of public measures, from the public prints, from correspondences with their representatives, and with other persons who reside at the place of their deliberation. This does not apply to Montgomery county only, but to all the counties, at any considerable distance from the seat of government.

It is equally evident that the same sources of information would be open to the people, in relation to the conduct of their representatives in the general government; and the impediments to a prompt communication which distance may be supposed to create, will be overballanced by the effects of the vigilance of the state governments. The executive and legislative bodies of each state will be so many centinels over the persons employed in every department of the national administration; and as it will be in their power to adopt and pursue a regular and effectual system of intelligence, they can never be at a loss to know the behaviour of those who represent their constituents in the national councils, and can readily communicate the same knowledge to the people. Their disposition to apprise the community of whatever may prejudice its interests from another quarter, may be relied upon, if it were only from the rivalship of power. And we may conclude with the fullest assurance, that the people, through that channel, will be better informed of the conduct of their national representatives, than they can be by any means they now possess of that of their state representatives.

It ought also to be remembered, that the citizens who inhabit the country at and near the seat of government, will in all questions that affect the general liberty and prosperity, have the same interest with those who are at a distance; and that they will stand ready to sound the alarm when necessary, and to point out the actors in any pernicious project. The public papers will be expeditious messengers of intelligence to the most remote inhabitants of the union.

Among the many extraordinary objections which have appeared against the proposed constitution, the most extraordinary and the least colourable one, is derived from the want of some provision respecting the debts due *to* the United States. This has been represented as a tacit relinquishment of those debts, and as a wicked contrivance to screen public defaulters. The newspapers have teemed with the most inflammatory railings on this head; and yet there is nothing clearer than that the suggestion is entirely void of foundation, and is the offspring of extreme ignorance or extreme dishonesty. In addition to the remarks I have made upon the subject in another place,[3] I shall only observe, that as it is a plain dictate of common sense, so it is also an established doctrine of political law, that *"States neither lose any of their rights, nor are discharged from any of their obligations by a change in the form of their civil government."**

The last objection of any consequence which I at present recollect, turns upon the article of expence. If it were even true that the adoption of the proposed government would occasion a considerable increase of expence, it would be an objection that ought to have no weight against the plan. The great bulk of the citizens of America, are with reason convinced that union is the basis of their political happiness. Men of sense of all parties now, with few exceptions, agree that it cannot be preserved under the present system, nor without radical alterations; that new and extensive powers ought to be granted to the national head, and that these require a different organization of the federal government, a single body being an unsafe depository of such ample authorities. In conceding all this, the question of expence must be given up, for it is impossible, with any degree of safety, to narrow the foundation upon which the system is to stand. The two branches of the legislature are in the first instance, to consist of only sixty-five persons, which is the same number of which congress, under the existing confederation, may be composed. It is true that this number is intended to be increased; but this is to keep pace with the increase of the population and resources of the country. It is evident, that a less number would, even in the first instance, have been unsafe; and that a continuance of the present number would, in a more advanced stage of population, be a very inadequate representation of the people.

Whence is the dreaded augmentation of expence to spring? One source pointed out, is the multiplication of offices under the new government. Let us examine this a little.

It is evident that the principal departments of the administration under the present government, are the same which will be required under the new. There are now a secretary at war, a secretary for foreign affairs, a secretary for domestic affairs, a board of treasury consisting of three persons, a treasurer, assistants, clerks, &c. These offices are indispensable under any system, and will suffice under the new as well as under the old. As to ambassadors and other ministers and agents in

---

[3] *in another place: Federalist* 43, not included in this text.
*Vide Rutherford's Institutes, vol. 2. book II, chap. x. sect. xiv, and xv.—Vide also Grotius, book II, chap. ix, sect. viii, and ix.

foreign countries, the proposed constitution can make no other difference, than to render their characters, where they reside, more
respectable, and their services more useful. As to persons to be
employed in the collection of the revenues, it is unquestionably true
that these will form a very considerable addition to the number of federal officers; but it will not follow, that this will occasion an increase of
public expence. It will be in most cases nothing more than an exchange
of state officers for national officers. In the collection of all duties, for
instance, the persons employed will be wholly of the latter description.
The states individually will stand in no need of any for this purpose.
What difference can it make in point of expence, to pay officers of the
customs appointed by the state, or those appointed by the United
States? There is no good reason to suppose, that either the number or
the salaries of the latter, will be greater than those of the former.

Where then are we to seek for those additional articles of expence
which are to swell the account to the enormous size that has been represented to us? The chief item which occurs to me, respects the support of the judges of the United States. I do not add the president,
because there is now a president of congress, whose expences may
not be far, if any thing, short of those which will be incurred on
account of the president of the United States. The support of the
judges will clearly be an extra expence, but to what extent will depend
on the particular plan which may be adopted in practice in regard to
this matter. But it can upon no reasonable plan amount to a sum which
will be an object of material consequence.

Let us now see what there is to counterballance any extra expences
that may attend the establishment of the proposed government. The
first thing that presents itself is, that a great part of the business,
which now keeps congress sitting through the year, will be transacted
by the president. Even the management of foreign negociations will
naturally devolve upon him according to general principles concerted
with the senate, and subject to their final concurrence. Hence it is evident, that a portion of the year will suffice for the session of both the
senate and the house of representatives: We may suppose about a
fourth for the latter, and a third or perhaps a half for the former. The
extra business of treaties and appointments may give this extra occupation to the senate. From this circumstance we may infer, that until
the house of representatives shall be increased greatly beyond its
present number, there will be a considerable saving of expence from
the difference between the constant session of the present, and the
temporary session of the future congress.

But there is another circumstance, of great importance in the view of economy. The business of the United States has hitherto occupied the state legislatures as well as congress. The latter has made requisitions which the former have had to provide for. Hence it has happened that the sessions of the state legislatures have been protracted greatly beyond what was necessary for the execution of the mere local business of the states. More than half their time has been frequently employed in matters which related to the United States. Now the members who compose the legislatures of the several states amount to two thousand and upwards; which number has hitherto performed what under the new system will be done in the first instance by sixty-five persons, and probably at no future period by above a fourth or a fifth of that number. The congress under the proposed government will do all the business of the United States themselves, without the intervention of the state legislatures, who thenceforth will have only to attend to the affairs of their particular states, and will not have to sit in any proportion as long as they have heretofore done. This difference, in the time of the sessions of the state legislatures, will be all clear gain, and will alone form an article of saving, which may be regarded as an equivalent for any additional objects of expence that may be occasioned by the adoption of the new system.

The result from these observations is, that the sources of additional expence from the establishment of the proposed constitution are much fewer than may have been imagined, that they are counterbalanced by considerable objects of saving, and that while it is questionable on which side the scale will preponderate, it is certain that a government less expensive would be incompetent to the purposes of the union.

PUBLIUS.

[HAMILTON]

Federalist 85

Conclusion, May 28, 1788

Seven months and eighty-four essays after first evoking the opportunity for "reflection and choice," Hamilton closes The Federalist *by confessing that two of the topics it had meant to consider independently had already been effectively covered in the preceding essays. Instead, he uses this final essay to remind readers that Publius has adhered to the basic tone and mode of address he promised to maintain at the outset. But rather than end on this valedictory note, Hamilton's final paragraphs warn against a new proposal that New York Anti-Federalists were advancing: to insist either on the calling of a second constitutional convention to consider the project anew, taking into account the criticisms of the imperfections of the Constitution, or on the prior adoption of amendments before the Constitution could be deemed conclusively ratified. Not only would such schemes prove politically impractical, Hamilton warns; they would compound the risk of disunion in the interval while the new project went forward, its fate even more uncertain than that of the proposed Constitution. Hamilton thus ends* The Federalist *by linking the cause of the Constitution with the security of the Union.*

According to the formal division of the subject of these papers, announced in my first number, there would appear still to remain for discussion, two points, "the analogy of the proposed government to your own state constitution," and "the additional security, which its adoption will afford to republican government, to liberty and to property." But these heads have been so fully anticipated and exhausted in the progress of the work, that it would now scarcely be possible to do any thing more than repeat, in a more dilated form, what has been heretofore said; which the advanced stage of the question, and the time already spent upon it conspire to forbid.

It is remarkable, that the resemblance of the plan of the convention to the act which organizes the government of this state holds, not less with regard to many of the supposed defects, than to the real excellencies of the former. Among the pretended defects, are the re-eligibility of the executive, the want of a council, the omission of a formal bill of rights, the omission of a provision respecting the liberty of the press: These and several others, which have been noted in the course of our inquiries, are as much chargeable on the existing constitution of this state, as on the one proposed for the Union. And a man must have slender pretensions to consistency, who can rail at the latter for imperfections which he finds no difficulty in excusing in the former. Nor indeed can there be a better proof of the insincerity and affectation of some of the zealous adversaries of the plan of the convention among us, who profess to be the devoted admirers of the government under which they live, than the fury with which they have attacked that plan, for matters in regard to which our own constitution is equally, or perhaps more vulnerable.

The additional securities to republican government, to liberty and to property, to be derived from the adoption of the plan under consideration, consist chiefly in the restraints which the preservation of the union will impose on local factions and insurrections, and on the ambition of powerful individuals in single states, who might acquire credit and influence enough, from leaders and favorites, to become the despots of the people; in the diminution of the opportunities to foreign intrigue, which the dissolution of the confederacy would invite and facilitate; in the prevention of extensive military establishments, which could not fail to grow out of wars between the states in a disunited situation; in the express guarantee of a republican form of government to each; in the absolute and universal exclusion of titles of nobility; and in the precautions against the repetition of those practices on the part of the state governments, which have undermined the foundations of property and credit, have planted mutual distrust in the breasts of all classes of citizens, and have occasioned an almost universal prostration of morals.

Thus have I, my fellow citizens, executed the task I had assigned to myself; with what success, your conduct must determine. I trust at least you will admit, that I have not failed in the assurance I gave you respecting the spirit with which my endeavours should be conducted. I have addressed myself purely to your judgments, and have studiously avoided those asperities which are too apt to disgrace political disputants of all parties, and which have been not a little provoked by the language and conduct of the opponents of the constitution. The charge of a conspiracy against the liberties of the people, which has been indiscriminately brought against the advocates of the plan, has something in it too wanton and too malignant not to excite the indignation of every man who feels in his own bosom a refutation of the calumny.[1] The perpetual charges which have been rung upon the wealthy, the well-born and the great, have been such as to inspire the disgust of all sensible men. And the unwarrantable concealments and misrepresentations which have been in various ways practiced to keep the truth from the public eye, have been of a nature to demand the reprobation of all honest men. It is not impossible that these circumstances may have occasionally betrayed me into intemperances of expression which I did not intend: It is certain that I have frequently felt a struggle between sensibility and moderation, and if the former has in some instances prevailed, it must be my excuse that it has been neither often nor much.

Let us now pause and ask ourselves whether, in the course of these papers, the proposed constitution has not been satisfactorily vindi-

---

[1] *calumny:* a false charge or malicious accusation.

cated from the aspersions thrown upon it, and whether it has not been shewn to be worthy of the public approbation, and necessary to the public safety and prosperity. Every man is bound to answer these questions to himself, according to the best of his conscience and understanding, and to act agreeably to the genuine and sober dictates of his judgment. This is a duty, from which nothing can give him a dispensation. 'Tis one that he is called upon, nay, constrained by all the obligations that form the bands of society, to discharge sincerely and honestly. No partial motive, no particular interest, no pride of opinion, no temporary passion or prejudice, will justify to himself, to his country or to his posterity, an improper election of the part he is to act. Let him beware of an obstinate adherence to party. Let him reflect that the object upon which he is to decide is not a particular interest of the community, but the very existence of the nation. And let him remember that a majority of America has already given its sanction to the plan, which he is to approve or reject.

I shall not dissemble, that I feel an intire confidence in the arguments, which recommend the proposed system to your adoption; and that I am unable to discern any real force in those by which it has been opposed. I am persuaded, that it is the best which our political situation, habits and opinions will admit, and superior to any the revolution has produced.

Concessions on the part of the friends of the plan, that it has not a claim to absolute perfection, have afforded matter of no small triumph to its enemies. Why, say they, should we adopt an imperfect thing? Why not amend it, and make it perfect before it is irrevocably established? This may be plausible enough, but it is only plausible. In the first place I remark, that the extent of these concessions has been greatly exaggerated. They have been stated as amounting to an admission, that the plan is radically defective; and that, without material alterations, the rights and the interests of the community cannot be safely confided to it. This, as far as I have understood the meaning of those who make the concessions, is an intire perversion of their sense. No advocate of the measure can be found who will not declare as his sentiment, that the system, though it may not be perfect in every part, is upon the whole a good one, is the best that the present views and circumstances of the country will permit, and is such an one as promises every species of security which a reasonable people can desire.

I answer in the next place, that I should esteem it the extreme of imprudence to prolong the precarious state of our national affairs, and to expose the union to the jeopardy of successive experiments, in the chimerical pursuit of a perfect plan. I never expect to see a perfect work from imperfect man. The result of the deliberations of all collective bodies must necessarily be a compound as well of the errors and prejudices, as of the good sense and wisdom of the individuals of whom they are composed. The compacts which are to embrace thirteen distinct states, in a common bond of amity and union, must as necessarily be a compromise of as many dissimilar interests and inclinations. How can perfection spring from such materials?

The reasons assigned in an excellent little pamphlet lately published in this city* are unanswerable to shew the utter improbability of assembling a new convention, under circumstances in any degree so favourable to a happy issue, as those in which the late convention met, deliberated and concluded. I will not repeat the arguments there used, as I presume the production itself has had an extensive circulation. It is certainly well worthy the perusal of every friend to his country. There is however one point of light in which the subject of amendments still remains to be considered; and in which it has not yet been exhibited to public view. I cannot resolve to conclude, without first taking a survey of it in this aspect.

It appears to me susceptible of absolute demonstration, that it will be far more easy to obtain subsequent than previous amendments to the constitution. The moment an alteration is made in the present plan, it becomes, to the purpose of adoption, a new one, and must undergo a new decision of each state. To its complete establishment throughout the union, it will therefore require the concurrence of thirteen states. If, on the contrary, the constitution proposed should once be ratified by all the states as it stands, alterations in it may at any time be effected by nine states. Here then the chances are as thirteen to nine† in favour of subsequent amendments, rather than of the original adoption of an intire system.

This is not all. Every constitution for the United States must inevitably consist of a great variety of particulars, in which thirteen independent states are to be accommodated in their interests or opinions of interest. We may of course expect to see, in any body of men charged with its original formation, very different combinations of the parts upon different points. Many of those who form the majority on one question may become the minority on a second, and an associa-

---

* Intitled "An Address to the people of the state of New-York."
† It may rather be said TEN, for though two-thirds may set on foot the measure, three-fourths must ratify.

tion dissimilar to either may constitute the majority on a third. Hence the necessity of moulding and arranging all the particulars which are to compose the whole in such a manner as to satisfy all the parties to the compact; and hence also an immense multiplication of difficulties and casualties in obtaining the collective assent to a final act. The degree of that multiplication must evidently be in a ratio to the number of particulars and the number of parties.

But every amendment to the constitution, if once established, would be a single proposition, and might be brought forward singly. There would then be no necessity for management or compromise, in relation to any other point, no giving nor taking. The will of the requisite number would at once bring the matter to a decisive issue. And consequently whenever nine* or rather ten states, were united in the desire of a particular amendment, that amendment must infallibly take place. There can therefore be no comparison between the facility of effecting an amendment, and that of establishing in the first instance a complete constitution.

In opposition to the probability of subsequent amendments it has been urged, that the persons delegated to the administration of the national government, will always be disinclined to yield up any portion of the authority of which they were once possessed. For my own part I acknowledge a thorough conviction that any amendments which may, upon mature consideration, be thought useful, will be applicable to the organization of the government, not to the mass of its powers; and on this account alone, I think there is no weight in the observation just stated. I also think there is little weight in it on another account. The intrinsic difficulty of governing THIRTEEN STATES at any rate, independent of calculations upon an ordinary degree of public spirit and integrity, will, in my opinion, constantly *impose* on the national rulers the *necessity* of a spirit of accommodation to the reasonable expectations of their constituents. But there is yet a further consideration, which proves beyond the possibility of doubt, that the observation is futile. It is this, that the national rulers, whenever nine states concur, will have no option upon the subject. By the fifth article of the plan the congress will be *obliged,* "on the application of the legislatures of two-thirds of the states, (which at present amounts to nine) to call a convention for proposing amendments, which *shall be valid* to all intents and purposes, as part of the constitution, when ratified by the legisla-

---

* It may rather be said TEN, for though two-thirds may set on foot the measure, three-fourths must ratify.

tures of three-fourths of the states, or by conventions in three-fourths thereof." The words of this article are peremptory. The congress "*shall* call a convention." Nothing in this particular is left to the discretion of that body. And of consequence all the declamation about their disinclination to a change, vanishes in air. Nor however difficult it may be supposed to unite two-thirds or three-fourths of the state legislatures, in amendments which may affect local interests, can there be any room to apprehend any such difficulty in a union on points which are merely relative to the general liberty or security of the people. We may safely rely on the disposition of the state legislatures to erect barriers against the encroachments of the national authority.

If the foregoing argument is a fallacy, certain it is that I am myself deceived by it; for it is, in my conception, one of those rare instances in which a political truth can be brought to the test of mathematical demonstration. Those who see the matter in the same light with me, however zealous they may be for amendments, must agree in the propriety of a previous adoption, as the most direct road to their own object.

The zeal for attempts to amend, prior to the establishment of the constitution, must abate in every man, who, is ready to accede to the truth of the following observations of a writer, equally solid and ingenious: "To balance a large state or society (says he) whether monarchial or republican, on general laws, is a work of so great difficulty, that no human genius, however comprehensive, is able by the mere dint of reason and reflection, to effect it. The judgments of many must unite in the work: EXPERIENCE must guide their labour: TIME must bring it to perfection: And the FEELING of inconveniences must correct the mistakes which they *inevitably* fall into, in their first trials and experiments."* These judicious reflections contain a lesson of moderation to all the sincere lovers of the union, and ought to put them upon their guard against hazarding anarchy, civil war, a perpetual alienation of the states from each other, and perhaps the military despotism of a victorious demagogue, in the pursuit of what they are not likely to obtain, but from TIME and EXPERIENCE. It may be in me a defect of political fortitude, but I acknowledge, that I cannot entertain an equal tranquillity with those who affect to treat the dangers of a longer continuance in our present situation as imaginary. A NATION without a NATIONAL GOVERNMENT is, in my view, an awful spectacle. The establishment of a constitution, in time of profound peace, by the voluntary

---

* Hume's Essays, vol. I, page 128.—The rise of arts and sciences.

consent of a whole people, is a PRODIGY, to the completion of which I look forward with trembling anxiety. I can reconcile it to no rules of prudence to let go the hold we now have, in so arduous an enterprise, upon seven out of the thirteen states; and after having passed over so considerable a part of the ground to recommence the course. I dread the more the consequences of new attempts, because I KNOW that POWERFUL INDIVIDUALS, in this and in other states, are enemies to a general national government, in every possible shape.

PUBLIUS.

A Constitutional Chronology
(1786–1791)

1786

September 11–14 Commissioners from five states meet at Annapolis and issue call for a general convention to meet at Philadelphia in May to consider changes to the Articles of Confederation.

December 4 Virginia elects delegation to the Convention at Philadelphia.

1787

February 10 James Madison returns to Continental Congress in New York.

February 21 Congress adopts resolution endorsing the Convention.

April Madison completes his preparation for the Convention.

May Delegates to the Convention slowly assemble in Philadelphia.

May 29 Governor Edmund Randolph presents Virginia Plan to those assembled.

June 15 William Paterson presents New Jersey Plan favoring interests of small states.

June 18 Alexander Hamilton presents his plan for a vigorous national government.

July 16 Delegates narrowly approve equal vote for states in the Senate.

August 6 Committee of Detail reports a draft constitution to the Convention.

September 12 Committee of Style reports a completed constitution to the Convention.

September 17 Delegates sign the Constitution, adjourn *sine die,* and transmit Constitution to Congress.

September 26–28 Congress agrees to submit proposed Constitution to the state legislatures, which in turn are asked to arrange for the election of ratification conventions.

October   Hamilton, Madison, and Jay discuss joint authorship of essays supporting ratification of the Constitution.

October 6   James Wilson gives widely reported speech rejecting early criticisms of the Constitution.

October 27   *Federalist* 1 appears in the *Independent Journal* of New York City.

November 5–8(?)   *Letters from a Federal Farmer,* a leading Anti-Federalist pamphlet, probably written by Melancton Smith of New York, published.

November 22   *Federalist* 10 published; George Mason's "Objections to the Constitution" first printed in the *Virginia Journal* of Alexandria.

December 7   Delaware becomes first state to ratify Constitution, 30–0.

December 12   Pennsylvania convention ratifies Constitution, 46–23.

December 18   New Jersey convention ratifies Constitution, 38–0.

December 31   Georgia convention ratifies Constitution, 26–0.

1788

January 8   Connecticut convention ratifies Constitution, 128–40.

February 6   Massachusetts convention ratifies Constitution, 187–168; Massachusetts becomes first state to recommend amendments for future consideration.

March 1–4   Madison publishes final essay as Publius, *Federalist* 63, and leaves New York City for Virginia to seek election to the state ratification convention.

March 6   Rhode Island rejects Constitution by popular referendum.

March 22   Volume I of *The Federalist,* containing 36 essays, published in New York City by John and Archibald McLean.

April 26   Maryland convention ratifies Constitution, 63–11.

May 23   South Carolina convention ratifies Constitution, 149–73, and also proposes amendments.

May 28   Volume II of the McLean edition of *The Federalist,* with 49 additional essays, published.

June 21   Second session of New Hampshire convention ratifies Constitution, 57–47, and proposes amendments, ensuring that the Constitution will take effect.

June 25   Virginia convention ratifies Constitution, 89–79, and proposes amendments.

July 26   New York convention ratifies Constitution, 30–27, and proposes amendments.

August 2 North Carolina convention rejects Constitution, pending prior adoption of amendments and a second constitutional convention.

1789

June 8 Madison introduces proposed constitutional amendments in the House of Representatives.

August 24 House of Representatives submits its version of amendments to the Senate.

September 9–25 Senate reports its revised version of the amendments, and conference committee of both houses produces final text of amendments to be submitted to the states.

November 21 Second North Carolina ratification convention approves the Constitution, 194–77.

1790

May 29 Second session of Rhode Island ratification convention approves the Constitution, 34–32.

1791

December Ratification of ten of the twelve amendments proposed by the Congress adds Amendments I–X, commonly known as the Bill of Rights, to the Constitution.

Questions for Consideration

1. In *Federalist* 1 and 37, Hamilton and Madison respectively lay down general principles for reasoning about politics. What are those principles, and which essays best illustrate how Publius applies these principles in practice?

2. Montesquieu was "the celebrated oracle" whose authority Anti-Federalists liked to invoke to argue against the very idea of a national republic and in favor of strict separation of powers. How does Publius attempt to deal with the problem that Anti-Federalist appeals to Montesquieu pose?

3. The argument of *Federalist* 10 rests on a series of definitions, distinctions, and comparisons. What are they, and can they be outlined as a coherent set of propositions and hypotheses?

4. On several occasions, Publius distinguishes a democracy from a republic, suggesting that the former depends on the direct participation of the people in deliberation and decision making, the latter on representation. What advantages does Publius attribute to preferring a system of representation to one of popular participation? Does this distinction justify the conclusion that *The Federalist* is itself an anti-democratic text?

5. Does Publius have a consistent theory of the role of public opinion in republican government, and if so, what is it? How do individual essays apply that theory to describe such problems as the competition between national and state governments, or of institutions within the national government, for power and influence, or the danger of allowing the people at large to resolve constitutional disputes?

6. How does Madison apply the general rules of reasoning about politics he lays down in *Federalist* 37 to the task of describing the national and federal characteristics of the Constitution in *Federalist* 39?

7. Some commentators have detected a tension between the argument about the extended republic in *Federalist* 10 and the approach to the problem of separated powers in *Federalist* 47–51. If the former essay is correct about the advantages of selecting representatives from

large districts, they suggest, then why should a Congress so elected develop into the "impetuous vortex" that Madison warns about in *Federalist* 48? Is there a real tension between these important arguments, or is Madison simply trying to answer all possible objections?

8. In defending the three-fifths clause in *Federalist* 54, Madison presumably could have taken a different approach, and simply said the decision to count slaves for purposes of apportioning representation was an expedient political compromise. Why would he adopt the different rhetorical strategy he uses here, and should eighteenth-century readers imbued with the right spirit of moderation be persuaded by his reasoning?

9. Hamilton faces an especially difficult task in *Federalist* 70 and 78: to defend the less representative branches of the executive and judiciary against the charge that the powers they will wield under the Constitution are still consistent with the spirit and principles of republican government. What arguments does he adduce on this score, and how well can they be reconciled with the idea that authority flows properly from the people?

Selected Bibliography

OTHER EDITIONS OF *THE FEDERALIST*

Numerous complete editions of *The Federalist* are readily available in libraries or for purchase. The standard scholarly edition is Jacob Cooke, ed., *The Federalist* (Middletown, Conn.: Wesleyan University Press, 1961). Other respectable editions include those edited by Benjamin F. Wright (Cambridge, Mass.: Harvard University Press, 1961); Isaac Kramnick (Harmondsworth, Eng.: Penguin Books, 1987); and Charles R. Kesler (New York: Mentor Books, 1999). The last is a reissuing, with a new introduction, of the extremely popular paperback edition prepared by the late Clinton Rossiter, a distinguished scholar at Cornell University, in 1961. It is this edition that wrongly convinced lay readers and scholars alike that the proper title of the collected essays of Publius is *The Federalist Papers.* Those who wish to read the essays exactly as they appeared in 1787–88 should use the versions printed in John P. Kaminski and Gaspare J. Saladino, eds., *The Documentary History of the Ratification of the Constitution,* vols. XIII–XVIII (Madison: State Historical Society of Wisconsin, 1981–95). The essays respectively written by Hamilton and Madison can also be found in the individual editions of their papers: Harold C. Syrett and Jacob Cooke, eds., *The Papers of Alexander Hamilton,* vol. IV (New York and London: Columbia University Press, 1962); Joanne Freeman, ed., *Alexander Hamilton: Writings* (New York: Library of America, 2001); Robert A. Rutland et al., eds., *The Papers of James Madison,* vol. 10 (Chicago and London: University of Chicago Press, 1977); and Jack N. Rakove, ed., *James Madison: Writings* (New York: Library of America, 1999).

OTHER PRIMARY SOURCES

The Federalist should not be read or interpreted in isolation from other sources illuminating the constitutional debates of the late 1780s. These, too, have been amply published in modern scholarly editions. The standard source for the deliberations at the Convention that framed the Constitution is Max Farrand, ed., *The Records of the Federal Convention of 1787,* 4 vols. (New Haven, Conn.: Yale University Press, 1966), along with James H.

Hutson, ed., *Supplement to Max Farrand's* The Records of the Federal Convention of 1787 (New Haven, Conn.: Yale University Press, 1987). A vast array of public and private documents relating to the ensuing debate over ratification can be found in Kaminski and Saladino, eds., *Documentary History of Ratification.* Bernard Bailyn, ed., *The Debate on the Constitution,* 2 vols. (New York: Library of America, 1993), is a handy compilation of major Federalist and Anti-Federalist writings, including most of the essays of *Publius.* Philip Kurland and Ralph Lerner, eds., *The Founders' Constitution,* 5 vols. (Chicago and London: University of Chicago Press, 1987), contains an introductory volume organized around broad themes in early American political and constitutional thinking, and four additional volumes providing clause-by-clause commentary on the entire text of the Constitution and the Bill of Rights. Herbert Storing, ed., *The Complete Anti-Federalist,* 7 vols. (Chicago and London: University of Chicago Press, 1987), is the most useful compilation of Anti-Federalist writings—although the title is inaccurate, and the whole contents, including the introductory volume, *What the Anti-Federalists Were For,* could have been published in two volumes instead of seven.

SECONDARY SOURCES

Modern scholarly commentary on *The Federalist* has devoted extraordinary attention to Madison's Tenth essay, which is widely regarded as the paradigmatic statement of a general theory of the new political order the Constitution was conceived to establish. This interest in *Federalist* 10 can be traced in significant measure to Charles A. Beard, *An Economic Interpretation of the Constitution* (New York: Macmillan, 1913), which, for all its flaws, remains one of the most important works of American history ever published. But interest in this essay also reflected the concerns of a distinct group of early-twentieth-century scholars, the founders of "pluralist" theory, as brilliantly explored in an essay by the late Australian scholar Paul Bourke, "The Pluralist Reading of James Madison's Tenth *Federalist,*" *Perspectives in American History,* 9 (1975): 271–95. In a different key, the use made of *The Federalist* in constitutional jurisprudence is examined in Ira C. Lupu, "Time, the Supreme Court, and *The Federalist,*" *George Washington Law Review,* 66 (1998): 1324–36.

The truly seminal era for *Federalist* scholarship—again focused on *Federalist* 10—was the decade and a half following the end of the Second World War. The most important pioneer was the historian Douglass Adair, who, in a series of sprightly and incisive articles, raised important questions about the intellectual context within which Publius could be located. Adair's leading essays included "The Authorship of the Disputed Federalist Papers," *William and Mary Quarterly,* 3rd ser., 1 (1944): 97–122, 235–64; "The Tenth Federalist Revisited," ibid., 8 (1951), 48–67; and "'That Politics

May Be Reduced to a Science': David Hume, James Madison, and the Tenth Federalist," *Huntington Library Quarterly,* 20 (1957): 343–60. All are reprinted in Trevor Colbourn, ed., *Fame and the Founding Fathers: Essays by Douglass Adair* (New York: W. W. Norton, 1974), 27–106. Other important interpretative essays from this period include Alpheus T. Mason, "The Federalist—A Split Personality," *American Historical Review,* 57 (1952): 625–43; the opening chapter on "Madisonian Democracy," in Robert A. Dahl, *A Preface to Democratic Theory* (Chicago and London: University of Chicago Press, 1956), 1–33, which attempted to recast *Federalist* 10 as a set of theoretical propositions akin to the hypotheses of contemporary social science; and Martin Diamond, "Democracy and *The Federalist:* A Reconsideration of the Framers' Intent," *American Political Science Review,* 53 (1959): 52–68. Interest in the study of the ratification debates was also enhanced by the portrait of the Anti-Federalists sketched in Cecilia Kenyon, "Men of Little Faith: The Anti-Federalists on the Nature of Representative Government," *William and Mary Quarterly,* 3rd ser., 12 (1955): 3–43.

Together, these essays called attention to the hypothesis about the liberty-preserving benefits of an extended national republic that Madison advanced in *Federalist* 10. In the last of his essays cited above, Adair suggested that Madison derived key inspiration from his reading of the political essays of the Scottish philosopher-historian David Hume. Adair's hypothesis about Madison's hypothesis has generated a continuing discussion of the potential intellectual influences that shaped this one essay and Madison's approach to the problems of republicanism more generally. Contributors to this debate include two journalist-historians: Garry Wills, *Explaining America: The Federalist* (Garden City, N.Y.: Doubleday, 1981); and Theodore Draper, "Hume and Madison: The Secrets of Federalist Paper No. 10," *Encounter,* 58 (1982); as well as Edmund S. Morgan, "Safety in Numbers: Madison, Hume, and the Tenth Federalist," *Huntington Library Quarterly,* 49 (1986): 95–112; and most thoroughly, Morton White, *Philosophy, The Federalist, and the Constitution* (New York: Oxford University Press, 1987). A recent essay by Mark Spencer, "Hume and Madison on Faction," *William and Mary Quarterly,* 3rd ser., 59 (2002), suggests that Madison drew more from Hume's account in his multivolume *History of England* of the disruptive effects of religious factions than from the scattered political essays. There are, of course, other intellectual contexts within which to locate *The Federalist* in general and Madison's Tenth essay in particular. A brilliant exploration of one of these broader contexts is Daniel W. Howe, "The Political Psychology of *The Federalist,*" *William and Mary Quarterly,* 3rd ser., 44 (1987): 485–509. In a contrarian vein, a few skeptics have questioned how well Madison's ideas represented the broader debates over the Constitution or how deeply they were absorbed. On this point, see especially Larry D. Kramer, "Madison's Audience," *Harvard Law Review,* 112 (1999): 611–79.

Commentary on *The Federalist* is not, of course, restricted to this one essay, which in any case would need to be correlated with the remaining eighty-four numbers. Broader efforts to assess the arguments of *Publius* and their impact on ratification include David F. Epstein, *The Political Theory of* The Federalist (Chicago and London: University of Chicago Press, 1984); the essays collected in Charles R. Kesler, ed., *Saving the Revolution:* The Federalist Papers *and the American Founding* (New York: Free Press, 1987); Albert Furtwangler, *The Authority of Publius: A Reading of the Federalist Papers* (Ithaca, N.Y., and London: Cornell University Press, 1984); Edward Millican, *One United People: The Federalist Papers and the National Idea* (Lexington: University Press of Kentucky, 1990); and Gottfried Dietze, *The Federalist: A Classic on Federalism and Free Government* (Baltimore: The Johns Hopkins University Press, 1960). Bernard Grofman and Donald Wittman, eds., *The Federalist Papers and the New Institutionalism* (New York: Agathon Press, 1989), is a collection of essays examining *The Federalist* from the vantage point of contemporary political science.

The Federalist may be the most important work of political theory produced during the American revolutionary era, but this period of rich political discourse has been extensively analyzed by numerous scholars. A short list of relevant works, many of which discuss *The Federalist,* would include Willi Paul Adams, *The First American Constitutions: Republican Ideology and the Making of the State Constitutions in the Revolutionary Era,* trans. Rita and Robert Kember, expanded edition (Lanham, Md.: Rowman & Littlefield, 2001); Bernard Bailyn, *The Ideological Origins of the American Revolution,* enlarged edition (Cambridge, Mass.: Harvard University Press, 1992); Samuel F. Beer, *To Make a Nation: The Rediscovery of American Federalism* (Cambridge, Mass.: Harvard University Press, 1993); Michael Lienesch, *New Order of the Ages: Time, the Constitution, and the Making of Modern American Political Thought* (Princeton, N.J.: Princeton University Press, 1988); Jackson Turner Main, *The Anti-Federalists: Critics of the Constitution, 1781–1788* (Chapel Hill: University of North Carolina Press, 1961); Cathy D. Matson and Peter S. Onuf, *A Union of Interests: Political and Economic Thought in Revolutionary America* (Lawrence: University Press of Kansas, 1985); Forrest McDonald, *Novus Ordo Seclorum: The Intellectual Origins of the Constitution* (Lawrence: University Press of Kansas, 1985); Jennifer Nedelsky, *Private Property and the Limits of American Constitutionalism: The Madisonian Framework and Its Legacy* (Chicago and London: University of Chicago Press, 1990); Jack N. Rakove, *Original Meanings: Politics and Ideas in the Making of the Constitution* (New York: Alfred A. Knopf, 1996); William H. Riker, *The Strategy of Rhetoric: Campaigning for the American Constitution* (New Haven, Conn.: Yale University Press, 1996); and perhaps most important, the pathbreaking book by Gordon S. Wood, *The Creation of the American Republic, 1776–1787* (Chapel Hill: University of North Carolina Press, 1969). A number of collections of essays also cover important constitutional topics: Terence Ball and J. G. A. Pocock, eds., *Conceptual Change and the Constitution* (Lawrence: University Press of Kansas, 1988); Richard Beeman et al., eds., *Beyond Confederation: Origins of the Constitution and American National Identity* (Chapel Hill: University of North Carolina Press, 1987); Herman Belz et al., eds., *To Form a More Perfect Union: The Critical Ideas of the Constitution* (Charlottesville: University Press of Virginia, 1992); and Leonard Levy and Dennis J. Mahoney, eds., *The Framing and Ratification of the Constitution* (New York: Macmillan, 1987). For narratives of the Federal Convention, see the classic work by Max Farrand, *The Framing of the Constitution of the United States* (New Haven, Conn.: Yale University Press, 1913), and the recent fetching account by Carol Berkin, *A Brilliant Solution: Inventing the American Constitution* (New York: Harcourt Brace, 2002).

Finally, political biographies offer another context in which to locate the evolving ideas and concerns of the authors. Richard B. Morris, *Witnesses at the Creation: Hamilton, Madison, Jay, and the Constitution* (New York: Holt, Rinehart, and Winston, 1985), is a good place to begin. Important studies of Hamilton include John C. Miller, *Alexander Hamilton: Portrait in Paradox* (New York: Harper and Brothers, 1959); Gerald Stourzh, *Alexander Hamilton and the Idea of Republican Government* (Stanford, Calif.: Stanford University Press, 1970); and Karl-Friedrich Walling, *Republican Empire: Alexander Hamilton on War and Free Government* (Lawrence: University Press of Kansas, 1999). For Madison, the necessary work is Lance Banning, *The Sacred Fire of Liberty: James Madison and the Founding of the Federal Republic* (Ithaca, N.Y., and London: Cornell University Press, 1995). Also useful are Ralph Ketcham, *James Madison: A Biography* (Charlottesville: University Press of Virginia, 1971); Jack N. Rakove, *James Madison and the Creation of the American Republic*, 2nd ed. (New York: Longman, 2001); and Gary Rosen, *American Compact: James Madison and the Problem of Founding* (Lawrence: University Press of Kansas, 1999).

Index